NEW BLACK PLAYWRIGHTS

NEW
BLACK

PLAYWRIGHTS

An Anthology EDITED
AND WITH AN INTRODUCTION BY
William Couch, Jr.

LOUISIANA STATE UNIVERSITY PRESS · BATON ROUGE

Copyright © 1968 by
LOUISIANA STATE UNIVERSITY PRESS

Library of Congress Catalog Card Number 68-31137
Manufactured in the United States of America by
The Seeman Printery, Durham, North Carolina
Designed by Jules B. McKee

To the Memory of W. E. B. D.

Contents

Introduction

It has been more than fifty years since W. E. B. Du Bois appealed to his fellow Negro writers to "set the black man before the world as both a creative artist and a strong subject for artistic treatment." And it has been several decades since Langston Hughes, at the height of the Harlem Renaissance, formulated his challenge echoing Du Bois: "We young Negro artists who are creating now intend to express our individual dark-skinned selves without fear or shame. If white people are pleased we are glad. If they are not, it does not matter . . . if colored people are pleased we are glad. If they are not, their displeasure does not matter either. We build our temples for tomorrow." Although today's black militants and revolutionaries were not born when Hughes and Du Bois (who now is one of the patron saints of the Black Left) proclaimed their independence, the spirit of their manifestoes is renascent.

As in most endeavor, assertion preceded the act. Langston Hughes's "temples for tomorrow" were built slowly, book by book, as gifted Negro writers arrived on the scene: Jean Toomer, Richard Wright, Chester Himes, Willard Motley, Ralph Ellison, James Baldwin. The list of sterling literary achievements in which these writers "set the black man before the world"—and the list could be extended—shows at a glance the mounting success of the Negro writer as novelist. An equally impressive roster could be made of Negro poets. Three years before Ralph Ellison received the 1953 National Book Award for *Invisible Man*, Gwendolyn Brooks—coming out of a tradition that dates from Jupiter Hammond, whose poems were published in 1760, and continuing through Phyllis Wheatley, Paul Lawrence Dunbar, Georgia Douglas Johnson, Countee Cullen, and Robert Hayden—became the first Negro to be awarded the Pulitzer Prize for poetry.

When we turn to the Negro as playwright, however, there is a noticeable difference. Very few plays written by Negroes have received major or even serious production, and fewer still have enjoyed a good run on Broadway—a neglect which appears all the more strange when we consider how closely Negroes have been allied with the major fields of entertainment in this country.

As early as the mid-eighteenth century, Negro minstrel companies like the Congo Melodists, the Ethiopian Serenaders, and the Georgia Minstrels were delighting American audiences. Bob Cole's *A Trip to Coontown* (1898) was probably the first show to be organized, produced, and managed by Negroes. By the turn of the century Paul Lawrence Dunbar, in collaboration with Will Marion Cook, was producing such successful Broadway theatricals as *Clorindy—the Origin of the Cakewalk* and *Jes Lak White Folks*, titles which clearly bespeak the era. The 1920's saw a spurt in the Negro's success in the field of musical comedy, with Broadway productions of Noble Sissle's *Chocolate Dandies* and Miller and Lyle's *Shuffle Along*, *Runnin' Wild*, and *The Black Birds*. That same period saw the rise to fame of such authentic stars of vaudeville as Bert

Williams, Florence Mills, Miller and Lyle, Sissle and Blake, and Bill "Bojangles" Robinson. Though discriminated against, black theatrical entertainers nevertheless found it possible to participate in a sector of the American theater, where they gained considerable prominence and acclaim.

This of course does not mean that Negroes did not desire to bring to the more serious side of the theater the same talents that they have demonstrated in the novel, in poetry, and in the lighter side of the theater. In fact, there is a considerable amount of history to attest to the black man's determination to establish himself in the great world of the theater. As early as 1821 an actor named James Hewlett formed the African Company in New York, where he became famous for his performances in Shakespearean roles. In 1833 Ira Aldridge, who entered the theater in this country as a handyman, was appearing on the London stage as Othello opposite Ellen Terry.

Charles Gilpin, who made drama history in 1920 playing the title role of Eugene O'Neill's *The Emperor Jones*, was selected by the New York Drama League, along with David Belasco and Eugene O'Neill, as one of the ten persons who contributed most to the American theater during the year. Paul Robeson, Rutgers University's four-letter man, a member of Phi Beta Kappa, and a graduate of the Columbia University Law School, later won fame in the Gilpin-created role and in O'Neill's *All God's Chillun*. "The Negro is a born actor," wrote George Jean Nathan, and "Robeson, with relatively little experience, and with no training to speak of, is one of the most thoroughly eloquent, impressive, and convincing actors that I have looked at and listened to in the past twenty years of theater going."

Similar accolades went to Leigh Whipper for his Broadway successes in John Steinbeck's *Of Mice and Men* and in George Sklar and Paul Peters' *Stevedore*, to Frank Wilson for his role in Paul Green's Pulitzer Prize–winning drama *In Abraham's Bosom*, and to Richard B. Harrison for his masterful portrayal of De Lawd in Marc Connelly's *Green Pastures.* Today the stage artistry of Robert Hooks, Sidney Poitier, and James Earl Jones forms a link with the accomplishments of the great Negro performers of the past.

Alain Locke, who in 1927 published an anthology entitled *Plays of Negro Life,* was optimistic about the rise of a national Negro theater "where the black playwright and the black actor will interpret the soul of their people in a way to win the attention and admiration of the world." Through the 1920's and 1930's Negroes, in the spirit of Langston Hughes, did seem to redouble their efforts to "build temples." In 1921 the Howard Players at Howard University in Washington, D. C., were organized, with the hope of establishing a basis for a Little Theater movement among Negroes. The Morgan College Players in Baltimore, Maryland, formed by playwright-teacher Randolph Edmonds in 1930, became a distinguished theatrical group. Edmonds also founded a Negro Intercollegiate Dramatic Association which included such predominately Negro schools as Morgan College, Howard University, Virginia State College, Shaw University, North Carolina College at Durham, Lincoln University in Pennsylvania, and A & T College at Greensboro, North Carolina. At the same time Fannin Belcher, drama coach at West Virginia State College, was organizing play tournaments among Negro high schools in the state "to cultivate in our students a more genuine enthusiasm for drama."

The contagion to perform and write for, to become an integral part of, the theater spread from black college campuses to black communities across the nation. Drama groups began to spring up—the Gilpin Players in Cleveland; the Krigwa Players with ensembles in Washington, in New York, and on the West Coast; Langston Hughes's Suitcase Theater in New York; the Rose McClendon Players; the Little Theater of Columbus, Ohio; The Neighborhood Players in Atlantic City, New Jersey, under the direction of Montgomery Gregory, who with Alain Locke founded the Howard University Players; and, currently, LeRoi Jones's Spirit House in Newark, New Jersey; and the Robert Hooks Negro Ensemble Company which operates in the Village on New York's Lower East Side under a $100,000 Ford Foundation grant. All such enterprises, despite their sometimes phoenix existence, provided Negroes with the opportunity for apprenticeship and expression in the field of drama.

But, as the Chicago *Defender* observed in 1930, the lot of the Negro in the theater continued to be "hard and the path more than unusually difficult. Work was uncertain, and wages more so." And the reality of the present, unfortunately, is that Negro actors have difficulty finding nonracial parts. A Negro actor cannot look forward to playing a lead role in a university theatrical production, where some of our best actors are receiving their training today; he still finds himself cast in plays written by white writers whose perception of Negro life, however sympathetic, often strikes one as false and superficial. Frederick O'Neal, Negro president of Actor's Equity Association, notes that there has been some improvement in the employment of Negro actors, but admits that the situation is far from acceptable. There was, in fact, a slight decrease between 1964 and 1965 in the number of Negroes employed in Broadway and off-Broadway shows. Also there is only a small handful of Negro producers and directors, and very few stage managers (Charles Blackwell, who was formerly with David Merrick Productions and now works with Harry Belafonte; James Wall, who works in television; and one or two others). Among theater talent agents the list is even shorter, probably the only successful one being Ernestine McClendon, whose clientele is integrated and who holds franchises from the major performer unions. An accurate estimate of the black actor's achievement must fall somewhere between, on the one hand, Locke's hopeful predictions and the brilliant instances that seem to bear out his judgment, and, on the other hand, the sobering comment recently made by James Baldwin: "It is a sad fact that I have rarely seen a Negro actor really well used on the American stage and screen, or on television."

As for black playwrights, it is possible that George Jean Nathan, in acclaiming Negroes as "born actors" and praising Paul Robeson for his ability to act without any training, inadvertently put his finger on the source of the problem. Actors, perhaps, may be "born," but the experience and craftsmanship necessary for successful playwrighting is more likely to come through close contact with the stage. Denied access to the full ambience of the theater, yet driven by an understandable urgency to make public their protests, Negro playwrights too often have suffered from the twin disasters of racial discrimination and hastily done work. Moreover, the relative preeminence of the black actor over the black playwright is in some degree the result of the public's tendency to regard actors as entertainers, a role traditionally "acceptable" for Negroes. Certainly it could be speculated that the kinds of social involvement attending the function of the playwright, the various contacts in the steps to Opening Night—the whole sociology of the theater world—restrict the opportunities of a black man. Poets and novelists work in solitude, their task being accomplished when they have had their say; but in the world of the theater, which demands relationships and interaction, the national ritual of race predominates.

From the start Negro writers have resisted the restrictions forced on black men. William Wells Brown's *The Escape, or a Leap to Freedom* (1858), the first play written in America by a Negro, satirized slavery. This play is not known to have been produced, although Brown did give numerous lyceum readings from it. Significantly, while Brown's plays (it is difficult to say how many he wrote, but he read from at least three in his lectures) languished unproduced in America, Victor Séjour, a Negro who was born in New Orleans in 1817, achieved a notable success in Europe as playwright and actor.

Le Théâtre Français presented Séjour's first play, *Diegarias*, in 1844, and it is believed that the theaters of Paris presented in all some twenty-one of this black expatriate's works.

Apparently the first successful drama written by a Negro and interpreted on the stage by Negro actors was Angeline Grimke's *Rachel*, a play in three acts dealing with the lynching of a girl's father, which was produced in 1916 by the Drama Committee of the NAACP in Washington, D.C. The tendentious character of the play was evident from the program announcement: "This is the first attempt to use the stage for race propaganda in order to enlighten the American people relative to the lamentable condition of ten millions of colored citizens in this free republic." In April, 1917, on the day of America's entrance into World War I, Broadway for the first time witnessed Negro actors performing in serious drama, when at the Garden City Theater the all-Negro Hapgood Players presented Ridgley Torrence's three one-act plays "written for the Negro theatre" (*Granny Maumee, The Rider of Dreams,* and *Simon the Cyrenian*). The event marked the beginning of public interest in the legitimate drama of Negro life as interpreted by Negroes. Five years later, in May, 1923, the Colored Folk Theatre, later known as the Ethiopian Art Theater, was organized by Raymond O'Neil in cooperation with Mrs. Sherwood Anderson. It offered such varied theater fare as Oscar Wilde's *Salome*, a jazz interpretation of Shakespeare's *A Comedy of Errors,* and *The Chip Woman's Fortune,* by Willis Richardson, a Negro government clerk who between 1921 and 1927 wrote six plays which were produced.

One of the most talented writers associated with the Harlem Renaissance was Jean Toomer, best known as a writer of fiction (*Cane*), whose almost tragic attempts to turn playwright were frustrated because the techniques he used were regarded as too advanced for the times. *Kabnis* (1923), a play that demonstrates his modernist methods, found no producer. *Balo, A Sketch of Negro Life* (1922), a less mature work dealing with

Negro peasants in Georgia, was performed by the Howard Players during the 1923–24 season.

Drama contests sponsored in the twenties by *Opportunity, A Journal of Negro Life* brought to light several new Negro playwrights: Frank Wilson, already well-known as an actor, who won first prize in 1925 with *Sugar Cane*; John Matheus, a promising literary talent who later turned to college teaching, who won first prize in 1926 with *'Cruiter*, a play which dealt with migrant Negro labor from the South after the First World War; and Georgia Douglas Johnson, the poet, whose *Plumes* won first prize in 1927.

Almost half the plays contributed to Alain Locke's *Plays of Negro Life* in 1927 were written by Negroes. That most of the white authors in the anthology (Eugene O'Neill, Paul Green, Ridgley Torrence) were better known than their Negro counterparts (Willis Richardson, Frank Wilson, or even Jean Toomer) neither obscured the Negroes' determination to succeed as playwrights nor concealed the progress these black writers had been making in spite of discouraging obstacles. Their achievement could be measured in light years from the days of minstrelsy and coon shows not too many decades before.

The following year, 1928, audiences at the Princess Theater on Broadway were captivated by Frank Wilson's *Meek Mose*, a serious study of Negro life. It had been a long journey for Wilson, from postal clerk to the *Opportunity* contests to Broadway as both playwright and actor. In 1929 Wallace Thurman's *Harlem* (written with assistance from William Rapp), which attempted to give an actual reproduction of the average Negro's existence in New York City, enjoyed a short run on Broadway before moving to Canada. In 1933 Hall Johnson's *Run Little Chillun* opened on Broadway. A folk play, it was a mixture of fantasy and realism, music and drama, and it revealed Johnson, whose reputation was already high as a composer and choir director, as a dramatist of genuine promise. In spite of weaknesses of plot and the overuse of melodramatic effects, *Run Little Chillun* is still probably one of the best theater works by an American Negro.

Creation of a Federal Theater Project in 1935 gave Negroes a laboratory for experiment in all areas of the theater. Plays of varying degrees of success devoted to the plight of the Negro were numerous and enjoyed a popularity which was reinforced by the general preoccupation with proletarian art in the thirties. Project productions of *The Hot Mikado, Haiti,* and *Macbeth* with black casts are still exciting memories. Of the contributions by Negro playwrights, perhaps the most notable in retrospect were Frank Wilson's *Walk Together Children* (1936), which focused on the race riots and friction that develop when southern Negro laborers come North, and Augustus Smith and Peter Morrell's powerful depiction in *Turpentine* (1936) of the struggles of workmen, black and white, in the Florida pines. When the Federal Theater Project ended in 1939, it had already served the purposes of revitalizing the interest of Negro communities in plays, especially in the larger cities, and had increased the knowledge and interest of black writers and actors in the techniques of the theater.

But it is not until we come to Langston Hughes that we find what, without any doubt, has been the most successful and enduring career of any Negro playwright. Hughes's *Mulatto,* a study of illicit relationships in the South which centers on the conflict between a mulatto son and his white father, is the first (and only) long-run Broadway hit by a Negro dramatist. Opening at the Vanderbilt Theatre on October 24, 1935, *Mulatto* played continuously until December 9, 1937. Encouraged by this success and loyal to a creative bent which embraced drama, poetry, and the novel, Hughes, unlike many of his contemporaries who after a few militant forays in the theater succumbed to what can only be described as the almost insurmountable difficulties of being a black playwright, continued to write plays for the rest of his life. Thirty years after his first Broadway success, and two years before his death in 1967,

Hughes's play *Tambourines to Glory* was running on Broadway. During the intervening years he had courageously accepted the writer's risk of never letting his pen remain idle, and he had steadfastly lived up to his credo that Negro artists should express themselves "without fear or shame." The results, in terms of artistry, were not always even. But the passionate confirmation of black life in America in such plays as *Trouble Island, Scottsboro Limited, Angela Herndon Jones,* and *Don't You Want to Be Free?*, not to mention dozens of lesser plays, comprises an honorable legacy to the proletarian drama of this country. Few American playwrights have surpassed the total achievement of Langston Hughes.

Ossie Davis, author of *Purlie Victorious* and an astute commentator on the theater, recently remarked that "No one can deny that integration has come to Broadway . . . that the Negro is now included, meaningfully, in more aspects of Broadway life." *Anna Lucasta* still remains one of the all-time record-holders for Broadway runs of straight plays, and Paul Robeson's *Othello* holds the record for the Broadway run of a Shakespearean play. Yet Mr. Davis is quick to confess "that while there are no impediments to plays about the truth of Negro experiences being produced on Broadway, such productions so far have not succeeded—have not been 'hits' in the sense that *Anna Lucasta* was." The hope that Negroes would be included in the mainstream of American theater, Mr. Davis confesses, "has been realized in form, but defeated in substance." Mr. Davis discloses that his own play, *Purlie Victorious*, which is a stunning comedy-satire on race nonrelations, was kept on Broadway for seven and one-half months with money out of his own pocket and that of his sympathetic producer. Lorraine Hansberry's *A Raisin in the Sun* did make money, but her *The Sign in Sidney Brustein's Window* was a financial failure. James Baldwin's much talked about, and little supported, *Blues for Mister Charlie* drained the author's friends and financial backers in the unsuccessful attempt to keep it in production.

The conclusion seems inescapable: Plays about Negroes, especially plays that deal candidly with the harsher realities of the Negro's existence in America, are not attractive to the general theater audience, and the bulk of the theatergoing audience is white.

Juxtaposed with this discouraging fact of our cultural life is the Negro's growing insistence that his story be told, and told in terms compatible with his own experience and self-awareness, told like it is. This conflict may force more and more Negro playwrights into an alliance with a revolutionary theater which already finds its expression in such plays as LeRoi Jones's *Dutchman, The Slave,* and *The Toilet.* "It is a political theatre," Mr. Jones has written, "a weapon to help in the slaughter of these dim-witted fat-bellied white guys who somehow believe that the rest of the world is here for them to slobber on." Mr. Jones goes on to claim for the revolutionary theater the task of "taking dreams" and "giving them a reality." It must "isolate the ritual and historical cycles of reality." Here he is on solid ground; a criticism of American life for its chronic and destructive necessity to substitute ritual for reality, and in far more areas than race, is entirely relevant and is indeed very hard to refute.

Ed Bullins, whose work is represented in this anthology, is similarly motivated by a consciousness of the "new roles, new themes and new definitions" that are waiting to be created and explored by the black writer. In fact, for men like Jones, Bullins, and William Wellington Mackey, this is the arresting and inescapable vocation of the black playwright today.

Such writers are, of course, aware of the problems facing them in the immediate future. Mr. Bullins, for instance, foresees a time when the black playwright may be told that his work is too "experimental" and "obscene" if it uses too much of the idiom of the black ghetto. Even where black theater groups are concerned we should not be surprised "when Negroes of flesh and blood are depicted on the stage, that this is verging upon revolution and is too drastic." Such groups, Mr. Bullins reflects, like their white counterparts, will perhaps for some time to come prefer the classics or the work of proven Negro writers like Langston Hughes to that of the "revolutionary" playwright. But the net result of the new black playwright's estrangement, in spite of a certain amount of confusion and vituperation which in the circumstances probably cannot be avoided, could be the emergence, in time, of a more sharply defined, and badly needed, sense of the white and the black dramatist's true function in this society. After all, the revolutionary's urgency to bring into being a theater where, as LeRoi Jones claims, "the nakedness of the human spirit is paraded" is certainly in accord with the profoundest requirements of dramatic art and is open very little to challenge in good faith. When we consider the vacuum that exists in the American theater today, which is largely the result of a nearly wholesale rejection of the vital uses of the theater by most established American playwrights, the current dispute of black playwrights with a public which seems to insist upon regarding the theater as a Fun House gains a better perspective, and we are inclined to believe that those playwrights who come forth with legitimate claims, however "revolutionary" they may be, ought to be warmly encouraged.

The plays in this book are a good sample of the concerns, in subject matter and treatment, of modern black consciousness. Douglas Turner Ward's *Day of Absence* and *Happy Ending* superbly combine thesis with theater farce, establishing a real, and sometimes half surreal world in which whites get their comeuppance from black folks whose sardonic cunning is mordant proof that they, like people in general, though less than angels are far more than fools. Mr. Ward's effects derive chiefly from his access to a brand of realism that is geared to the tempo and style of the absurd theater.

Adrienne Kennedy's *The Owl Answers* (not included) and *A Rat's Mass*, on the other hand, are richly symbolic, poetic pieces. Her plays, structured in interplays of lights and shadows of meaning, achieve a delicately muted resonance. Images like shapes beneath a surface transform the black man's social and moral tragedies into an iconography of the universal quest for selfhood and identity. Satiric wit crackles like live current through Mr. Ward's plays, but in the plays of Miss Kennedy there is an evocative and mystical sense of being.

Awareness of an inherent validity in the drab lives that most people lead is the significance of Lonne Elder's *Ceremonies in Dark Old Men*, which probes the substratum of Harlem culture and finds in plain, prosaic characters a powerful and explosive energy. What the reader gains from the experience is the terrifying and necessary knowledge of what it is like, if one happens to be black, to take one's life in one's hands just by being alive in the U.S.A. Or, as Mr. Elder puts it, how people bear up under "the hazardous and interminable crime of being a Negro." Or better still, as one of his characters expresses it, "Don't let nobody tell you nothing about no communist, Chinese or anything—there ain't nothing on this earth meaner and dirtier than an American born cracker." Traditional realism, in this case, is a suitable vehicle as it is used by Mr. Elder to convey the groping heroism of ordinary but persecuted people.

In *Goin'a Buffalo* Ed Bullins brings us fully into the revolutionary theater or, as Mr. Bullins prefers to call it, "the theatre of reality." "The revolutionary nature of this theater is not of style and technique but of theme and character." Honesty, Mr. Bullins writes, "is what the writer should be after." The black playwright performs his function "by uncovering the reality of his art, his humanity, his existence as an intelligent and moral entity in the universe, and makes the entire universe an audience of this transformation of the psyche and spirit." Mr. Bullins, who could be called "an angry young man," is gifted with extraordinary imagination and ability. His play reflects the dramaturgy of Antonin

Artaud yet brandishes the ideology of the current Black Left.
Mama Too Tight, one of the main characters, displays an amaz-
ing element of the comic and pathetic, the sacred and profane.
One of society's New Waifs, she is surely one of the least for-
gettable creatures likely to be encountered in contemporary
plays. *Goin'a Buffalo* (the title is deceptive) must be seen,
or read, to be believed.

The pursuit of new ideology, and a redefinition of social
roles, preoccupies all thoughtful black Americans today. The
result is a proliferation of viewpoints that mirrors the circumstances enjoyed, or endured, by black men and women across
the nation. The conflict that exists between the middle-class,
successful Negro and his numerous less fortunate brothers is a
subject that interests William Wellington Mackey. Mr. Mackey
has written one play (*Requiem for Brother X, A Homage to
Malcolm X*) to be "a spit at the black middle class for turning
their backs on the black masses still in bondage." Indeed Mr.
Mackey shares a rapidly growing belief among the black masses
that the cynicism of white Americans toward black Americans
is total and intransigent, and has infected the minds of many
Negroes themselves. In this conviction Mr. Mackey has found
the matrix of his reality—namely, that black people must,
through supreme acts of self-reevaluation and efforts of the will,
rescue themselves from a malignant history, and through their
own energy and genius must recover their stolen humanity. It
is precisely this fiery protest and affirmation, joined with a perfect grasp of the black idiom and a superb use of irony, that
elevates Mr. Mackey's *Family Meeting* to a level at which his
polemics become irresistible.

Other black writers today would include Woodie King, Jr.,
Alice Childress, William Branch, Loftin Mitchell, Errol John,
Abram Hill, Irving Burgie, Ann Flagg, Louis Peterson, and
William Hairston.

Black writers, of course, differ among themselves in their
outlook on the world and society, as well as in their views on

the purposes of drama. Out of such diversity come many of the instances of beauty and honesty to be found in this collection. Because there are vast tracts of unrecorded American experience, uncharted regions of the heart, we are fortunate that black playwrights today with renewed strength are undertaking to reveal us to ourselves more clearly than we have been able to perceive in our troubled history.

WILLIAM COUCH, JR.

North Carolina College at Durham
March 4, 1968

NEW BLACK PLAYWRIGHTS

Happy Ending

Short One-Act Play

DOUGLAS TURNER WARD

Cast of Characters (in order of appearance)

ELLIE

VI

JUNIE

ARTHUR

TIME: The present; an early weekday evening around 5 or 6 P.M.

PLACE: The spotless kitchen of a Harlem tenement apartment. At stage left is a closed door providing entry to the outside hallway. On the opposite side of the stage is another door leading into the interior of the railroad flat. Sandwiched between this door and a window facing the brick walls of the apartment's inner shaft is a giant, dazzling white refrigerator. Positioned center stage is a gleaming, porcelain-topped oval table. Directly behind is a modern stove. To the left of the

3

stove, another window looks out upon a backyard court. The window is flanked on its left by a kitchen sink. Adjacent to the sink, upstage left, a bathroom door completes the setting.

As curtain rises, waning rays of daylight can be seen streaming through the courtyard window. Two handsome women, both in their late thirties or early forties, are sitting at opposite ends of the kitchen table. They are dressed as if recently entered from work. Hats and coats are still worn; handbags lie on floor propped against legs of respective chairs. They remain in dejected poses, weeping noiselessly.

ELLIE. Let me have your handkerchief, Vi . . .

(VI *hands it to her absently.* ELLIE *daubs eyes, then rests hankie on table. It lies there until* VI *motions for it to be handed back.*)

VI. What we gon do, Ellie?

ELLIE. Don' know . . . Don't seem like there's much more we kin do . . .

VI. This time it really might happen . . .

ELLIE. I know . . .

ELLIE. Lord, this may be the limit . . .

VI. End of the line . . .

VI. Persons kin go but just so far . . .

ELLIE. Hear us, Savior!

VI. Think it might help if I prayed a novena to him first thing tomorrow morning?

ELLIE. Certainly couldn't do no harm . . . .

(*They lapse into silence once again, passing hankie back and forth on request. Suddenly* JUNIE, *a tall, slender, sharply handsome, tastefully dressed youth in his early twenties, bursts upon the scene, rushing through hallway door.*)

JUNIE (*rapidly crossing, shedding coat in transit*). Hey Vi, Ellie . . . (*Exits through interior door, talking offstage*)

Ellie, do I have any more pleated shirts clean . . . ? Gotta make fast impression on new chick tonight . . . . (*Thrusting head back into view*) One of them foxy, black "Four Hundred" debutantes, you dig! All class and manners, but nothing underneath but a luscious, V-8 chassis!—which is a-o-reeet wit me since that's all I'm after. You hear me talking to ya! Now, tell me what I say! Hah, hah, hah! (*Withdraws head back offstage*) Sure got them petty tyrants straight at the unemployment office today. (*Dripping contempt*) Wanted me to snatch up one of them jive jobs they try to palm off on ya. I told 'em no thanks!—Shove it! (*Re-entering, busily buttoning elegantly pleated shirt*) If they can't find me something in my field, up to my standards, forgit it! . . . Damn, act like they payin you money out their own pockets . . . Whatcha got to eat, Ellie? . . . I'm scarfy as a bear. In fact—with a little salt 'n pepper, I could devour one of you—or both between a double-decker! (*Descends upon them to illustrate playfully. Pulls up short on noticing their tears for the first time*) Hey? . . . What'sa matter . . . ? What's up? (*They fail to respond.*) Is it the kids? (*They shake heads negatively.*) Somebody sick down home? (*Fearfully*) Nothing's wrong wit mother? (*They shake heads again.*) Roy or Jim in jail? . . . Arthur or Ben lose their jobs? (*Another double headshake.*) Tell me, I wanta know! Everything was fine this morning. Somp'um musta happened since. Come on, what is it?

ELLIE. Should we tell him, Vi?

VI. I don't know . . . No use gitting him worried and upset . . .

ELLIE (*Sighing heavily*). Maybe we better. He's got to find out sooner or later.

JUNIE. What are you crying for?

ELLIE. Our bosses—Mr. and Mrs. Harrison, Junie . . .

JUNIE. Mr. and Mrs. Harrison . . . ? (*Suddenly relieved; amused and sardonic*) What happened? They escape from a car wreck—UNHURT?

ELLIE (*failing to grasp sarcasm*). No.

JUNIE (*returning to shirt-buttoning*). Did you just git disappointing news flashes they gon live forever?

VI (*also misreading him*). No, June.

JUNIE. Well, what then? . . . I don't get it.

ELLIE. They's getting a divorce . . .

JUNIE. A what—?

VI. A divorce.

JUNIE. Why?

ELLIE. 'Cause Mr. Harrison caught her wit a man.

JUNIE. Well, it's not the first time 'cording to you.

ELLIE. The other times wasn't wit his best friend.

JUNIE. His best friend? Wheeee! Boy, she really did it up this time . . . Her previous excursions were restricted to his casual acquaintances! . . . But why the hell should he be so upset? He's put up wit all the rest. This only means she's gitting closer to home. Maybe next time it'll be him, ha, ha, ha . . .

ELLIE (*reprimandingly*). It's no joke, Junie.

JUNIE (*exiting into bathroom*). How'd it happen?

ELLIE. (*flaring at the memory*). Just walked in and caught 'em in his own bedroom!

VI. (*even more outraged*). Was that dirty dog, Mr. Heller, lives on the nineteenth floor of the same building!

ELLIE (*anger mounting*). I warned her to be careful when she first started messing with him. I told her Mr. Harrison was really gon kick her out if he found out, but she'd have the snake sneak in sometimes soon as Mr. Harrison left! Even had nerve to invite him to chaperone his wife back later in the evening for a lil after-dinner snack!

JUNIE (*re-entering*). What's a little exchange of pleasantries among rich friends, bosom buddies? Now, all Harrison has to do is return the favor and even things up.

VI. She really cooked her goose this time.

JUNIE. Good for her.

ELLIE. Good . . . ?

JUNIE. Sure—What'd she 'spect? To wait 'till she hauled some cat into bed right next to her old man befo' he got the message?

VI. They is gitting a *divorce*, Junie!

JUNIE (*sauntering over to fruit bowl atop refrigerator*). That's all? . . . I'm surprised I didn't read headlines 'bout a double murder and one suicide . . . But I forgot!—that's our soul folk's method of clearing up little gummy problems like that—that is, *minus* the suicide bit.

ELLIE. *They's breaking up their home, Junie!*

JUNIE (*biting into apple selected from bowl*). They'll learn to live wit it . . . Might even git to like the idea.

VI. And the chillun?

JUNIE. Delicate lil boobies will receive nice fat allowances to ease the pain until they grow up to take over the world.

ELLIE. Is that all you feel at a time like this, boy?

VI. Disastrous, that's what it is!

ELLIE. Tragicull 'n unfair!

JUNIE. Is this what you boohooing 'bout?

ELLIE. Could you think of anything worser?

JUNIE. But, why?

ELLIE. 'Cause this time we *know he means business, Junie!* Ain't no false alarm like them other times. We were there, right there! . . . Had a feeling somp'um was gon happen soon as I answered the door and let Mr. Heller in! Like chilly pneumonia on top a breeze . . . Miss Harrison tole me she didn't wanta be disturbed for the rest of the afternoon. Well, she was disturbed all right! They musta fell asleep 'cause Mr. Harrison even got home late and still caught 'em . . .

JUNIE. Couldn't you have interrupted their togetherness and sounded a timely danger warning?

ELLIE. We didn't hear him. I was in the kitchen, Vi down

in the basement ironing. I didn't know Mr. Harrison had come in 'till I heard screaming from the bedroom. But soon as I did, I called Vi and me and her tipped down the hall and heard Mr. Harrison order Mr. Heller to put his clothes back on and stop considering hisself a friend for the rest of his life! " 'N you—slut! Pack up and git out soon as you find a suitable apartment." . . . Then he invited me and Vi into the room and told us he was divorcing her . . . That man was hurt, Junie, hurt deep! Could see it in his eyes . . . Like a little boy, so sad he made you wanta grab hold his head and rock him in your arms like a baby.

VI. Miss Harrison looked a sight herself, po' thing! Like a lil girl caught stealing crackers out the cookie jar.

ELLIE. I almost crowned ole back-stabber Heller! Brushing 'gainst me on his way out!

JUNIE. Shoulda pinned a medal on him as he flew by. Escaping wit head still on shoulder and no bullet holes dotting his chest.

ELLIE. The skunk really left us all too high and dry for that, Junie . . . Oh, don't think it wouldn't broke your heart, too, nephew . . . Sneaky rascal gone, rest of us in sorrow, tears pouring down our faces 'n me and Vi jist begging and begging . . . "Y'all please think twice befo' you act rash and do anything you'll be sorry for. You love each other—and who's in better position than Vi and me to know how much you love each other—"

VI. 'Course she love him, just can't help herself.

ELLIE. "—When two hearts love each other as much as we know y'all do, they better take whole lots of time befo' doing something so awful as breaking up a marriage—even if it ain't hunert-percent perfect. Think about your reputation and the scandal this will cause Mr. Harrison. Jist 'bout kill your po' mother—her wit her blood pressure, artritis, gout, heart tickle 'n everything. But most of all, don't orphan the kids! Kids come first. Dear lil angels! Just innocents looking on gitting hurt in ways they can't understand."

JUNIE. You told 'em this, Ellie?

ELLIE. Love conquers all, Junie.

JUNIE. Wit your assistance, Vi?

VI. As much as I could deliver, Junie.

JUNIE. And what impression did your tender concern have on the bereaved couple?

ELLIE. Mr. Harrison said he understood 'n appreciated our feelings and was very grateful for our kindly advice—but he was sorry, his mind was made up. She'd gone too far and he couldn't forgive her—not EVER! . . . We might judge him a harsh, vindicty man, he said, but he couldn't bring hisself to do it. Even apologized to us for being so cruel.

JUNIE (*continuing his slow boil*). You accepted his apology, Vi?

VI. I should say not. I pleaded wit him agin to think it over for sake of home, family and good name!

JUNIE. Well of all the goddamn things I ever heard!

ELLIE. (*heartened by his support*). I'm telling ya!

VI. I knew it was gon happen if she kept on like she did!

ELLIE. Just wouldn't listen!

JUNIE. It's a disgrace!

ELLIE. Ain't the word!

VI. Lot worse than that!

JUNIE. Did you both plop to your knees begging him to give her another chance?

VI. NO!—but we woulda if we'd thought about it! Why didn't we, Ellie?

ELLIE. Things happened so fast—

JUNIE. Never have I been so humiliated in all my life—!

VI. (*self-disgusted by their glaring omission*). No excuse not thinking 'bout it, Ellie!

ELLIE. Certainly ain't

JUNIE. What about your pride—?

VI. You right! Musta been false pride kept us from dropping to our knees!

JUNIE. Acting like imbeciles! Crying your heart out 'cause Massa and Mistress are gon break up housekeeping! Maybe I oughta go beat up the adulterous rat crawling in between the sheets! (*Pacing up and down in angry indignation as they sit stunned*) Here we are—Africa rising to its place in the sun wit prime ministers and other dignitaries taking seats around the international conference table—us here fighting for our rights like never before, changing the whole image, dumping stereo-types behind us and replacing 'em wit new images of dignity and dimension—and I come home and find my own aunts, sisters of my mother, daughters of my grandpa who never took crap off no cracker even though he did live on a plantation—drowning themselves in tears jist 'cause boss man is gonna kick boss lady out on her nose! Maybe *Gone With the Wind* was accurate! Maybe we jist can't help "Miss Scarrrrrlet-ing" and "Oh Lawdying" every time mistress white gets a splinter in her pinky. That's what *I'm* talking about.

VI. Ain't you got no feelings, boy?

JUNIE. Feelings? . . . So you work every day in their kitchen, Ellie, and every Thursday you wash their stinky clothes, Vi. But that don't mean they're paying you to bleed from their scratches! . . . Look—don't get me wrong—I'm not blaming you for being domestics. It's an honorable job. It's the only kind available sometimes, and it carries no stigma in itself—but that's all it is, *a job*! An exchange of work for pay! *Bad pay at that*! Which is all the more reason why you shouldn't give a damn whether the Harrisons kick, kill or mangle each other!

ELLIE. You gotta care, Junie—

JUNIE. "Breaking up home and family!"—Why I've seen both of you ditch two husbands apiece and itching to send third ones packing if they don't toe the line. You don't even cry over that!

ELLIE. Don't have time to—

JUNIE. Boy, if some gray cat was peeping in on you, he'da sprinted back home and wrote five *Uncle Tom's Cabins* and ten "Old Black Joes"!

ELLIE. Wait a minute, now—

JUNIE. I never heard you shedding such tragic tears when your own lil crumb-crushers suffered through fatherless periods! All you grumbled was "good riddance, they better off wit'out the sonsabitches!" . . . Maybe Harrisons' tots will make out just as well. They got puny lil advantages of millions of dollars and slightly less parched skins!

VI. Show some tenderness, boy. Ain't human not to trouble over our bosses' sorrows—

JUNIE. That's what shames me. I gave you credit for more integrity. Didn't figger you had chalk streaks in ya. You oughta be shamed for *yourselves*!

ELLIE. And done what?

JUNIE. NOTHING!—Shoulda told 'em their sticky mess is their own mud puddle. You neutrals. Just work there. Aren't interested in what they do!

ELLIE. That wouldn't be expressing our deepest sentiments—

JUNIE. I'm ashamed you even had any "sentiments"! . . . Look, it's hopeless, I'm not getting anywhere trying to make you understand . . . I'm going out for a whiff of fresh air! (*Rushes to exit.*)

ELLIE. Come back here, boy!

JUNIE (*stopping at door*). What? To watch you blubber over Massa? No thanks!

ELLIE. I said come here, you hear me talking to you!

VI. You still ain't too big to git yourself slapped down!

ELLIE. Your ma gave us right any time we saw fit!

(*He returns reluctantly. An uneasy silence prevails.*)

ELLIE. Better git yourself somp'um to eat. (*rises, taking off coat.*)

JUNIE (*sulking*). I lost my appetite.

ELLIE (*hanging coat up*). What you want?

JUNIE. I told you I'm not hungry anymore.

VI. *We* made you lose your appetite . . . ?

(*He doesn't reply.*)

ELLIE. What did you crave befo' you lost it?

JUNIE. Anything you had cooked. Didn't have anything special in mind . . .

ELLIE (*offhandedly*). Steak? . . . T-Bone? . . . Porterhouse? . . . Filet . . . ?

JUNIE. No . . . I didn't particularly have steak in mind.

VI. Been eating too many lately, huh?

JUNIE. Just kinda tired of 'em, that's all.

ELLIE. How bout some chicken then . . . ? Roast beef? . . . Lobster? . . . Squab? Duck, or something?

JUNIE (*nettled*). All I wanted was some food, Ellie! . . . In fact, I really had a hankering for some plain ole collard greens, neck bones or ham hocks . . .

ELLIE. Good eatin', boy. Glad to hear that. Means that high-class digestion hasn't spoiled your taste buds yet . . . But if you want that rich, choice food, you welcome to it—

JUNIE. I know that, Ellie!

ELLIE. It's in the freezer for you, go and look.

JUNIE. I don't hafta, Ellie, I know—

ELLIE. Go look anyway.

JUNIE (*goes and opens refrigerator door*). It's there, Ellie, I didn't need to look.

VI. Come here for a second, Junie, got something on your pants leg. (*He obeys. She picks a piece of lint off trousers, then rubs material admiringly.*) Pants to your suit, ain't they? . . . Sure is a fine suit to be trotting off to the unemployment office . . . Which one-r the other you gon wear tonight when you try to con that girl outa her virginity—if she still got it?—The gray one? Brown one? The tweed? Or maybe you gon git sporty and strut that snazzy plaid jacket and them tight light pants? If not—which jacket and which pants?

ELLIE. Slept good last night, nephew? Or maybe you gitting tired of that foam rubber mattress and sheep fur blanket?

VI. How do them fine college queens and snooty office girls like the furniture they half see when you sneak 'em in here late at night? Surprised to see such fancy stuff in a beat-up ole flat, ain't they? But it helps you put 'em at ease, don't it? I bet even those sweet lil white ones are impressed by your class?

JUNIE (*indignantly*). That's not fair, Vi—

ELLIE. When last time you bought any food in this house, boy?

JUNIE. Ellie, you know—

ELLIE. When, Junie?

JUNIE. Not since I been here, but—

VI. And your last piece of clothes?

JUNIE (*more indignant*). I bought some underwear last week, Vi!

VI. I mean clothes you wear on top, Junie. Shirts, pants, jackets, coats?

JUNIE (*squirming*). You—you know I haven't, Vi—

ELLIE. Buy anything else in your room besides that tiny, midget frame for your mama's picture?

JUNIE. All right. I know I'm indebted to ya. You don't have to rub it in. I'll make it up to you when I git on my feet and *fulfill* my potential . . . But that's not the point!

ELLIE. You ain't indebted to us, Junie.

JUNIE. Yes, I am, I know it, I thank you for it.

ELLIE. Don't hafta thank us—

JUNIE. But that's not the issue! Despite your benevolence, I refuse to let you blackmail my principle, slapping me in the face wit how good you been to me during my temporary outta work period! I'm talking to you now, 'bout something above our personal relationship. Pride—Race—Dignity—

ELLIE. What's gon happen to me and Vi's dignity if Mr. Harrison throws Mrs. Harrison out on her nose as you put it?

JUNIE. Git another job! You not dependent on them. You young, healthy, in the prime of life . . . In fact—I've always wondered why you stagnate as domestics when you're trained and qualified to do something better and more dignified.

ELLIE. Glad you brought that up. Know why I'm not breaking my back as a practical nurse and Vi's not frying hair—'cept on the side? . . . Cause the work's too hard, the money ain't worth it and there's not much room for advancement—

JUNIE. Where kin you advance as a domestic? From kitchen to closet?

ELLIE (*refusing to be provoked, continuing evenly*). Besides, when I started working for the Harrisons, Junie, Mr. Harrison vowed that he would support me for life if I stayed with 'em until his daughter Sandy, his oldest child, reached ten years old.

JUNIE. Bully for him! He'll build ya a little cottage backa the penthouse garage!

ELLIE (*still unruffled*). Mr. Harrison is strictly a man of his word, Junie. Which means that even if I left one day after Sandy made ten, he owes me some money every week or every month as long as I live . . . . Sandy is *nine*, Junie, N-I-N-E! If I don't last another year, the deal is off.

JUNIE. Don't need no handouts! Even hearing you say you want any makes me shame!

ELLIE. Done used that word quite a lot, boy. You shamed of us? . . . Well, git slapped in the face wit this! How shame you gon be when you hafta git outta here and hustle yourself a job?—*any job*?

JUNIE. Huh?

ELLIE. How shame you gon be when you start getting raggedy and all them foxy girls are no longer impressed bout how slick, smooth and pretty you look? When you stop being one-r the best dressed black boys in New York City?

JUNIE. Don't get you, Ellie.

ELLIE. I know you went to college for a coupler years, boy, but I thought you still had some sense, or I woulda told you . . .

VI. Every time you bite into one of them big tender juicy steaks and chaw it down into your belly, ever think where it's coming from?

ELLIE. The Harrisons.

VI. Every time you lay one of them young gals down in that plush soft bed of yours and hear her sigh in luxury, ever think 'bout who you owe it to?

ELLIE. The Harrisons.

VI. When you swoop down home to that run-down house your ma and pa rent, latch eyes on all that fine furniture there, you ever think who's responsible?

ELLIE. The Harrisons.

VI. You ain't bought a suit or piece of clothes in five years and none of the other four men in this family have . . . . Why not?

ELLIE. Mr. Harrison

VI. Junie, you is a fine, choice hunk of chocolate pigmeat, pretty as a new-minted penny and slick 'nuff to suck sugar outta gingerbread wit'out it losing its flavor—but the Harrisons ain't hardly elected you no favorite pinup boy to introduce to Santa Claus. Took a heap of pow'ful coaxing to win you such splendid sponsorship and wealthy commissions, 'cause waiting for the Harrisons to voluntarily *donate* their Christian charity is one sure way of landing headfirst in the poorhouse dungeon . . . Who runs the Harrison's house, Junie?

JUNIE. Ellie . . . I guess . . . ?

ELLIE. From top to bottom. I cook the food, scrub the floor, open the doors, serve the tables, answer the phones, dust the furniture, raise the children, lay out the clothes, greet the guests, fix the drinks and dump the garbage—all for bad pay as you said . . . You right, Junie, money I git in my envelope ain't worth the time 'n the headache. . . . *But—God Helps Those Who Help Themselves* . . . I also *order* the food, estimate the credit, *pay* the bills and *balance* the budget. Which means that each steak I order for them, befo' butcher carves cow, I done reserved *two* for myself. Miss Harrison wouldn't know how much steak cost and Mr. Harrison so loaded, he writes me a check wit'out even looking . . . Every once in a full moon they git so good-hearted and tell me take some leftovers home, but by that time my freezer and pantry is already fuller than theirs . . . Every one of them high-price suits I lay on you haven't been worn more than once and some of 'em not at all. You lucky to be same size as Mr. Harrison, Junie. He don't know how much clothes he got in his wardrobe, which is why *yours* is as big as *his*. Jim, Roy, Arthur and Ben can't even fit into the man's clothes, but that still don't stop 'em from cutting, shortening, altering and stretching 'em to fit. Roy almost ruined his feet trying to wear the man's shoes . . . Now, I've had a perfect record keeping y'all elegantly dressed and stylishly fashion-plated—'cept that time Mr. Harrison caught me off guard asking: "Ellie, where's my brown suit?" "In the cleaners," I told him and had to snatch it off your hanger and smuggle it back—temporarily.

VI. If y'all warn't so lucky and *Mrs.* Harrison so skinny and tacky-flashy, Ellie and I would also be best dressed domestics of the year.

ELLIE. Which, if you didn't notice, is what your Aunt Doris was—rest her soul—when we laid her in her grave, decked out in the costliest, ritziest, most expensest nightgown the good Lord ever waited to feast his eyes on . . . As for furniture, we could move out his whole house in one day if we had to.

VI. Which is what we did when they moved from the old penthouse and we hired us a moving van to haul 'nuff pieces to furnish both our own apartments and still had enough to ship a living room set down home to your ma. Mr. Harrison told us to donate the stuff to charity. We did—US!

ELLIE. And all our bills I add on to their bills—Jim even tried to git me to sneak in his car note, but that was going too far—all the deluxe plane tickets your ma jet up here on every year, weekly prescriptions filled on their tab, tons of laundry cleaned along wit theirs and a thousand other services and I'm earning me quite a bonus along with my bad pay. It's the BONUS that counts, Junie. Total it up for nine years and I'd be losing money on any other job. Now Vi and I, after cutting cane, picking rice and shucking corn befo' we could braid our hair in pigtails, figure we just gitting back what's owed us . . . But, if Mr. Harrison boots Mrs. Harrison out on her tocus, the party's over. He's not gon need us. Miss Harrison ain't got a copper cent of her own. Anyway, the setup won't be as ripe for picking. My bonus is suddenly cut off and out the window go my pension.

VI. Suppose we did git us another job wit one-r them penny-pinching old misers hiding behind cupboards watching whether you stealing sugar cubes? Wit our fringe benefits choked off, we'd fall down so quick to a style of living we ain't been used to for a long time, it would make your head swim. I don't think we could stand it . . . Could you?

ELLIE. So when me and Vi saw our pigeons scampering out the window for good today, tears started flowing like rain. The first tear trickle out my eyes had a roast in it.

VI. Mine was a chicken.

ELLIE. Second had a crate of eggs.

VI. Mine a whole pig.

ELLIE. Third an oriental rug.

VI. A continental couch.

ELLIE. Fourth an overcoat for Arthur.

VI. A bathrobe for Ben.

ELLIE. The fifth one had my gas, electric and telephone bills in it.

VI. Three months' rent, Lord!

ELLIE. The faster the stream started gushing, the faster them nightmares crowded my eyes until I coulda flooded 'em 'nuff water to swim in. Every time I pleaded "Think of your love!"—

VI. She meant think 'bout our bills.

ELLIE. Every time I begged "Don't crack up the home!"—

VI. It meant please keep *ours* cemented together!

ELLIE. "Don't victim the chillun!"—

VI. By all means insure the happiness of *our* lil darlings!

ELLIE. They didn't know 'bout these eyeball visions—they only see what they see 'n hear what they hear—and that's okey-dokey wit me—but I was gitting these watery pictures in my mind 'n feeling a giant-size sickness in my gut! Few seconds longer and I woulda been down on my knees witout even thinking 'bout it.

VI. If I didn't beat ya to the floor!

ELLIE. Junie—maybe we shoulda given a little more thought to that—whatchamacallit?—"image" of yours. Maybe we did dishonor Africa, embarrass the NAACP, are hopelessly behind time and scandalously outdated. But we didn't have too much time to think . . . Now that you know the whole truth, you have a right to disown us. We hardly worthy of your respect . . . But when I thought 'bout that new topcoat wit the velvet-trimmed collar I jest packed to bring you (*tears begin to re-form.*) . . . coupler new cashmere sweaters, brand new slacks, a shiny new attaché case for your appointments, and a scrumptious new collapsible swimming pool I promised your ma for her backyard—I couldn't help but cry.

(VI *has joined her in a double torrent.*)

JUNIE (*back turned to audience*). Vi?

VI. What?

JUNIE. Pass me the handkerchief . . .

(*He receives it and joins the table—a moist-faced trio.* AR-THUR, ELLIE's *husband, walks in finding them thus.*)

ARTHUR (*beelining for bathroom*). Even' everybody . . . (*Hearing no response, stops before entering john*) Hey, what's the matter? What you three looking like somebody died for?

ELLIE. It's the Harrisons, Arthur. Mr. Harrison getting a divorce.

ARTHUR. Aww, not agin!

VI. He really means it this time, Arthur.

ARTHUR. He does?

ELLIE. Yes, Jesus.

ARTHUR. You sure?

VI. Caught her dead to rights.

ARTHUR (*indignant*). But he can't do that!

VI. He is.

ARTHUR. What 'bout us?

JUNIE. What you think we grieving bout?

ARTHUR. Well, just don't sit there! What we gon do?

ELLIE. Done it, didn't work.

ARTHUR. Not at all?

ELLIE. Nope.

ARTHUR. Not even a little bit?

ELLIE. Not one lousy inch.

ARTHUR (*crestfallen*). Make room for me.

(*They provide space. He sits, completing the depressed quartet.*)

JUNIE (*suddenly jolted with an idea*). Ellie! Wait! Why don't you tell him to take her on a private ocean cruise, just the two of 'em, so they kin recapture the thrill for one another!

ELLIE. He did that already, until somebody told him she was cuddling up with the ship stoker in the engine room.

JUNIE (*undaunted*). Advise him to spend less time wit his business and more with her. She wouldn't need to look outside for satisfaction!

ELLIE. Tried that too, but his business like to fell apart and he caught her making eyes at the messenger bringing him the news.

JUNIE (*desperate*). Convince him she's sick! It's not her fault, he should send her to a psychiatrist!

ELLIE. Already did . . . till he found out she was doing more than talking on the couch.

JUNIE. What 'bout a twenty-four hour guard on her? That won't give her so many opportunities!

ELLIE. What about guards? They men too.

JUNIE (*in angry frustration*). Well, damn, git her a chastity belt and lock her up!

ELLIE. Locks, also, have been known to be picked.

ARTHUR (*inspired by a brilliant solution*). Wait! I got it! I got it! . . . Tell him you know of some steady-ready goofer dust . . . or jooger-mooger saltpeter to cool her down. And you'll slip it in her food every day!

ELLIE. Wouldn't work . . . Way her glands function, probably jazz her up like a spanish fly.

VI. Let's face it, it's all over. We just gotta tuck in our belts, stare the future square in the eye and git ready for depression. It's not gon do us no good to whine over spilt clabber . . . . You jist better start scrounging 'round for that job, Junie. Befo' you git chance to sneeze, we will have had it. And call up—No! Write your ma and tell her not to come up this year.

ELLIE. Arthur, best you scrape up another job to moonlight wit the one you got. We facing some scuffling days 'head us.

VI. Well . . . I better git out of here and go warn my own crew bout Satan's retribution . . . Well . . . it was good while it lasted, Ellie . . .

ELLIE. Real good.

(*They glance at each other and another deluge starts. The phone interrupts, but no one bothers to answer. Finally,* AR-

THUR *rises and exits in the direction of peals. During his absence, the disconsolate trio remains silent.*)

ARTHUR (*re-entering slowly, treading each step with the deliberateness of a man fearful of cracking eggs*). That—was—Mr. Harrison—He said—thank both of you for desperately trying to —shock him to his senses—pry open his eyes to the light—and rescue his house from collapsing—He and Mrs. Harrison, after stren'ous consideration, are gonna stick it out together! (*A stunned moment of absolute silence prevails, finally broken by an earsplitting, exultant whoop which erupts simultaneously from each member of the quartet. They spring to their feet, embracing and prancing around the room, crying through laughter.* ARTHUR *simmers down first, tries to recapture their attention.*) Ellie . . . Ellie, Mr. Harrison requests if it's not too much trouble, he'd like for you to come over and stay wit Sandy and Snookie while he and Mrs. Harrison go out and celebrate their reunion, and it's too late to git a baby-sitter.

ELLIE. If it's all right? . . . Tell him I'm climbing on a broomstick, then shuttling to a jet! (ARTHUR *starts to exit.*) Wait a minute! Waaaait a minute! Hold on!—I must be crazy! Don't tell him that . . . Tell him he knows very well it's after my working hours and I'm not paid to baby-sit and since I've already made plans for the evening, I'll be glad to do it for double overtime, two extra days' pay and triple time off to recuperate from the imposition . . . . And, Arthur! . . . Kinda suggest that *you* is a little peeved 'cause he's interrupting me from taking care of something important for you. He might toss in a day for your suffering.

ARTHUR. He'll swear he was snatching you away from my deathbed, guarding my door 'gainst Lucifer busting through! (*Exits.*)

ELLIE. I'd better throw on some more clothes. (*Exits.*)

JUNIE. Vi, what you s'pose granpa would say bout his chillun if he got a breathing spell in between dodging pitchforks and sidestepping the fiery flames?

VI. Shame on you, boy, Papa ain't near 'bouts doing no ducking 'n dodging. Why he's right up there plunked down safe, snuggled up tight besides the good Lord's righteous throne.

ARTHUR (re-entering). He was real sorry. 'If it wasn't such a special occasion, he wouldn't bother us!' (They guffaw heartily.)

JUNIE. This IS a special occasion! . . . (Grandly) Arthur, break out a flagon of the latest champagne Ellie brought us.

ARTHUR. At your service, Massa Junie.

JUNIE. The 1947! That was a good year. Not the fifty, which was bad! (ARTHUR moves to refrigerator. ELLIE returns, ready to depart.) Wait for a drink, auntie. We've gotta celebrate our resurrection. A toast of deliverance. (ARTHUR presents JUNIE with champagne, points out 1947 label, then gets goblets from shelf. JUNIE pours. They lift goblets.) First! . . . To the victors and the vanquished, the top dog and the bottom dog! Sometimes it's hard to tell which is which . . . !

VI. If nothing else, boy, education did teach you how to sling around some choice conversation.

ARTHUR. Ain't hardly the way I heard the slinging described. (They all laugh.)

JUNIE. Second! . . . To my two cagey aunts. May they continue to prevail in times of distress! . . . Third! . . . To the Harrisons . . . . May they endure forever in marital bliss! Cheers to 'em! (After finishing drink, ELLIE moves to exit through hallway door. JUNIE stops her.) Oh, Ellie . . . Why don't you start fattening Mr. Harrison up. Please slip some more potatoes and starch into his menu. I've gained a few pounds and the clothes are gitting a little tight. Don't you think it's time for him to plumpen up a bit, stick on a little weight? . . .

ELLIE. Would ten pounds do?

JUNIE. Perfect! (Again she moves to exit.) And Ellie! . . .

Kinda hint 'round to him that fashions is changing. I wouldn't want him to fall behind in the latest styles . . .

VI (*lifting goblet, along with* ARTHUR *and* ELLIE, *in a final toast*). There's hope, Junie. You'll make it, boy, you'll make it . . .

CURTAIN

Day of Absence

A Satirical Fantasy

DOUGLAS TURNER WARD

The time is now.

Play opens in unnamed Southern town of medium popula-tion on a somnolent cracker morning—meaning no matter the early temperature, it's gonna get hot. The hamlet is just be-ginning to rouse itself from the sleepy lassitude of night.

NOTES ON PRODUCTION: No scenery is necessary—only actors shifting in and out on an almost bare stage and freezing into immobility as focuses change or blackouts occur.

Play is conceived for performance by a Negro cast, a reverse minstrel show done in white face. Logically, it might also be performed by whites—at their own risk. If any producer is faced with choosing between opposite hues, author strongly suggests: "Go 'long wit the blacks—besides all else, they need the work more."

If acted by the latter, race members are urged to go for broke, yet cautioned not to ham it up too broadly. In fact—it just might be more effective if they aspire to serious tragedy. Only qualification needed for Caucasian casting is that the company fit a uniform pattern—insipid white.

Before any horrifying discrimination doubts arise, I hasten to add that a bona fide white actor should be cast as the ANNOUNCER *in all productions, likewise a Negro thespian in pure native black as* RASTUS. *This will truly subvert any charge that the production is unintegrated.*

All props, except essential items (chairs, brooms, rags, mop, debris) should be imaginary (phones, switchboard, mikes, eating utensils, food, etc.). Actors should indicate their presence through mime.

The cast of characters develops as the play progresses. In the interest of economical casting, actors should double or triple in roles wherever possible

*PRODUCTION CONCEPT: This is a red-white-and-blue play—meaning that the entire production should be designed around the basic color scheme of our patriotic trinity. Lighting should illustrate, highlight, and detail time, action, and mood—opening scenes stage-lit with white rays of morning, transforming to panic reds of afternoon, flowing into ominous blues of evening. Costuming should be orchestrated around the same color scheme. In addition, subsidiary usage of grays, khakis, yellows, pinks, and patterns of stars and bars should be employed. All actors (*ANNOUNCERS *and* RASTUS *excepted, of course) should wear white shoes or sneakers, and all women characters clothed in knee-length frocks should wear white stockings. Blond wigs, both for males and females, can be used in selected instances. Makeup should have uniform consistency, with individual touches thrown in to enhance personal identity.*

SAMPLE MODELS OF MAKEUP AND COSTUMING:

MARY: *Kewpie-doll face, ruby-red lips painted to valentine pursing, moon-shaped rough circles implanted on each cheek, blond wig of fat flowing ringlets, dazzling ankle-length snow-white nightie.*

MAYOR:*Seersucker white ensemble, ten-gallon hat, red string tie, and blue belt.*

CLEM: *Khaki pants, bareheaded, and blond.*

LUKE: *Blue work jeans, strawhatted.*

CLUB WOMAN: *Yellow dress patterned with symbols of Dixie, gray hat.*

CLAN: *A veritable, riotous advertisement of red-white-and-blue combinations with stars and bars tossed in.*

PIOUS: *White ministerial garb with black cleric's color topping his snow-white shirt.*

OPERATORS: *All in red with different color wigs.*

All other characters should be carefully defined through costuming which typifies their identity.

SCENE: Street.

TIME: Early morning.

CLEM (*sitting under a sign suspended by invisible wires and bold-printed with the lettering:*"STORE"). Morning, Luke . . .

LUKE (*sitting a few paces away under an identical sign*). Morning, Clem . . .

CLEM. Gon be a hot day.

LUKE. Looks that way . . .

CLEM. Might rain though . . .

LUKE. Might.

CLEM. Hope it does . . .

LUKE. Me too . . .

CLEM. Farmers could use a little wet spell for a change . . . How's the Missis?

LUKE. Same.

CLEM. 'N the kids?

LUKE. Them too . . . How's yourns?

CLEM. Fine, thank you . . . (*They both lapse into drowsy silence, waving lethargically from time to time at imaginary passersby.*) Hi, Joe . . .

LUKE. Joe . . .

CLEM. How'd it go yesterday, Luke?

LUKE. Fair.

CLEM. Same wit me . . . Business don't seem to git no better or no worse. Guess we in a rut, Luke, don't it 'pear that way to you?—Morning, Ma'm.

LUKE. Morning . . .

CLEM. Tried display, sales, advertisement, stamps—everything —yet merchandising stumbles 'round in the same old groove. . . . But—that's better than plunging downwards, I reckon.

LUKE. Guess it is.

CLEM. Morning, Bret. How's the family? . . . That's good.

LUKE. Bret—

CLEM. Morning, Sue.

LUKE. How do, Sue.

CLEM (*staring after her*). Fine hunk of woman.

LUKE. Sure is.

CLEM. Wonder if it's any good?

LUKE. Bet it is.

CLEM. Sure like to find out!

LUKE. So would I.

CLEM. You ever try?

LUKE. Never did . . .

CLEM. Morning, Gus . . .

LUKE. Howdy, Gus.

CLEM. Fine, thank you. (*They lapse into silence again.* CLEM *rouses himself slowly, begins to look around quizzically.*) Luke . . . ?

LUKE. Huh?

CLEM. Do you . . . er, er—feel anything—funny . . . ?

LUKE. Like what?

CLEM. Like . . . er—something—strange?

LUKE. I dunno . . . haven't thought about it.

CLEM. I mean . . . like something's wrong—outta place, unusual?

LUKE. I don't know . . . What you got in mind?

CLEM. Nothing . . . just that—just that—like somp'um's outta
kilter. I got a funny feeling somp'um's not up to snuff. Can't
figger out what it is . . .

LUKE. Maybe it's in your haid . . .

CLEM. No, not like that . . . Like somp'um's happened—or
happening—gone haywire, loony.

LUKE. Well, don't worry 'bout it, it'll pass.

CLEM. Guess you right (*attempts return to somnolence but
doesn't succeed*). I'm sorry, Luke, but you sure you don't feel
nothing peculiar . . . ?

LUKE (*slightly irked*). Toss it out your mind, Clem! We got
a long day ahead of us. If something's wrong, you'll know 'bout
it in due time. No use worrying about it 'till it comes and if
it's coming, it will. Now, relax!

CLEM. All right, you right . . . Hi, Margie . . .

LUKE. Marge.

CLEM (*unable to control himself*). Luke, I don't give a damn
what you say. Somp'um's topsy-turvy, I just know it!

LUKE (*increasingly irritated*). Now look here, Clem—it's a
bright day, it looks like it's gon git hotter. You say the wife
and kids are fine and the business is no better or no worse?
Well, what else could be wrong? . . . If somp'um's gon happen,
it's gon happen anyway and there ain't a damn fool thing you
kin do to stop it! So you ain't helping me, yourself or nobody
else by thinking 'bout it. It's not gon be no better or no worse
when it gits here. It'll come to you when it gits ready to come
and it's gon be the same whether you worry about it or not.
So stop letting it upset you! (LUKE *settles back in his chair.*
CLEM *does likewise.* LUKE *shuts his eyes. After a few moments,*

they reopen. He forces them shut again. They reopen in greater curiosity. Finally, he rises slowly to an upright position in the chair, looks around frowningly. Turns slowly to CLEM.) Clem? . . . You know something? . . . Somp'um is peculiar . . .

CLEM (*vindicated*). I knew it, Luke! I jist knew it! Ever since we been sitting here, I been having that feeling!

(*Scene is blacked out abruptly. Lights rise on another section of the stage where a young couple lie in bed under an invisible wire-suspension sign lettered* "HOME." *Loud, insistent sounds of baby yells are heard.* JOHN, *the husband, turns over trying to ignore the cries;* MARY, *the wife, is undisturbed.* JOHN'S *efforts are futile; the cries continue until they cannot be denied. He bolts upright, jumps out of bed, and disappears offstage. Returns quickly and tries to rouse* MARY.)

JOHN. Mary . . . (*Nudges her, pushes her, yells into her ear, but she fails to respond*) Mary, get up . . . Get up!

MARY. Ummm . . . (*Shrugs away, still sleeping.*)

JOHN. GET UP!

MARY. Ummmmmmmmmm!

JOHN. Don't you hear the baby's bawling? . . . NOW GET UP!

MARY (*mumbling drowsily*). What baby . . . whose baby . . . ?

JOHN. Yours!

MARY. Mine? That's ridiculous . . . what'd you say . . . ? Somebody's baby bawling? . . . How could that be so? (*Hearing screams*) Who's crying? Somebody's crying! . . . What's crying? . . . *Where's Lula?*

JOHN. I don't know. You better get up.

MARY. That's outrageous! . . . What time is it?

JOHN. Late 'nuff! Now rise up!

MARY. You must be joking . . . I'm sure I still have four or five hours' sleep in store—even more after that head-splittin' blowout last night . . . (*Tumbles back under covers.*)

JOHN. Nobody told you to gulp those last six bourbons—

MARY. Don't tell me how many bourbons to swallow, not

after you guzzled the whole stinking bar! . . . Get up? . . . You must be cracked . . . Where's Lula? She must be here, she always is . . .

JOHN. Well, she ain't here yet, so get up and muzzle that brat before she does drive me cuckoo!

MARY (*springing upright, finally realizing gravity of situation*). Whaddaya mean Lula's not here? She's always here, she must be here . . . Where else kin she be? She supposed to be . . . She just can't *not* be here—call her!

(*Blackout as* JOHN *rushes offstage. Scene shifts to a trio of* TELEPHONE OPERATORS *perched on stools before imaginary switchboards. Chaos and bedlam are taking place to the sound of buzzes. Effect of following dialogue should simulate rising pandemonium.*)

FIRST OPERATOR. The line is busy—
SECOND OPERATOR. Line is busy—
THIRD OPERATOR. Is busy—
FIRST OPERATOR. Doing best we can—
SECOND OPERATOR. Having difficulty—
THIRD OPERATOR. Soon as possible—
FIRST OPERATOR. Just one moment—
SECOND OPERATOR. Would you hold on—
THIRD OPERATOR. Awful sorry, madam—
FIRST OPERATOR. Would you hold on, please—
SECOND OPERATOR. Just a second, please—
THIRD OPERATOR. Please hold on, please—
FIRST OPERATOR. The line is busy.
SECOND OPERATOR. The line is busy—
THIRD OPERATOR. The line is busy—
FIRST OPERATOR. Doing best we can—
SECOND OPERATOR. Hold on, please—
THIRD OPERATOR. Can't make connections—
FIRST OPERATOR. Unable to put it in—
SECOND OPERATOR. Won't plug through—
THIRD OPERATOR. Sorry, madam—

FIRST OPERATOR. If you'd wait a moment—
SECOND OPERATOR. Doing best we can—
THIRD OPERATOR. Sorry—
FIRST OPERATOR. One moment—
SECOND OPERATOR. Just a second—
THIRD OPERATOR. Hold on—
FIRST OPERATOR. *Yes—*
SECOND OPERATOR. *Stop it!—*
THIRD OPERATOR. *How do I know—*
FIRST OPERATOR. *You another one!*
SECOND OPERATOR. *Hold on, Dammit!*
THIRD OPERATOR. *Up yours, too!*
FIRST OPERATOR. *The line is busy—*
SECOND OPERATOR. *The line is busy—*
THIRD OPERATOR. *The line is busy—*
(*The switchboard clamors a cacaphony of buzzes as* OPERA-
TORS *plug connections with the frenzy of a Chaplin movie.
Their replies degenerate into a babble of gibberish. At the
height of frenzy, the* SUPERVISOR *appears.*)
SUPERVISOR. *What's the snarl-up?*
FIRST OPERATOR. Everybody calling at the same time, Ma'am!
SECOND OPERATOR. Board can't handle it!
THIRD OPERATOR. Like everybody in big New York City is
trying to squeeze a call through to lil ole us!
SUPERVISOR. God! . . . Somp'um terrible musta happened! . . .
Buzz the emergency frequency hookup to the Mayor's office and
find out what the hell's going on!
(*Scene blacks out quickly to* CLEM *and* LUKE.)
CLEM (*something slowly dawning on him*). Luke . . . ?
LUKE. Yes, Clem?
CLEM (*eyes roving around in puzzlement*). Luke . . . ?
LUKE (*irked*). I said what, Clem!
CLEM. Luke . . . ? Where—where is—the—the—?
LUKE. The *what?*
CLEM. Nigras . . . ?

LUKE. What . . . ?

CLEM. Nigras . . . Where is the Nigras, where is they, Luke . . . ? *All the Nigras!* . . . I don't see no Nigras . . . !

LUKE. Whatcha mean . . . ?

CLEM (*agitatedly*). Luke there ain't a darkey in sight . . . . And if you remember, we ain't seen a nappy hair all morning . . . The Nigras, Luke! We ain't laid eyes on nary a coon this whole morning!

LUKE. You must be crazy or something, Clem!

CLEM. Think about it, Luke, we been sitting here for an hour or more—try and recollect if you remember seeing jist *one* go by!

LUKE (*confused*). I don't recall . . . But . . . but there musta been some . . . The heat musta got you, Clem! How in hell could that be so?

CLEM (*triumphantly*). Just think, Luke! . . . Look around ya . . . Now, every morning mosta people walkin 'long this street is colored. They's strolling by going to work, they's waiting for the buses, they's sweeping sidewalks, cleaning stores, starting to shine shoes and wetting the mops—Right? . . . Well, look around you, Luke—Where is they? (LUKE *paces up and down, checking.*) I told you, Luke, they ain't nowheres to be seen.

LUKE. This . . . this . . . some kind of holiday for 'em—or something?

CLEM. I don't know, Luke . . . but . . . but what I do know is they ain't here'n we haven't seen a solitary one . . . It's scarifying, Luke . . . !

LUKE. Well . . . Maybe they's jist standing 'n walking and shining on other streets—Let's go look!

(*Scene blacks out to* JOHN *and* MARY. *Baby cries are as insistent as ever.*)

MARY (*at end of patience*). Smother it!

JOHN (*beyond his*). That's a hell of a thing to say 'bout your own child! You should know what to do to hush her up!

MARY. Why don't you try?

JOHN. You had her!

MARY. You shared in borning her!

JOHN. Possibly not!

MARY. Why, you lousy—!

JOHN. What good is a mother who can't shut up her own daughter?

MARY. I told you she yells louder every time I try to lay hands on her—Where's Lula? Didn't you call her?

JOHN. I told you I can't get the call through!

MARY. Try agin—

JOHN. It's no use! I tried numerous times and can't even git through to the switchboard. You've got to quiet her down yourself. (*Firmly*) Now, go in there and clam her up 'fore I lose my patience! MARY *exits. Soon, we hear the yells increase. She rushes back in.*)

MARY. She won't let me touch her, just screams louder!

JOHN. Probably wet 'n soppy!

MARY. Yes! Stinks something awful! Phooooey! I can't stand that filth and odor!

JOHN. That's why she's screaming! Needs her didee changed —go change it!

MARY. How you 'spect me to when I don't know how? Suppose I faint?

JOHN. Well let her blast away. I'm getting outta here.

MARY. You can't leave me here like this!

JOHN. Just watch me! . . . See this nice split-level cottage, peachy furniture, multicolored T.V., hi-fi set n' the rest? . . . Well, how you think I scraped 'em together while you curled up on your fat lil fanny? . . . By gitting outta here—not only *on time* . . . but *earlier*!—Beating a frantic crew of nice young executives to the punch—gitting there fustest with the mostest brown-nosing you ever saw! Now if I goof one day—just ONE DAY!—you reckon I'd stay ahead? NO! . . . There'd be a wolf pack trampling over my prostrate body, racing to replace my smiling face against the boss's left rump! . . . *No, mam!* I'm zooming outta here on time, just as I always have, and what's more—you gon fix me some breakfast. *I'm hungry!*

MARY. But—

JOHN. No buts about it! (*Flash blackout as he gags on a mouthful of coffee.*) What you trying to do, STRANGLE ME? (*Jumps up and starts putting on jacket.*)

MARY (*sarcastically*). What did you expect?

JOHN (*in biting fury*). That you could possibly boil a pot of water, toast a few slices of bread and fry a coupler eggs! . . . It was a mistaken assumption!

MARY. So they aren't as good as Lula's!

JOHN. That is an overstatement. Your efforts don't result in anything that could possibly be digested by man, mammal, or insect! . . . When I married you, I thought I was fairly acquainted with your faults and weaknesses—I chalked 'em up to human imperfection . . . But now I know I was being extremely generous, overoptimistic and phenomenally deluded!—You have no idea how useless you really are!

MARY. Then why'd you marry me?

JOHN. Decoration!

MARY. You shoulda married Lula!

JOHN. I might've if it wasn't 'gainst the segregation law! . . . But for the sake of my home, my child and my sanity, I will even take a chance on sacrificing my slippery grip on the status pole and drive by her shanty to find out whether she or someone like her kin come over here and prevent some ultimate disaster. (*Storms toward door, stopping abruptly at exit*) Are you sure you kin make it to the bathroom wit'out Lula backing you up?

(*Blackout. Scene shifts to* MAYOR's *office where a cluttered desk stands center stage amid paper debris.*)

MAYOR (*striding determinedly toward desk; stopping midway, bellowing*). Woodfence! . . . Woodfence! . . . Woodfence!

(*Receiving no reply, completes distance to desk*) Jack-son! . . . Jackson!

JACKSON (*entering worriedly*). Yes, sir . . . ?

MAYOR. Where's Vice-Mayor Woodfence, that no-good brother-in-law of mine?

JACKSON. Hasn't come in yet, sir.

MAYOR. *Hasn't come in?* . . . Damn bastard! Knows we have a crucial conference. Soon as he staggers through that door, tell him to shoot in here! (*Angrily focusing on his disorderly desk and littered surroundings*) And git Mandy here to straighten up this mess—Rufus too! You know he shoulda been waiting to knock dust off my shoes soon as I step in. Get 'em in here! . . . What's the matter wit them lazy Nigras? . . . Already had to dress myself because of J. C., fix my own coffee without May-Belle, drive myself to work 'counta Bubber, feel my old bag's tits after Sapphi—*Never Mind!*—Git 'em in here—*Quick!*

JACKSON (*meekly*). They aren't . . . they aren't here, sir . . .

MAYOR. Whaddaya mean they aren't here? Find out where they at. We got important business, man! You can't run a town wit laxity like this. Can't allow things to git snafued jist because a bunch of lazy Nigras been out gitting drunk and living it up all night! Discipline, man, discipline!

JACKSON. That's what I'm trying to tell you, sir . . . they didn't come in, can't be found . . . none of 'em.

MAYOR. Ridiculous, boy! Scare 'em up and tell 'em scoot here in a hurry befo' I git mad and fire the whole goddamn lot of 'em!

JACKSON. But we can't find 'em, sir.

MAYOR. Hogwash! Can't nobody in this office do anything right? Do I hafta handle every piddling little matter myself? Git me their numbers, I'll have 'em here befo' you kin shout to—

(THREE MEN *burst into room.*)

ONE. Henry—they vanished!

TWO. Disappeared into thin air!

THREE. Gone wit'out a trace!

TWO. Not a one on the street!

THREE. In the house!

ONE. On the job!

MAYOR. Wait a minute! . . . Hold your water! Calm down—!

ONE. But they've gone, Henry—GONE! All of 'em!

MAYOR. What the hell you talking 'bout? Gone? Who's gone—?

ONE. The Nigras, Henry! They gone!

MAYOR. Gone? . . . Gone where?

TWO. That's what we trying to tell ya—they just disappeared! The Nigras have disappeared, swallowed up, vanished! All of 'em! Every last one!

MAYOR. Has everybody 'round here gone batty? . . . That's impossible, how could the Nigras vanish?

THREE. Beats me, but it's happened!

MAYOR. You mean a whole town of Nigras just evaporated like that—poof!—overnight?

ONE. Right!

MAYOR. Y'all must be drunk! Why, half this town is colored. How could they just sneak out?

TWO. Don't ask me, but there ain't one in sight!

MAYOR. Simmer down 'n put it to me easy-like.

ONE. Well . . . I first suspected somp'um smelly when Sarah Jo didn't show up this morning and I couldn't reach her—

TWO. Dorothy Jane didn't 'rive at my house—

THREE. Georgia Mae wasn't at mine neither—and SHE sleeps in!

ONE. When I reached the office, I realized I hadn't seen nary one Nigra all morning! Nobody else had either—Wait a minute —Henry, have you?

MAYOR. Now that you mention it . . . no, I haven't . . .

ONE. They gone, Henry . . . Not a one on the street, not a one in our homes, not a single, last living one to be found no-wheres in town. What we gon' do?

MAYOR (*thinking*). Keep heads on your shoulders 'n put clothes on your back . . . They can't be far . . . Must be 'round somewheres . . . Probably playing hide 'n seek, that's it! . . . *Jackson!*

JACKSON. Yessir?

MAYOR. Immediately mobilize our Citizens Emergency Distress Committee!—order a fleet of sound trucks to patrol streets urging the population to remain calm—situation's not as bad as it looks—everything's under control! Then, have another squadron of squawk buggies drive slowly through all Nigra alleys, ordering them to come out wherever they are. If that don't git 'em, organize a vigilante search squad to flush 'em outta hiding! But most important of all, track down that lazy goldbricker Woodfence and tell him to git on top of the situation! By God, we'll find 'em even if we hafta dig 'em outta the ground!

(*Blackout. Scene shifts back to* JOHN *and* MARY *a few hours later. A funereal solemnity pervades their mood.*)

JOHN. Walked up to the shack, knocked on door, didn't git no answer. Hollered: "Lula? Lula . . . ?—not a thing. Went 'round the side, peeped in window—nobody stirred. Next door —nobody there. Crossed other side of street and banged on five or six other doors—not a colored person could be found! Not a man, neither woman or child—not even a black dog could be seen, smelt or heard for blocks around . . . They've gone, Mary.

MARY. What does it all mean, John?

JOHN. I don't know, Mary . . .

MARY. I always had Lula, John. Never missed a day at my side . . . That's why I couldn't accept your wedding proposal until I was sure you'd welcome me and her together as a package. How am I gonna git through the day? Baby don't know *me*, I ain't acquainted wit *it*. I've never lifted cover off pot, swung a mop or broom, dunked a dish or even pushed a dustrag. I'm lost wit'out Lula, I need her, John, I need her. (*Begins to weep softly.* JOHN *pats her consolingly.*)

JOHN. Courage, honey . . . Everybody in town is facing the same dilemma. We mustn't crack up . . .

(*Blackout. Scene shifts back to* MAYOR's *office later in day. Atmosphere and tone resembles a wartime headquarters at the front.* MAYOR *is perched on ladder checking over huge map.*)

INDUSTRIALIST. Half the day is gone already, Henry. On behalf of the factory owners of this town, you've got to bail us out! Seventy-five percent of all production is paralyzed. With the Nigra absent, men are waiting for machines to be cleaned, floors to be swept, crates lifted, equipment delivered and bathrooms deodorized. Why, restrooms and toilets are so filthy until they not only cannot be sat in, but it's virtually impossible to get within hailing distance because of the stench!

MAYOR. Keep your shirt on, Jeb—

BUSINESSMAN. Business is even in worse condition, Henry. The volume of goods moving 'cross counters has slowed down to a trickle—almost negligible. Customers are not only not purchasing—but the absence of handymen, porters, sweepers, stockmovers, deliverers and miscellaneous dirty-work doers is disrupting the smooth harmony of marketing!

CLUBWOMAN. Food poisoning, severe indigestitis, chronic diarrhea, advanced diaper chafings and a plethora of unsanitary household disasters dangerous to life, limb and property! . . . As a representative of the Federation of Ladies' Clubs, I must sadly report that unless the trend is reversed, a complete breakdown in family unity is imminent . . . Just as homosexuality and debauchery signaled the fall of Greece and Rome, the downgrading of Southern Bellesdom might very well prophesy the collapse of our indigenous institutions . . . . Remember— it has always been pure, delicate, lily-white images of Dixie femininity which provided backbone, inspiration and ideology for our male warriors in their defense against the onrushing black horde. If our gallant men are drained of this worship and idolatry—God knows! The cause won't be worth a Confederate nickel!

MAYOR (*jumping off ladder*). Stop this panicky defeatism, y'all hear me! All machinery at my disposal is being utilized. I assure you wit great confidence the damage will soon repair itself—Cheerful progress reports are expected any moment now —Wait! See, here's Jackson . . . Well, Jackson?

JACKSON. As of now, sir, all efforts are fruitless. Neither hide nor hair of them has been located. We have not unearthed a single one in our shack-to-shack search. Not a single one has heeded our appeal. Scoured every creek and cranny inside their hovels, turning furniture upside down and inside out, breaking down walls and tearing through ceilings. We made determined efforts to discover where'bouts of our faithful Uncle Toms and informers—but even they have vanished without a trace . . . Searching squads are on the verge of panic and hysteria, sir, wit hotheads among 'em campaigning for scorched earth policies. Nigras on a whole lack cellars, but there's rising sentiment favoring burning to find out whether they're underground-dug in!

MAYOR. Absolutely counter such foolhardy suggestions! Suppose they are tombed in? We'd only accelerate the gravity of the situation using incendiary tactics! Besides, when they're rounded up where will we put 'em if we've already burned up their shacks—*in our own bedrooms*?

JACKSON. I agree, sir, but the mood of the crowd is becoming irrational. In anger and frustration, they's forgetting their original purpose was to *find* the Nigras!

MAYOR. At all costs! Stamp out all burning proposals! Must prevent extremist notions from gaining ascendancy. Git wit it . . . Wait—'n for Jehovah's sake, find out where the hell is that trifling slacker, *Woodfence*!

COURIER (*rushing in*). Mr. Mayor! . . . We've found some! We've found some!

MAYOR (*excitedly*). Where?

COURIER. In the—in the—(*Can't catch breath*).

MAYOR (*impatiently*). Where, man? Where?

COURIER. In the colored wing of the city hospital!

MAYOR. The hos—? The hospital! I shoulda known! How could those helpless, crippled, cut and shot Nigras disappear from a hospital? Should thought of that! . . . Tell me more, man!

COURIER. I—I didn't wait, sir . . . I—I ran in to report soon as I heard—

MAYOR. Well git back on the phone, you idiot! Don't you know what this means?

COURIER. Yes, sir. (*Races out*).

MAYOR. Now we gitting somewhere! . . . Gentlemen, if one sole Nigra is among us, we're well on the road to rehabilitation! Those Nigras in the hospital must know somp'um 'bout the others where'bouts . . . Scat back to your colleagues, boost up their morale and inform 'em that things will zip back to normal in a jiffy! (*They start to file out, then pause to observe the* COURIER *re-entering dazedly.*) Well . . . ? Well, man . . . ? What's the matter wit you, ninny? Tell me what else was said!

COURIER. They all . . . they all . . . they all in a—in a—a coma, sir . . .

MAYOR. They all in a what . . . ?

COURIER. In a coma, sir . . .

MAYOR. Talk sense, man! . . . Whaddaya mean, they all in a coma?

COURIER. Doctor says every last one of the Nigras are jist laying in bed . . . *still* . . . not moving . . . neither live or dead . . . laying up there in a coma . . . every last one of 'em . . .

MAYOR (*sputters, then grabs phone*). Get me Confederate Memorial . . . Put me through to the Staff Chief . . . YES, this is the Mayor . . . Sam? . . . What's this I hear? . . . But how could they be in a coma, Sam? . . . You don't know! Well, what the hell you think the city's paying you for! You've got 'nuff damn hacks and quacks there to find out! . . . How could it be somp'um unknown? You mean Nigras know somp'um 'bout drugs your damn butchers don't? . . . Well, what the crap good are they? . . . All right, all right, I'll be calm. . . . Now, tell me . . . Uh huh, uh huh . . . Well, can't you give 'em some injections or somp'um . . . ?—You did . . . uh huh . . . *Did you try a lil rough treatment?*— that too, huh . . . All right, Sam, keep trying . . . (*Puts phone down deliberately, continuing absently.*) Can't wake 'em up. Just lay there. Them that's sick won't git no sicker, them that's half-well won't git no better, babies that's due won't be born and them that's come won't show no life. Nigras wit cuts won't bleed and them which need blood won't be transfused . . . He say dying Nigras is even refusing to pass away! (*Is silently perplexed for a moment, then suddenly breaks into action.*) Jackson? . . . Call up the police—*the jail!* Find out what's going on there! Them Nigras are captives! If there's one place we got darkies under control, it's there! Them sonsabitches too onery to act right either for colored or white! (JACKSON *exits.*) Keep your fingers crossed, citizens, them Nigras in jail are the most important Nigras we got!

(*All hands are raised conspicuously aloft, fingers prominently crossed. Seconds tick by. Soon* JACKSON *returns crestfallen.*)

JACKSON. Sheriff Bull says they don't know whether they still on premises or not. When they went to rouse Nigra jailbirds this morning, cell block doors refused to swing open. Tried everything—even exploded dynamite charges—but it just wouldn't budge . . . Then they hoisted guards up to peep through barred windows, but couldn't see good 'nuff to tell whether Nigras was inside or not. Finally, gitting desperate, they power-hosed the cells wit water but had to cease 'cause Sheriff Bull said he didn't wanta jeopardize drowning the Nigras since it might spoil his chance of shipping a record load of cotton pickers to the State Penitentiary for cotton-snatching jubilee . . . Anyway—they ain't heard a Nigra-squeak all day.

MAYOR. That so . . . ? *What 'bout trains 'n busses passing through?* There must be some dinges riding through?

JACKSON. We checked . . . not a one on board.

MAYOR. Did you hear whether any other towns lost their Nigras?

JACKSON. Things are status quo everywhere else.

MAYOR (*angrily*). Then what they picking on us for?

COURIER (*rushing in*). Mr. Mayor! Your sister jist called— *hysterical*! She says Vice-Mayor Woodfence went to bed wit her last night, but when she woke up this morning he was gone! Been missing all day!

MAYOR. Could Nigras be holding him hostage?

COURIER. No, sir. Besides him—investigations reveal that dozens or more prominent citizens—two City Council members, the chairman of the Junior Chamber of Commerce, our City College All-Southern halfback, the chairlady of the Daughters of the Confederate Rebellion, Miss Cotton Sack Festival of the Year and numerous other miscellaneous nobodies—are absent wit'out leave. Dangerous evidence points to the conclusion that they been infiltrating!

MAYOR. Infiltrating?

COURIER. Passing all along!

MAYOR. *What?*

COURIER. Secret Nigras all the while!

MAYOR. *Naw!*

(CLUBWOMAN *keels over in faint.* JACKSON, BUSINESSMAN *and* INDUSTRIALIST *begin to eye each other suspiciously.*)

COURIER. Yessir!

MAYOR. *Passing?*

COURIER. Yessir!

MAYOR. *Secret Nig—?*

COURIER. Yessir!

MAYOR (*momentarily stunned to silence*). The dirty mongrel-izers! . . . Gentlemen, this is a grave predicament indeed . . . It pains me to surrender priority of our states rights credo, but it is my solemn task and frightening duty to inform you that we have no other recourse but to seek outside help for deliverance.

(*Blackout. Lights rise again on Huntley-Brinkley-Murrow-*

Severeid-Cronkite- Reasoner-type ANNOUNCER *grasping a hand-held microphone [imaginary] a few hours later. He is vigorously, excitedly mouthing his commentary, but no sound escapes his lips. During this dumb, wordless section of his broadcast, a bedraggled assortment of figures marching with picket signs occupies his attention. On their picket signs are inscribed various appeals and slogans.* "CINDY LOU UNFAIR TO BABY JOE" . . . "CAP'N SAM MISS BIG BOY" . . . "RETURN LIL BLUE TO MARS JIM" . . . "INFORMATION REQUESTED BOUT MAMMY GAIL" . . . "BOSS NATHAN PROTEST TO FAST LEROY." *Trailing behind the* MARCHERS, *forcibly isolated, is a* WOMAN *dressed in widow black holding a placard which reads:* "WHY DIDN'T YOU TELL US—YOUR DEFILED WIFE AND 11 ABSENT MONGRELS.")

ANNOUNCER (*who has been silently mouthing his delivery during the picketing procession, is suddenly heard as if caught in the midst of commentary*). Factories standing idle from the loss of nonessential workers. Stores remaining shuttered from the absconding of uncrucial personnel. Fruit, vegetables and other edible foodstuffs rotting in warehouses, with uncollected garbage threatening pestilence and pollution . . . Also, each second somewhere in this former utopia below the Mason and Dixon, dozens of decrepit old men and women usually tended by faithful nurses and servants are popping off like flies—abandoned by sons, daughters and grandchildren whose refusal to provide these doddering souls with bedpans and other soothing necessities results in their hasty, nasty, messy departures . . .

An equally wretched fate lurks in wait for juveniles of the town as hundreds of new born infants HUNGER for the comforting embraces of devoted nannies while being forced to endure the presence of strange parents . . .

But most critically affected of all by this complete drought of Afro-American resources are policemen and other public safety guardians denied their daily quota of Negro arrests. One officer known affectionately as "Two-a-Day-Pete" because of his unblemished record of TWO Negro headwhippings per day has already been carted off to the County Insane Asylum—strait jacketed, screaming and biting, unable to withstand the shock of having his spotless slate sullied by interruption . . . It is feared that similar attacks are soon expected among municipal judges prevented for the first time in years of distinguished bench-sitting from sentencing one single Negro to corrective institutions . . .

Ladies and gentlemen, as you trudge in from the joys and headaches of workday chores and dusk begins to descend on this sleepy Southern hamlet, we *repeat*—today—before early morning dew had dried upon magnolia blossoms, your comrade citizens of this lovely Dixie village awoke to the realization that some—pardon me! not some but *all*—of their Negroes were missing . . . Absent, vamoosed, departed, at bay, fugitive, away, gone and so far unretrieved . . .

In order to dispel your incredulity, gauge the temper of your suffering compatriots and just possibly prepare you for the likelihood of an equally nightmarish eventuality, we have gathered a cross section of this city's most distinguished leaders for exclusive interviews . . . First, Mr. Council Clan, grand dragoon of this area's most active civic organizations and staunch bellwether of the political opposition . . . Mr. Clan, how do you *account* for this incredible disappearance?

CLAN. A *plot*, plain and simple, that's what it is, as plain as the corns on your feet!

ANNOUNCER. Whom would you consider responsible?

CLAN. I could go on all night.

ANNOUNCER. Cite a few.

CLAN. Too numerous.

ANNOUNCER. Just one?

CLAN. Name names when time comes.

ANNOUNCER. Could you be referring to native Negroes?

CLAN. Ever try quaranteening lepers from their spots?

ANNOUNCER. Their organizations?

CLAN. Could you slice a nose off a mouth and still keep a face?

ANNOUNCER. Commies?

CLAN. Would you lop off a titty from a chest and still have a breast?

ANNOUNCER. Your city government?

CLAN. Now you talkin'!

ANNOUNCER. State administration?

CLAN. Warming up!

ANNOUNCER. Federal?

CLAN. Kin a blind man see?

ANNOUNCER. The Court?

CLAN. Is a pig clean?

ANNOUNCER. Clergy?

CLAN. Do a polecat stink?!

ANNOUNCER. Well, Mr. Clan, with this massive complicity, how do you think the plot could've been prevented from succeeding?

CLAN. If I'da been in office, it never woulda happened.

ANNOUNCER. Then you're laying major blame at the doorstep of the present administration?

CLAN. Damn tooting!

ANNOUNCER. But from your oft-expressed views, Mr. Clan, shouldn't you and your followers be delighted at the turn of events? After all—isn't it one of the main policies of your society to *drive* the Negroes away? *Drive* 'em back where they came from?

CLAN. Drivvve, boy! Driiiivvve! That's right! . . . When we say so and not befo'. Ain't supposed to do nothing 'til we tell 'em. Got to stay put until we exercise our God-given right to tell 'em when to git!

ANNOUNCER. But why argue if they've merely jumped the gun? Why not rejoice at this premature purging of undesirables?

CLAN. The time ain't ripe yet, boy . . . The time ain't ripe yet.

ANNOUNCER. Thank you for being so informative, Mr. Clan— Mrs. Aide? Mrs. Aide? Over here, Mrs. Aide . . . Ladies and gentlemen, this city's Social Welfare Commissioner, Mrs. Handy Anna Aide . . . Mrs. Aide, with all your freeloading Negroes seemingly AWOL, haven't developments alleviated the staggering demands made upon your Welfare Department? Reduction of relief requests, elimination of case loads, removal of chronic welfare dependents, et cetera?

AIDE. Quite the contrary. Disruption of our pilot projects among Nigras saddles our white community with extreme hardship . . . You see, historically, our agencies have always been foremost contributors to the Nigra Git-A-Job movement. We pioneered in enforcing social welfare theories which oppose coddling the fakers. We strenuously believe in helping Nigras help themselves by participating in meaningful labor. "Relief is Out, Work is In," is our motto. We place them as maids, cooks, butlers, and breast-feeders, cesspool-diggers, wash-basin maintainers, shoeshine boys, and so on—mostly on a volunteer self-work basis.

ANNOUNCER. Hired at prevailing salaried rates, of course?

AIDE. God forbid! Money is unimportant. Would only make 'em worse. Our main goal is to improve their ethical behavior. "Rehabilitation Through Positive Participation" is another motto of ours. All unwed mothers, loose-living malingering fathers, bastard children and shiftless grandparents are kept occupied through constructive muscle therapy. This provides 'em with less opportunity to indulge their pleasure-loving amoral inclinations.

ANNOUNCER. They volunteer to participate in these pilot projects?

AIDE. Heavens no! They're notorious shirkers. When I said the program is voluntary, I meant white citizens in overwhelming majorities do the volunteering. Placing their homes, offices, appliances and persons at our disposal for use in "Operation Uplift" . . . We would never dare place such a decision in the hands of the Nigra. It would never get off the ground! No, they have no choice in the matter. "Work or Starve" is the slogan we use to stimulate their awareness of what's good for survival.

ANNOUNCER. And a good one it is. Thank you, Mrs. Aide, and good luck . . . Rev? . . . Rev? . . . Ladies and gentlemen, this city's foremost spiritual guidance counselor, Reverend Reb Pious . . . How does it look to you, Reb Pious?

PIOUS (*continuing to gaze skyward*). It's in *His* hands, son, it's in *His* hands.

ANNOUNCER. How would you assess the disappearance, from a moral standpoint?

PIOUS. An immoral act, son, morally wrong and ethically indefensible. A perversion of Christian principles to be condemned from every pulpit of this nation.

ANNOUNCER. Can you account for its occurrence after the many decades of the Church's missionary activity among them?

PIOUS. It's basically a reversion of the Nigra to his deep-rooted primitivism . . . Now, at last, you can understand the difficulties of the Church in attempting to anchor God's kingdom among ungratefuls. It's a constant, unrelenting, no-holds-barred struggle against Satan to wrestle away souls locked in his possession for countless centuries! Despite all our aid, guidance, solace and protection, Old Beezlebub still retains tenacious grips upon the Nigras' childish loyalty—comparable to the lure of bright flames to an infant.

ANNOUNCER. But actual physical departure, Reb Pious? How do you explain that?

PIOUS. Voodoo, my son, voodoo . . . With Satan's assist, they have probably employed some heathen magic which we cultivated, sophisticated Christians know absolutely nothing about. However, before long we are confident about counteracting this evil witch-doctory and triumphing in our Holy Savior's name. At this perilous juncture, true believers of all denominations are participating in joint, 'round-the-clock observances, offering prayers for our Master's swiftiest intercession. I'm optimistic about the outcome of His intervention . . . Which prompts me—if I may, sir—to offer these words of counsel to our delinquent Nigras . . . I say to you without rancor or vengeance, quoting a phrase of one of your greatest prophets, Booker T. Washington: "Return your buckets to where they lay and all will be forgiven."

ANNOUNCER. A very inspirational appeal, Reb Pious. I'm certain they will find the tug of its magnet sincerity irresistible. Thank you, Reb Pious . . . All in all—as you have witnessed, ladies and gentlemen—this town symbolizes the face of disaster, suffering as severe a prostration as any city wrecked, ravaged and devastated by the holocaust of war. A vital, lively, throbbing organism brought to a screeching halt by the strange enigma of the missing Negroes . . .

We take you now to offices of the one man into whose hands has been thrust the final responsibility of rescuing this shuddering metropolis from the precipice of destruction . . . We give you the honorable Mayor, Henry R. E. Lee . . . Hello, Mayor Lee.

MAYOR (*jovially*). Hello, Jack.

ANNOUNCER. Mayor Lee, we have just concluded interviews with some of your city's leading spokesmen. If I may say so, sir, they don't sound too encouraging about the situation.

MAYOR. Nonsense, Jack! The situation's as well in hand as it could be under the circumstances. Couldn't be better in hand. Underneath every dark cloud, Jack, there's always a ray of sunlight, ha, ha, ha.

ANNOUNCER. Have you discovered one, sir?

MAYOR. Well, Jack, I'll tell you . . . Of course we've been faced wit a little crisis, but look at it like this—we've faced 'em befo': Sherman marched through Georgia—*once*! Lincoln freed the slaves—*momentarily*! Carpetbaggers even put Nigras in the Governor's mansion, state legislature, Congress and the Senate of the United States. But what happened? Ole Dixie bounced right on back up . . . At this moment the Supreme Court's trying to put Nigras in our schools and the Nigra has got it in his haid to put hisself everywhere . . . But what you spect gon happen? Ole Dixie will kangaroo back even higher. Southern courage, fortitude, chivalry and superiority always wins out. . . . SHUCKS! We'll have us some Nigras befo' daylight is gone!

ANNOUNCER. Mr. Mayor, I hate to introduce this note, but in an earlier interview one of your chief opponents, Mr. Clan, hinted at your own complicity in the affair—

MAYOR. *A lot of poppycock!* Clan is politicking! I've beaten him four times outta four and I'll beat him four more times outta four! This is no time for partisan politics! What we need now is level-headedness and across-the-board unity. This typical, rash, mealy-mouth, shooting-off-at-the-lip of Clan and his ilk proves their insincerity, and voters will remember that in the next election! Won't you, voters? (*Has risen to the height of campaign oratory.*)

ANNOUNCER. Mr. Mayor! . . . Mr. Mayor! . . . Please—

MAYOR. I tell you, I promise you—

ANNOUNCER. *Please, Mr. Mayor!*

MAYOR. Huh? . . . Oh—yes, carry on.

ANNOUNCER. Mr. Mayor, your cheerfulness and infectious good spirits lead me to conclude that startling new developments warrant fresh-found optimism. What concrete, declassified information do you have to support your claim that Negroes will reappear before nightfall?

MAYOR. Because we are presently awaiting the payoff of a masterful five-point supra-recovery program which can't help but reap us a bonanza of Nigras 'fore sundown! . . . First: Exhaustive efforts to pinpoint the where'bouts of our own missing darkies continue to zero in on the bull's-eye . . . Second: The President of the United States, following an emergency cabinet meeting, has designated us the prime disaster area of the century—National Guard is already on the way . . . Third: In an

unusual, but bold, maneuver we have appealed to the NAACP
'n all other Nigra conspirators to help us git to the bottom of
the vanishing act . . . Fourth: We have exercised our non-
reciprocal option and requested that all fraternal Southern
states express their solidarity by lending us some of their Nigras
temporarily on credit . . . Fifth and foremost: We have already
gotten consent of the Governor to round up all stray, excess and
incorrigible Nigras to be shipped to us under escort of the
state militia . . . That's why we've stifled pessimism and are
brimming wit confidence that this full-scale concerted mobilization will ring down a jackpot of jigaboos 'fore light vanishes
from sky!

ANNOUNCER. Congratulations! What happens if it fails?

MAYOR. Don't even think *that*! Absolutely no reason to sus-
pect it will . . . (*Peers over shoulder, then whispers confidential-
ly while placing hand over mouth by* ANNOUNCER's *imaginary
mike*) But speculating on the dark side of your question—if we
don't turn up some by nightfall, it may be all over. The harm
has already been done. You see the South has always been glued
together by the uninterrupted presence of its darkies. No telling how unstuck we might git if things keep on like they have
—Wait a minute, it musta paid off already! Mission accomplished 'cause here's Jackson 'head a time wit the word . . .
Well, Jackson, what's new?

JACKSON. Situation on the home front remains static, sir—
can't uncover scent or shadow. The NAACP and all other
Nigra front groups 'n plotters deny any knowledge or connec-
tion wit the missing Nigras. Maintained this even after appearing befo' a Senate Emergency Investigating Committee which
subpoenaed 'em to Washington posthaste and threw 'em in jail
for contempt. A handful of Nigras who agreed to make spec-
tacular appeals for ours to come back to us have themselves
mysteriously disappeared. But, worst news of all, sir, is our
sister cities and counties, inside and outside the state, have
changed their minds, fallen back on their promises and refused

to lend us any Nigras, claiming they don't have 'nuff for themselves.

MAYOR. What 'bout Nigras promised by the Governor?

JACKSON. Jailbirds and vagrants escorted here from chain gangs and other reservations either revolted and escaped en route or else vanished mysteriously on approaching our city limits . . . Deterioration rapidly escalates, sir. Estimates predict we kin hold out only one more hour before overtaken by anarchistic turmoil . . . Some citizens seeking haven elsewheres have already fled, but on last report were being forcibly turned back by armed sentinels in other cities who wanted no parts of 'em—claiming they carried a jinx.

MAYOR. That bad, huh?

JACKSON. Worse, sir . . . we've received at least five reports of plots on your life.

MAYOR. What?—We've gotta act quickly then!

JACKSON. Run out of ideas, sir.

MAYOR. Think harder, boy!

JACKSON. Don't have much time, sir. One measly hour, then all hell gon break loose.

MAYOR. Gotta think of something drastic, Jackson!

JACKSON. I'm dry, sir.

MAYOR. Jackson! Is there any planes outta here in the next hour?

JACKSON. All transportation's been knocked out, sir.

MAYOR. I thought so!

JACKSON. What were you contemplating, sir?

MAYOR. Don't ask me what I was contemplating! I'm still boss 'round here! Don't forgit it!

JACKSON. Sorry, sir.

MAYOR. Hold the wire! . . . Wait a minute . . . ! Waaaaait a minute—*goddammit*! All this time crapping 'round, diddling and fotsing wit puny lil solutions—all the while neglecting our ace in the hole, our trump card! Most potent weapon for digging Nigras outta the woodpile? All the while right befo' our eyes! . . . Ass! Why didn't you remind me?

JACKSON. What is it, sir?

MAYOR. *Me—That's what! Me!* a personal appeal from ME! *Directly to them!* . . . Although we wouldn't let 'em march to the polls and express their affection for me through the ballot box, we've always known I'm held highest in their esteem. A direct address from their beloved Mayor! . . . If they's anywheres close within the sound of my voice, they'll shape up! Or let us know by a sign they's ready to.

JACKSON. You sure *that'll* turn the trick, sir?

MAYOR. As sure as my ancestors befo' me who knew that when they puckered their lips to whistle, ole Sambo was gonna come a-lickey-splitting to answer the call! . . . That same chips-down blood courses through these Confederate gray veins of Henry R. E. Lee ! ! !

ANNOUNCER. I'm delighted to offer our network's facilities for such a crucial public interest address, sir. We'll arrange immediately for your appearance on an international hookup, placing you in widest proximity to contact them wherever they may be.

MAYOR. Thank you, I'm very grateful . . . Jackson, regrease the machinery and set wheels in motion. Inform townspeople what's being done. Tell 'em we're all in this together. The next hour is countdown. I demand absolute cooperation, citywide silence and inactivity. I don't want the Nigras frightened if they's nearby. This is the most important hour in the town's history. Tell 'em if one single Nigra shows up during the hour of decision, victory is within sight. I'm gonna git 'em that one— maybe all! Hurry and crack to it!

(ANNOUNCER *rushes out, followed by* JACKSON.

Blackout. Scene reopens, with MAYOR *seated, eyes front, spotlight illuminating him in semidarkness. Shadowy figures stand in the background, prepared to answer phones or aid in any other manner.* MAYOR *waits patiently until "Go" signal is given.*)

MAYOR (*voice combining elements of confidence, tremolo and gravity*). Good evening . . . Despite the fact that millions of you wonderful people throughout the nation are viewing and listening to this momentous broadcast—and I thank you for your concern and sympathy in this hour of our peril—I primarily want to concentrate my attention and address these remarks solely for the benefit of our departed Nigra friends who may be listening somewhere in our far-flung land to the sound of my voice . . . If you are—it is with heartfelt emotion and fond memories of our happy association that I ask—"Where are you . . . ?"

Your absence has left a void in the bosom of every single man, woman and child of our great city. I tell you—you don't know what it means for us to wake up in the morning and discover that your cheerful, grinning, happy-go-lucky faces are missing! . . . From the depths of my heart, I can meekly, humbly suggest what it means to me personally . . . You see—the one face I will never be able to erase from my memory is the face—not of my Ma, not of Pa, neither wife or child—but the image of the first woman I came to love so well when just a wee lad—the vision of the first human I laid clear sight on at childbirth—the profile—better yet the full face of my dear old . . . Jemimah—God rest her soul . . . Yes! My dear ole mammy, wit her round black moonbeam gleaming down upon me in the crib, teeth shining, blood-red bandana standing starched, peaked and proud, gazing down on me affectionately as she crooned me a Southern lullaby . . . Oh! It's a memorable picture I will eternally cherish in permanent treasure chambers of my heart, now and forever always . . .

Well, if this radiant image can remain so infinitely vivid to me all these many years after her unfortunate demise in the po' folks' home—*think* of the misery the rest of us must be suffering after being *freshly* denied your soothing presence!

We need ya. If you kin hear me, just contact this station 'n I will welcome you back personally. Let me just tell you that since you eloped, nothing has been the same. How could it? You're part of us, you belong to us. Just give us a sign and we'll be contented that all is well . . .

Now if you've skipped away on a little fun fest, we understand, ha, ha. We know you like a good time and we don't begrudge it to ya. Hell—er, er, we like a good time ourselves— who doesn't . . . In fact, think of all the good times we've had together, huh? We've had some real fun, you and us, yesiree! . . . Nobody knows better than you and I what fun we've had together. You singing us those old Southern coon songs and dancing those Nigra jigs and us clapping, prodding 'n spurring you on! Lots of fun, huh? . . . *Oh boy!* The times we've had together . . . If you've snucked away for a bit of fun by yourself, we'll go 'long wit ya—long as you let us know where you at so we won't be worried about you . . .

We'll go 'long wit you long as you don't take the joke too far. I'll admit a joke is a joke and you've played a *lulu!* . . . I'm warning you, we can't stand much more horsing 'round from you! Business is business 'n fun is fun! You've had your fun so now let's get down to business! Come on back, *you hear me!*

If you been hoodwinked by agents of some foreign government, I've been authorized by the President of these United States to inform you that this liberty-loving Republic is prepared to rescue you from their clutches. Don't pay no 'tention to their sireen songs and atheistic promises! You better off under our control and you know it! . . . If you been bamboozled by rabble-rousing nonsense of your own so-called leaders, we prepared to offer some protection. Just call us up! Just give us a sign! . . . Come on, give us a sign . . . give us a sign— even a teeny weeny one . . . ? (*Glances around checking on possible communications. A bevy of headshakes indicate no success.* MAYOR *returns to address with desperate fervor.*)

Now look—you don't know what you doing! If you persist in this disobedience, you know all too well the consequences! We'll track you to the end of the earth, beyond the galaxy, across the stars! We'll capture you and chastise you with all the vengeance we command! 'N you know only too well how stern we kin be when double-crossed! The city, the state and the entire nation will crucify you for this unpardonable defiance! (*Checks again*) No call . . . ? No sign . . . ? Time is running out! Deadline slipping past! They gotta respond! They gotta! (*resuming*) Listen to me! I'm begging y'all, you've gotta come back . . . ! *Look, George!* (*Waves dirty rag aloft*) I brought the rag you wax the car wit . . . Remember, George . . . ? Don't this bring back memories, George, of all the days you spent shining that automobile to shimmering perfection . . .? And you, Rufus! . . . Here's the polish and the brush! . . . 'Member, Rufus? . . . Remember the happy mornings you spent popping this rag and whisking this brush so furiously 'till it created music that was sympho-nee to the ear . . . ? And you—Mandy? . . . Here's the wastebasket you didn't dump this morning. I saved it just for you! . . . *Look*, all y'all out there . . . (*Signals and a three-person procession parades one after the other before the imaginary camera.*)

DOLL WOMAN (*brandishing a crying baby [doll] as she strolls past and exits*). She's been crying ever since you left, Caldonia . . .

MOP MAN (*flashing mop*). It's been waiting in the same corner, Buster . . .

BRUSH MAN (*flagging toilet brush*). It's been dry ever since you left, Washington . . .

MAYOR (*jumping in on the heels of the last exit*). Don't these things mean anything to y'all? By God! Are your memories so short? Is there nothing sacred to ya . . . Please come back, for my sake, please! All of you—even you questionable ones! I promise no harm will be done to you! Revenge is disallowed! We'll forgive everything! Just come on back and I'll git down on my knees— (*Immediately drops to knees*) I'll be kneeling in the middle of Dixie Avenue to kiss the first shoe of the first one to show up . . . I'll smooch any other spot you request . . . Erase this nightmare 'n we'll concede any demand you make, just come on back—please? . . . *Pleeeeeeeze!*

VOICE (*shouting*). Time!

MAYOR (*remaining on knees, frozen in a pose of supplication. After a brief, deadly silence, he whispers almost inaudibly.*) They wouldn't answer . . . they wouldn't answer . . .

(*Blackout as bedlam erupts offstage. Total blackness holds during a sufficient interval where offstage sound effects create the illusion of complete pandemonium, followed by a diminution which trails off into an expressionistic simulation of a city coming to a stricken standstill: industrial machinery clanks to halt, traffic blares to silence, etc. . . . The stage remains dark and silent for a long moment, then lights rise again on the* ANNOUNCER.)

ANNOUNCER. A pitiful sight, ladies and gentlemen. Soon after his unsuccessful appeal, Mayor Lee suffered a vicious pummeling from the mob and barely escaped with his life. National guardsmen and state militia were impotent in quelling the fury of a town venting its frustration in an orgy of destruction—a frenzy of rioting, looting and all other aberrations of a town gone berserk . . . Then—suddenly—as if a magic wand had been waved, madness evaporated and something more frightening replaced it: submission . . .

Even whimpering ceased. The city: exhausted, benumbed— Slowly its occupants slinked off into shadows, and by midnight the town was occupied exclusively by zombies. The fight and life had been drained out . . . Pooped . . . Hope ebbed away as completely as the beloved, absent Negroes . . . As our crew packed gear and crept away silently, we treaded softly—as if we were stealing away from a mausoleum . . . The face of a defeated city.

Blackout.

Lights rise slowly at the sound of rooster crowing, signaling the approach of a new day, the next morning. Scene is same as opening of play. CLEM *and* LUKE *are huddled over dazedly, trancelike. They remain so for a long count. Finally, a figure drifts on stage, shuffling slowly.*)

LUKE (*gazing in silent fascination at the approaching figure*). Clem . . . ? Do you see what I see or am I dreaming . . . ?

CLEM. It's a . . . a Nigra, ain't it, Luke . . . ?

LUKE. Sure looks like one, Clem—but we better make sure—eyes could be playing tricks on us . . . Does he still look like one to you, Clem?

CLEM. He still does, Luke—but I'm scared to believe—

LUKE. Why . . . ? It looks like Rastus, Clem!

CLEM. Sure does, Luke . . . but we better not jump to no hasty conclusion . . .

LUKE (*in timid softness*). That you, Rastus . . . ?

RASTUS (*Stepin Fetchit, Willie Best, Nicodemus, Butterfly McQueen and all the rest rolled into one*). Why . . . howdy . . . Mr. Luke . . . Mr. Clem . . .

CLEM. It is him, Luke! It is him!

LUKE. Rastus?

RASTUS. Yas . . .sah?

LUKE. Where was you yesterday?

RASTUS (*very, very puzzled*). Yes . . . ter . . .day? . . . Yester . . . day . . . ? Why . . . right . . . here . . . Mr. Luke . . .

LUKE. No you warn't, Rastus, don't lie to me! Where was you yestiddy?

RASTUS. Why . . . I'm sure I was . . . Mr. Luke . . . Remember . . . I made . . . that . . . delivery for you . . .

LUKE. That was *Monday*, Rastus, yestiddy was *Tuesday*.

RASTUS. Tues . . . day . . . ? You don't say . . . Well . . . well . . . well . . .

LUKE. Where was you 'n all the other Nigras yesterday, Rastus?

RASTUS. I . . . thought . . . yestiddy . . . was . . . Monday, Mr.

Luke—I coulda swore it . . . ! . . . See how . . . things . . . kin git all mixed up? . . . I coulda swore it . . .

LUKE. *Today* is *Wednesday*, Rastus. Where was you *Tuesday?*

RASTUS. Tuesday . . . huh? That's somp'um . . . I . . . don't remember . . . missing . . . a day . . . Mr. Luke . . . but I guess you right . . .

LUKE. Then where was you?

RASTUS. Don't rightly know, Mr. Luke. I didn't know I had skipped a day—But that jist goes to show you how time kin fly, don't it, Mr. Luke . . . Uuh, uuh, uuh . . . (*He starts shuffling off, scratching head, a flicker of a smile playing across his lips.* CLEM *and* LUKE *gaze dumbfoundedly as he disappears.*)

LUKE (*eyes sweeping around in all directions*). Well . . . There's the others, Clem . . . Back jist like they useta be . . . Everything's same as always . . .

CLEM. Is it . . . Luke . . . ?

(*Slow fade.*)

CURTAIN

A Rat's Mass

ADRIENNE KENNEDY

Cast of characters:

ROSEMARY
BROTHER RAT
SISTER RAT
JESUS, JOSEPH, MARY, TWO WISE MEN, SHEPHERD

BROTHER RAT *has a rat's head, a human body, a tail.* SISTER RAT *has a rat's belly, a human head, a tail.* ROSEMARY *wears a Holy Communion dress and has worms in her hair. Mass said in prayer voices that later turn to gnawing voices. They were two pale Negro children.*

Scene is the rat's house. The house consists of a red carpet runner and candles. The light is the light of the end of a summer day.
BROTHER RAT *is kneeling facing the audience.*
At the far left of the house stands a procession of JESUS,

JOSEPH, MARY, TWO WISE MEN *and a* SHEPHERD.
SISTER RAT *stands at the end of the red aisle.*

BROTHER RAT. Kay within our room I see our dying baby, Nazis, screaming girls and cursing boys, empty swings, a dark sun. There are worms in the attic beams. (*Stands*) They scream and say we are damned. I see dying and grey cats walking. Rosemary is atop the slide. Exalted! (*Kneels again*) Kay within our room I see a dying baby, Nazis, again they scream (*Stands again*) and say we are damned. Within our once Capitol I see us dying. Rosemary is atop the slide exalted.

SISTER RAT. We swore on Rosemary's Holy Communion book.

BROTHER RAT. Did you tell? Does anyone know?

(*The procession watches.*)

SISTER RAT. Blake, we swore on our father's Bible the next day in the attic.

BROTHER RAT. Did you tell Sister Rat, does anyone know? (*Kneels*) It was Easter and my fear of holy days, it was because it was Easter I made us swear.

SISTER RAT. Brother Rat, it was not Easter. It was night after Memorial Day.

BROTHER RAT. No, it was not after Memorial Day. It was the beginning of winter. Bombs fell. It was the War.

SISTER RAT. It was the War.

BROTHER RAT. Our fathers said everyone was getting hung and shot in Europe. America wouldn't be safe long. (*Remains kneeling; procession marches across the house to center.*)

SISTER RAT. Remember . . . we lived in a Holy Chapel with parents and Jesus, Joseph, Mary, our wise men and our Shepherd. People said we were the holiest children.

(BROTHER RAT *turns face front.* SISTER RAT *comes down the aisle. Procession is still.* SISTER RAT *walking*). Blake, our parents send me to Georgia. It is a house with people who say they are relatives and a garden of great sunflowers. Be my brother's keeper, Blake. I hide under the house, my rat's belly growing all day long I eat sunflower petals, I sit in the garden Blake and hang three grey cats. (*Stands before* BROTHER RAT) Blake, I'm going to have a baby. I got our baby on the slide. (*Falls*) Gray cats walk this house all summer I bury my face in the sand so I cannot bear the rats that hide in our attic beams. Blake, why did the War start? I want to hang myself.

BROTHER RAT. Kay, stop sending me the petals from Georgia. Stop saying our mother says you have to go to the State Hospital because of your breakdown. Stop saying you have a rat's belly.

(*Procession marches across sound of rats.*)

BROTHER AND SISTER RAT. The Nazis! (*Marching*) The Nazis have invaded our house. (*Softer*) Why did the War start? We want to hang ourselves. The rats. (*Sound*) The rats have invaded our Cathedral. (*They rapidly light more candles. Procession returns, marches to the center.*) Our old Rosemary songs. Weren't they beautiful! Our Rosemary Mass. (*Procession watches; silence.*) Yet we weren't safe long. (*They look at Procession.*) Soon we will be getting shot and hung. Within our house is a giant slide. Brother and Sister Rat we are.

SISTER RAT. Blake, remember when we lived in our house with Jesus and Joseph and Mary?

BROTHER RAT. Now there are rats in the church books behind every face in the congregation. They all have been on the slide. Every sister bleeds and every brother has made her bleed. The Communion wine.

BROTHER AND SISTER RAT. The Communion wine. Our father gives out the Communion wine and it turns to blood, a red aisle of blood. Too something is inside the alter listening. (SISTER RAT *kneels*.) When we were children we lived in our house, our mother blessed us greatly and God blessed us. Now they listen from the rat beams. (*Sound rats. They remain kneeling. Sound rats.*) It is our mother.

Rosemary, Rosemary was the first girl we ever fell in love

with. She lived next door behind a grape arbor her father had built. She often told us stories of Italy and read to us from her Holy Catechism book. She was the prettiest girl in our school. It is one of those midwestern neighborhoods, Italians, Negroes and Jews. Rosemary always went to Catechism and wore Holy Communion dresses.

BROTHER RAT. Where are you going Rosemary? we say. And she says, "I have to go to Catechism." Why do you always go to Catechism? "Because I am Catholic"; then thinking, she says, "Colored people are not Catholics, are they?"

SISTER RAT. I don't think many.

BROTHER RAT. "Well I am. I am a descendant of the Pope and Julius Caesar and the Virgin Mary." Julius Caesar? "Yes, Caesar was the Emperor of all Italia." And are you his descendant? "Yes," she said.

BROTHER AND SISTER RAT. We wish we were descendants of this Caesar, we said, how holy you are, how holy and beautiful. She smiled.

BROTHER RAT. Our school had a picnic in the country and she took my hand. We walked to a place of white birch trees. It is our Palestine, she said. We are sailing to Italy, I said. She was the prettiest girl—the only thing, she has worms in her hair.

SISTER RAT. Great Caesars my brother and I were. Behold us singing greatly walking across our Palestine, my brother holding my hand and I holding his and we are young before the War O Italia. Rosemary was our best friend and taught us Latin and told us stories of Italy. O Rosemary songs.

BROTHER AND SISTER RAT. My sister and I when we were young before the War, and Rosemary our best friend, O Rosemary songs. Now we live in Rat's Chapel. My sister and I.

(BROTHER RAT *stares down the aisle.*)

BROTHER RAT. It is Rosemary. (*Stares*) Did you tell? Does anyone know? Did you tell? Does anyone know? You started to cry Kay and I struck you in the face with our father's rifle. It was the beginning of summer. Just getting dark, we were playing and Rosemary said let's go to the playground. After you lay down on the slide so innocently Rosemary said if I loved her I would do what she said. Oh Kay. After that our hiding in the attic rats in the beam. Now there is snow on the playground, ambulances are on every street and within every ambulance is you Kay going to the hospital with a breakdown.

SISTER RAT. Blake, perhaps God will marry us in the State Hospital. Our fellow rats will attend us. Every day I look under our house to see who is listening. (*Aisle bright. Procession marches out.*) I cry all the time now . . . not sobbing . . . Blake, did we really go on that slide together? What were those things made us do while she watched?

BROTHER RAT. We hide in the attic like rats.

SISTER RAT. I cry all the time now.

BROTHER RAT. Within every ambulance is you, Kay. Sister, all the time.

SISTER RAT. (*Sound rats.*) I am waiting for you Blake under the hospital so the Nazis won't see me.

(*Procession marches to center.*)

BROTHER RAT. The rat comes to the attic crying softly within her head down. She thinks she's going to have a baby. If I were a Nazi I'd shoot her. On the slide she said, Blake I am bleeding. Now there is blood on the aisle of our church. Before rat blood came onto the slide we sailed. We did not swing in chains before blood, we sang with Rosemary. Now I must go to battle. (*Heil. Salutes procession*) Will you wait for me again at last spring?

(*Procession does not answer.* BROTHER *and* SISTER RAT *fall down and light candles.* BROTHER RAT *stands. Stares down aisle*) Will they wait for me at last spring Rosemary?

(ROSEMARY *comes down red aisle in her Holy Communion dress.*)

ROSEMARY. Blake the Nazis will get you on the battlefield.

(ROSEMARY *and* BROTHER RAT *stand before each other.* SISTER *remains kneeling.*)

BROTHER RAT. Rosemary atone us, take us beyond the Nazis. We must sail to the Capitol. Atone us. Deliver us unto your descendants.

ROSEMARY. The Nazis are going to get you.

BROTHER RAT. If you do not atone us Kay and I will die. We shall have to die to forget how every day this winter gray cats swing with sunflowers in their mouths because my sister thinks I am the father of a baby. Rosemary will you not atone us?

ROSEMARY. I will never atone you. Perhaps you can put a bullet in your head with your father's shotgun, then your holy battle will be done.

(*The procession is at the edge of the house.*)

SISTER RAT (*kneeling*). O Holy Music return.

(*The procession marches to center.*)

ROSEMARY. Come with me, Blake.

BROTHER RAT. How can I ever reach last spring again if I come with you, Rosemary? I must forget how every day this winter gray cats swing with sunflowers in their mouths.

ROSEMARY. Perhaps you can put a bullet in your head.

SISTER RAT. I have a rat's belly.

BROTHER RAT. How can I ever again reach last spring if I come with you, Rosemary?

ROSEMARY. You must damn last spring in your heart. You will never see last spring again.

BROTHER AND SISTER RAT. Then we must put a bullet in our heads.

(*Procession marches out. Silence. They stare at* ROSEMARY. *Procession returns.*)

PROCESSION. Goodbye Kay and Blake. We are leaving you.

BROTHER AND SISTER RAT. Jesus, Joseph, Mary, Wise Men and Shepherd, do not leave. Great Caesars, we will be again, you will behold us as we were before Rosemary with the worms in her hair, a spring can come after the War.

PROCESSION. What Kay and Blake?

BROTHER AND SISTER RAT. A spring can come after the War

when we grow up we will hang you so that we can run again, walk in the white birch trees. Jesus, Joseph, Wise Men, Shepherd, do not leave us.

PROCESSION. We are leaving because it was Easter.

BROTHER RAT. No, no, it was not Easter, it was the beginning of June.

PROCESSION. In our minds it was Easter. Goodbye Kay and Blake. (*They walk out. A gnawing sound.* SISTER RAT *kneels,* BROTHER RAT *and* ROSEMARY *face each other. A gnawing sound.*)

ROSEMARY. In my mind was a vision of us rats all.

BROTHER RAT. If only we could go back to our childhood.

SISTER RAT. Now there will always be rat blood on the rat walls of our rat house just like the blood that came onto the slide.

BROTHER RAT. Beyond my rat head there must remain a new Capitol where Great Kay and I will sing. But no within my hot head I see the dying baby Nazis and Georgia relatives screaming girls cursing boys a dark sun and my grave. I am damned. No . . . when I grow up I will swing again in white trees because beyond this dark rat run and gnawed petals there will remain a Capitol.

SISTER RAT. A Cathedral.

BROTHER RAT. Now within my mind I forever see dying rats. And gray cats walking. Rosemary worms in her hair atop the slide. Our Holy songs in our parents' house weren't they beautiful.

BROTHER AND SISTER RAT. Now it is our rat's mass. (*From now on their voices sound more like gnaws*) She said if you love me you will. It seemed so innocent. She said it was like a wedding. Now my sister Kay sends me gnawed petals from sunflowers at the State Hospital. She puts them in gray envelopes. Alone I go out to school and the movies. No more do I call by for Rosemary. She made me promise never to tell if you love me she screamed you'll never tell. And I do love her. I found my father's rifle in the attic. Winter time . . . gray time dark boys come laughing starting a game of horseshoes gnawing in the beams. The winter is a place of great gnawed sunflowers. I see them in every street in every room of our house. I pick up gnawed great yellow petals and pray to be atoned.

BROTHER RAT. I am praying to be atoned. I am praying to be atoned dear God. I am begging dear God to be atoned for the Holy Communion that existed between my sister and me and the love that I have for Rosemary. I am praying to be atoned. (*He kisses* ROSEMARY. *He comes down aisle, movements more rat-like . . . voice more like gnawing.*) Bombs fall I am alone in our old house with an attic full of dead rat babies. I must hide.

BROTHER AND SISTER RAT. God we ask you to stop throwing dead rat babies.

(BROTHER RAT *kneels.*)

BROTHER RAT. When I asked you yesterday the day they brought my sister Kay home from the State Hospital, you said God, Blake perhaps you must put a bullet in your head then your battle will be done. God, I think of Rosemary all the time. I love her. I told myself afterward it was one of the boys playing horseshoes who had done those horrible things on the slide with my sister. Yet I told Kay I am her keeper yet I told Rosemary I love her. It is the secret of my battlefield.

SISTER RAT. Here we are again in our attic where we once played games, but neither of us liked it because from time to time you could hear the rats. But it was our place to be alone, Blake now that I am home from the hospital we must rid our minds of my rat's belly. Can you see it? You did not visit me in the hospital Brother Rat. Blake I thought you were my brother's keeper.

BROTHER RAT. Everywhere I go I step in your blood. Rosemary I wanted you to love me. (*He turns—aisles bright—gnawing sound—battlefield sounds.*)

BROTHER AND SISTER RAT. God is hanging and shooting us.

SISTER RAT. Remember Brother Rat before I bled, before descending bombs and death on our capitol we walked the Palestine . . . we went to the movies. Now the Germans and Caesar's army are after us, Blake.

(*He goes back to* ROSEMARY *whose back is to him and starts.*)

ROSEMARY. The Nazis are after you. My greatest grief was your life together. My greatest grief.

BROTHER AND SISTER RAT (*look up*). Now every time we will go outside we will walk over the grave of our dead baby Red aisle runners will be on the street when we come to the playground Rosemary will forever be atop the slide exalted with worms in her hair. (*They kneel then rise, kneel, then rise.*) We must very soon get rid of our rat heads so dying baby voices on the beams will no more say we are our lost Caesars.

ROSEMARY. It is our wedding now, Blake.

BROTHER AND SISTER RAT. Brother and Sister Rat we are very soon we must.

SISTER RAT. We are rats in the beam now.

ROSEMARY. My greatest grief was your life together. The Nazis will come soon now.

BROTHER AND SISTER RAT. Every time we go out red blood runners will be on the street. (*They kneel, then rise, kneel, then rise.*) At least soon very soon we will get rid of our rat heads and rat voices in beams will say no more we are your lost Caesars.

ROSEMARY. It is our wedding, Blake. The Nazis have come. (*Marching*) Brother and Sister Rat you are now soon you will become headless and all will cease the dark sun will be bright no more and no more sounds of shooting in the distance. (*Marching procession appears bearing shotguns.*)

BROTHER AND SISTER RAT. We will become headless and all will cease the dark sun will be bright no more and no more sounds of shooting in the distance. It will be the end. (*The procession shoots, they scamper, more shots, they fall,* ROSEMARY *remains.*)

CURTAIN

Ceremonies in Dark Old Men

A Play in Two Acts

LONNE ELDER, III

Cast of Characters (*In Order Of Their Appearance*)

MR. RUSSELL B. PARKER

MR. WILLIAM JENKINS

THEOPOLIS PARKER

ADELE ELOISE PARKER

BOBBY PARKER

BLUE HAVEN

YOUNG GIRL

TIME: Early spring, about four-thirty in the afternoon, the present time.

PLACE: A small, poverty-stricken barber shop on 126th Street between Seventh and Lenox avenues, Harlem, U.S.A.

There is only one barber's throne in this barber shop. There is a not too lengthy mirror running along the wall and a high, broad shelf in the immediate, reachable area of the throne.

There are two decks of shelves of equal width projecting just below the main shelf. These shelves are covered by small sliding panels. To the far left corner of the shop is the street door, and to the far right corner of the shop is a door leading to a back room. Just to the right of this door, flush against the wall, is a card table with two chairs. Even farther right of this area is a clothes rack. Against the wall to the far left of the shop, near the door, are four chairs lined in uniformity.

The back room is as all back rooms are in poverty-stricken barber shops. It has an old refrigerator, an even older antique desk, and a medium-size bed. To the far right section of the room is a short group of stairs, in sight, suggesting that they lead upwards to a first-floor apartment.

The entire action of the play takes place in the two areas referred to in the above notes. There are no suggested lighting cues, other than those directly related to the intent and meaning of a given scene. There are sinks in both areas.

ACT I

Scene 1

As the curtain rises, MR. RUSSELL B. PARKER *is seated in the single barber's throne, reading a book. He is a man in his early or middle fifties. He rises nervously, moves to the window and peers outward with his right hand over the brows of his eyes. He returns to the throne and continues to read his book. He checks his watch, rises, and once again moves to the window to take a look-see. It appears that he recognizes the party he has been waiting for nearing him. He moves to the door and opens it. A man enters.* MR. WILLIAM JENKINS: *In his early fifties, dressed well in a complete suit, and carrying a newspaper under his arm.*

MR. PARKER (*moves away from* MR. JENKINS *toward the center of the barber shop and turns*). Where have you been?

MR. JENKINS. Whatcha mean? You know where I was . . .

MR. PARKER. I thought you said you was gon get up here as quick as you could?

MR. JENKINS. I'm here . . .

MR. PARKER. I talked to you at three o'clock . . . (*Checks his watch*)—it's now four-thirty.

MR. JENKINS. That's as quick as I could . . .

MR. PARKER. Now I *told* you Adele would be getting home *soon* . . .

MR. JENKINS. That's too bad, I just can't walk off and leave my job the moment you call me.

MR. PARKER. You want to play the game or not?

MR. JENKINS. That's what I came here for . . .

MR. PARKER. I wanted to get in at least three games, but this way, we'll be lucky if we get in one . . . (*Bends down by the barber's chair and opens up one of the sliding panels.*)

MR. JENKINS. Stop complaining and get the board out. I'll beat you, and that will be that.

MR. PARKER (*pulls out a checkerboard, and a small can. He moves and places the items on the table to the rear of the shop.*) I can do without your bragging . . . (*Shakes up the can*) Close your eyes and take a man . . .

MR. JENKINS (*closing his eyes*). You never learn . . . (*Reaches into the can and pulls out a checker*) It's red . . .

MR. PARKER. All right, I get the black . . . (*Sits at the table and rushes to place his men down in their respective spots*) Get your men down, Jenkins!

MR. JENKINS (*sitting at the table*). Aw man, take it easy, the checkers ain't gon run away! (*Setting up his men*) If you could play the game, I wouldn't mind it—but you can't play! (*His men are in order now.*) Your move . . .

MR. PARKER. I'll start here . . . (*Makes his move*) Ever since Doris died, Adele's been giving me a fit about getting a job, and I know she's gon start messing with me again tonight about it . . .

MR. JENKINS. Don't you think it's about time? In the five

years I've been knowing you, I can count the heads of hair you done cut in this shop on one hand . . . I'll do this . . .

MR. PARKER. This shop is gon work yet—I know it can—just give me one more year, and you'll see . . . Going out to get a job ain't gon solve nothing—all it's gon do is create a lot of bad feelings with everybody . . . I can't work! I don't know how to! . . . I'll go there . . .

MR. JENKINS. And I'll go there . . . I bet if you had take care of yourself and live alone like I do, you'd know how to. That's one thing I don't understand about you, Parker. How can you expect your daughter to go on supporting you and those two boys?

MR. PARKER. I don't expect that, man! I'll give you this man . . . I just want some time until I can straighten things out. My dear Doris understood that . . . She understood me like a book . . .

MR. JENKINS. You mean to tell me your wife enjoyed working for you?

MR. PARKER. Of course she didn't—but she never worried me. You been married, Jenkins—you know what happens to a man when a woman worries him all the time, and that's what Adele's been doing—worrying my head off!

MR. JENKINS. Whatcha gon do about it?

MR. PARKER. I'm gon get tough—that's the only sign a woman gets from a man . . . Get tough and evil, that's what you do— and you know me, Jenkins, when I get evil, I get greasy, rusty, dusty evil! (*Makes a move and rises*) You're trapped, Jenkins!

MR. JENKINS (*pondering*). Hmmmmmmm . . . It looks that way, don't it?

MR. PARKER (*moves for the door*). While you're moaning over the board, I'll just make a little check to see if Adele is coming —don't cheat now! (*He moves backwards towards the window to make certain that his adversary does not cheat on him. He gets to the window and quickly takes a look out.*) Uh uh! It's Adele! She's in the middle of the block talking to Miss Thomas!

(*Rushes back to the table*) We got to quit now! (*Rushes to the shelf, takes a towel, returns to the table and spreads it over the checkerboard*) Come on man! (*Grabbing* MR. JENKINS *by the arm and forcibly leading him to the barber's throne.*)

MR. JENKINS. *What are you doing, Parker?*

MR. PARKER (*forcing him into the throne*). You need a shave!

MR. JENKINS (*jumping out of the throne and onto the floor*). I don't need no shave!

MR. PARKER. Then you gon have to hide out in the back room, cause if Adele comes in here and sees you, she'll think that you and me have been playing checkers all day!

(*The lights come up full on the back room where* THEOPOLIS PARKER *is descending the stairs, carrying a square bundle wrapped in an army blanket. He is in his twenties, of medium height, and has a lean solid physique. He places the bundle on the old desk. He is followed by his younger brother,* BOBBY PARKER, *carrying a jug of liquid. He places the jug under the desk.* BOBBY *is a well-built boy in his early twenties.*)

MR. JENKINS. I don't care about that!

(*The two boys hear the fuss with the two men and tiptoe to the door to listen in.*)

MR. PARKER. You wan't to finish the game, don't you?

MR. JENKINS. Yeah, but—

MR. PARKER. All you have to do, Jenks, is just lay low for a minute. One minute and that's all—She'll stop in like she always do—she'll ask me what I want for supper, and then she'll go on upstairs. There won't be nobody . . . left here, but you and me, and maybe the boys, but them two lazy bums don't count for nothing. Whatcha say, Jenks?

MR. JENKINS (*pause*). All right I'll do it—I don't like it, but I'll do it, and you better not mention this to nobody—you hear?

MR. PARKER. Not a single soul in this world will know but you and me.

(*They move for the back room.* THEOPOLIS *and* BOBBY *rip away from the door and scamper under the bed.*)

MR. JENKINS (*moves just inside the room and stands to the side of the door against the wall*). This is the most ridiculous thing I ever heard—of hiding in somebody's back room just to finish up a checker game . . .

MR. PARKER. Stop fighting it man!

MR. JENKINS. All right, I'm not—now get away from this door.

MR. PARKER. Not there!

MR. JENKINS. (*moving briskly back into the shop*). What in the hell is it, now?

MR. PARKER. *You've got to get under the bed*!

MR. JENKINS. I'm not gettin' under *nobody's* bed!

MR. PARKER (*rushes to the window, takes a quick look, and turns back to* MR. JENKINS). Sometimes when Adele comes in, she goes through the back room, and up the basement stairs to the apartment. Now you want her to catch you standing behind that door, looking like a fool?

MR. JENKINS. No—I can take myself out of here, and go home! (*Starts towards the door.*)

MR. PARKER (*grabbing him by the arms*). No you don't!

MR. JENKINS. Are you crazy, Parker?

MR. PARKER. (*pushes his friend over to the table and lifts the towel from the checkerboard*). Look at this! Now you just take a good look at this board! (*Releases him.*)

MR. JENKINS. I'm looking, so what?

MR. PARKER. So what? I got you and you know it! There ain't no way in the world you'll ever get out of that little trap I got you in. *And it's your move.* How many years we been playing against each other?

MR. JENKINS. Three . . .

MR. PARKER. Never won a game from you in all that time, have I?

MR. JENKINS. That ain't the half of it—you ain't gon win one either.

MR. PARKER. Now that I finally got you, that's easy talk comin' from a running man . . . All right, go on—run . . . (*Moves away from him.*)

MR. JENKINS. Go on hell! All I gotta do is put my king here, give you this jump here, move this man over there, and you're dead!

MR. PARKER (*turns to him*). Try me then—try me or are you scared at last I'm gon beat you!

MR. JENKINS. I can't do it now—there ain't enough time!

MR. PARKER (*moves away from him, strutting like a sport*). Run rabbit, run . . .

MR. JENKINS. All right, I'll hide under your bed, but I swear, I'm gon beat you, Parker!

MR. PARKER. Under the bed then . . .

MR. JENKINS (*moves to the door and stops*). It's got to be under?

(*It is at this precise moment that the two boys are scrambling to get out from under the bed. They make their way to the stairs and stop about three or four steps up.*)

MR. PARKER. All the way under . . .

MR. JENKINS. You'll have to help me—I'm not used to crawling under people's beds . . .

MR. PARKER. I'll help you . . .

(*The two boys' heads can be seen projecting out slowly, peeping on the old men as they foolishly struggle on the floor near the bed. After a short while, they make it, and* MR. PARKER *hurriedly moves back out into the barber shop. He takes out a notebook and pencil. He sits in the throne as if he's working out some astronomical plan or idea.*)

ADELE (*Enters. She is in her late twenties, well dressed in the conventional New York female office worker's garb. She is carrying a smart-looking purse, and a brown office envelope in her right hand*). Hello, Father . . .

MR. PARKER. Oh—Hi honey . . .

ADELE (*moves to him and kisses him on the forehead*). How's business?

MR. PARKER (*answers her as if he is deeply involved*). Slow . . .

ADELE. In other words, as usual . . .

MR. PARKER. As usual, but I've been sitting here for the past two hours, working out some new ideas.

ADELE. Good! We could use some new ideas—in fact, we could use a few old ones. (*Sits at the table where the checkerboard is.*)

MR. PARKER (*cringes for a moment*). My birthday comes up on the tenth of next month, and I plan to celebrate it with that one big idea to capture the attention of everybody within twenty blocks of this neighborhood, and then, I'm gon really go to the country.

ADELE. Don't go to the country—just cut a few hairs, huh . . . Oh God, I'm tired!

MR. PARKER (*jumps down from the chair and pulls her up in his arms*). Come on and let me take you upstairs so you can get yourself some rest—I know you must've had yourself a real rough day at the office . . . (*Leading her away from the table*) And you can forget about cooking supper and all that stuff . . .

ADELE (*breaks away from him and moves to the window and stops*). Thank you, Father, but I've already given myself the privilege of not cooking your supper tonight.

MR. PARKER. You did?

ADELE. There are a few matters you and I are going to take time out for—now.

MR. PARKER. Oh yeah—like what, honey?

(THEOPOLIS *and* BOBBY *step down into the room and listen in on their conversation momentarily, then move out into the shop and stand next to the door, side by side. They have surreptitious grins on their faces.*)

ADELE. Mother's insurance policy, and—(*Catches sight of the two boys*) Well! From what cave did you fellows crawl out of? I had no idea you hung around barbershops—Want a haircut, boys.

THEO. For your information, this is the first time we been in this barbershop today. We been upstairs, thinking . . .

ADELE. With what?

THEO. With our *minds*, baby!

ADELE. If the two of you found that house upstairs so attractive to keep you in it all day, then I can think of only three things: the telephone, the bed, and the kitchen.

BOBBY. The kitchen, that's it—we been washing dishes all day!

ADELE. I don't like that, Bobby!

THEO. And I don't like your attitude!

ADELE. Do you like it when I go out of here every morning to work!?

THEO (*pause*). Mama understood—I don't know why you gotta give everybody a hard time . . .

ADELE. That was one of Mama's troubles: understanding everybody. (*Pause*) Bless her . . .

THEO. Now don't start that!

ADELE. I have got to start *that*, MR. THEOPOLIS PARKER!

MR. PARKER. Hold on now—there's no need for all this!

ADELE. There is a need for something—Mama's been dead for three months . . . (*She opens the envelope and goes through the papers.*) and you fellows have gone on as if nothing happened—the only difference being, that there is one woman working instead of two—but I want to tell you: I am tired, and I have made it up in my mind, that some quick and pretty changes are going to be made if we're going to live together in this place . . .

THEO. And who gives you the right to say that?

ADELE. Me, Adele Eloise Parker, black, over twenty-one, and the only working *person in this house*! (*Fingers through the bills*) Every one of these bills here are in the name of *Doris Alice Parker*, and since I am the only one that's working who else was she going to leave them to—Here's your policy Daddy . . . (*Hands him the policy.*)

MR. PARKER (*taking the policy from her*). I've been looking all over for this policy, where—

ADELE. Let's talk about these bills! (*Pause*) Now something's got to be done about this situation, Daddy. It was enough of a hard time with just me and Mama working, but with Mama gone, it will simply be impossible for me to carry all this weight alone—and I am not going to let the three of you drive me into the graveyard the way Mama was . . . And if you really want to know how I feel about that, I'll tell you. Mama killed herself because there was no kind of order in this house—there was nothing but her old fashion love for a bum like you, Theo . . . and this one . . . (*points to* BOBBY) who's got nothing better to do with his time but to idolize you . . . And you, Daddy—you and those fanciful stories you're always ready to tell, and all the talk of the good old days when you were the big vaudeville star, of hitting the numbers. How? How Daddy? The money you spent on the numbers, you got from Mama. In a way, you let Mama make a bum out of you—You let her kill herself!

MR. PARKER. That's a terrible thing to say, Adele, and I'm not going to let you put that off on me!

ADELE. But the fact remains that in the seven years you have been in this barbershop, you haven't earned enough money to buy seven hot dogs! (*She moves abruptly to the table and snatches the towel from the checkerboard.*) Most of your time is spent with *this*!

(MR. PARKER *indignantly moves to the table and gazes down sadly on the board.*)

THEO. I hope you know what you're doing . . .

ADELE (*turns on him*). You object? (THEO *turns his back on her.*) Bobby?

BOBBY. It's okay with me . . .

ADELE. Theo?

THEO. Theo, what?

ADELE. You just go right on and be a clown if you want to!

THEO. I don't need you, Adele . . . Why don't you get married or something, and stop using me and Bobby to make yourself feel important. We don't need you—Pop is here—it's *his house*!

(*Turns to his father*) We're your sons, ain't that right, Pop?

ADELE. You're lucky I don't get married and—

THEO. Nobody wants you, baby!

ADELE. (THEO's *remark stabs and stops her for a moment. She resettles herself*). All right—or you just let someone ask me, and I'll leave you here with *Pop*, to starve with *Pop*—but that wouldn't be right, soon you'd have him in his grave . . . Or there's another way—why don't you just leave and try making it on your own? Why don't we try that, Theo? (*Everyone looks to* THEO.) Well?

THEO (*pause*). I'll stay . . .

ADELE. Under whose conditions?

THEO (*pause*). Yours . . .

ADELE. And those conditions have to do with getting a job for the three of you, starting with you, Daddy . . .

MR. PARKER. Work?

ADELE. That's right, Daddy, work . . .

MR. PARKER. What's goin' to happen to my shop?

ADELE. There's going to be no more shop—it was a bad investment, and the whole of Harlem knows it!

MR. PARKER (*grabbing her by the arm desperately*). *I'm an old man!*

ADELE (*pulling away from him*). Don't touch me!

MR. PARKER (*waving the policy in his hand*). I have this!

ADELE. Hush, Daddy, please hush—the money Mama left you on that policy couldn't feed you for six months—

MR. PARKER. You go ahead and do what you want, but I'm not leaving this shop!

ADELE. Can't you understand, Father! *I'm a woma*n, I can't go on supporting three grown men! *That ain't right!*

MR. PARKER (*her remark shakes him up a bit*). No, it's not right— it's not right at all . . .

ADELE. Something has to be done, Father—you should realize that . . . (THEO *and* BOBBY *start for the exit. Catching sight of them*) Come back here you two!

THEO. Now what?

ADELE. Jobs boys, jobs . . . The two of you, out of here to-morrow morning. I'll give you two weeks, and if you haven't found anything by that time, out you go!

THEO. That ain't fair!

ADELE. I don't want to hear it—it's going to be *me* or *you*.

BOBBY. I'll do what I can, Adele . . .

ADELE. You'll do more than you can . . .

BOBBY. I'll do more than I can . . .

ADELE. Is that all right by you, Mr. Theopolis?

THEO. Yes!

ADELE. That's fine . . . Out of this house tomorrow morning, before I leave here or with me—suit your choice. And don't look so mournful boys . . . (*Gathers up her belongings at the shelf*) Smile—you're going to be happier than you think, earn-ing a living for a change . . . (*Moves through the back room and on up the stairs.*)

BOBBY. You do look pretty bad, Theo . . . A job might be just the thing for you . . .

THEO. Who the hell do she think she's kidding—nobody's happy in Harlem.

(MR. JENKINS *scrambles out from under the bed in the back room and rushes into the shop.*)

MR. JENKINS. I heard every word she said, and I'm getting out of here!

BOBBY (*kidding*). Mr. Jenkins! When did you get here?

MR. JENKINS. I let you make a fool out of me, Parker!

MR. PARKER. We can still play!

MR. JENKINS. We can't play nothing, I'm going home where I belong!

MR. PARKER. Okay okay, I'll come over to your place to-night . . .

MR. JENKINS. That's the only way—I ain't gon have my feel-ings hurt by that girl of yours.

MR. PARKER. I'll see you tonight—about eight . . .

MR. JENKINS (*at the door*). Parker, tell me something.

MR. PARKER. Yeah, Jenks?

MR. JENKINS. You sure Adele is your daughter?

MR. PARKER. Get out of here! (MR. JENKINS *rushes out.*) Now what made him ask such a silly question like that?

THEO. I think he was trying to tell you that you ain't supposed to be taking all that stuff from Adele.

BOBBY. Yeah Pop—he's right . . .

(MR. PARKER *starts to put his checkerboard together.*)

THEO. Why don't you be quiet. You had your chance a few minutes ago, but all you did was poke your eyes at me, and nod your head like a fool; mumbling, "Yes, yes Miss Adele!"

BOBBY. I don't have anything against Adele. I don't see why you gotta make a big thing out of her taking charge . . . Somebody's gotta do it—I think she's right!

THEO. But she wants us to go out and get jobs! We ain't hit a lick at a snake in years! Now how she gon ask somebody to just up and switch their lives around like that, and go out and work on some job?

BOBBY. She's not right!

THEO. She's crazy! I've got other things to do with my life . . . I'm a painter, an artist! That's what I am. I ain't got time for no job—I've got artistry to think about.

BOBBY. You don't say!

(MR. PARKER *is standing at the throne fingering a pair of scissors. He motions to* BOBBY *to get into the chair.* BOBBY *sits in the chair as his father starts setting him up for a trim.*)

THEO (*sits in one of the chairs*). I know what she's up to . . . She wants us to get jobs so she can fix the house up like she always wanted it, and then it's gon happen . . .

BOBBY. What's that?

THEO. She gon get married to some konk head out on the Avenue, and then she gon throw us out the door.

BOBBY. She wouldn't do that . . .

THEO. She wouldn't huh? Put yourself in her place—she's

busting thirty wide open . . . *Thirty years old*—that's a lot of years for a broad that's not married.

BOBBY. I never thought of it that way . . .

THEO (*in half-confidence*). You know what? I peeped her bank book one day, and you know what she's got stashed away?

MR. PARKER AND BOBBY (*both turning their heads in his direction at the same time*). How much?

THEO. Four thousand, two hundred and sixty five dollars!

BOBBY. WHAT!

MR. PARKER. I don't believe it!

THEO. You better—and don't let her hand you that business about how she been sacrificing all these years for the house . . . The only way she could've saved up that kind of money was by staying right here! She better watch out is all I gotta say, cause I know some birds out there on that Avenue, who practice and practice every day of their lives on how to run through working girls and their savings accounts.

MR. PARKER. You oughta know, cause you're one of them yourself. Adele can take care of herself.

THEO. I wouldn't bet on it . . .

MR. PARKER. The way I figure it, Theo—anybody that can handle you, the way she did, can very well take care of themselves.

THEO. That's mighty big talk coming from you, after the way she treated you a few minutes ago. But he don't care, Bobby, he's not like you and me. We heard you tell Mr. Jenkins we weren't nothing but a couple of bums. He can talk that way, he's got his—got himself a big ol' fat policy in his hand . . . How much is it, Pop?

MR. PARKER. None of your damn business . . .

THEO. You got all that money and you goin' out to look for a job?

MR. PARKER. I'm giving it some serious thought . . .

THEO. Well, I'm not . . .

BOBBY. You lied when you said you would look for a job?

THEO. Didn't you?

BOBBY. Yeah, I guess I was lying . . .

THEO. She ain't using me for something as low and dirty as a job. I got my paintings to think about.

BOBBY. Do you really think you're some kind of painter or something?

THEO. You've seen them . . .

BOBBY. Yeah, but how would I know?

THEO. Yeah, how would you . . .

MR. PARKER. You're going to get a job or Adele's gon throw you out.

THEO. I can get by that—there are plenty of ways to fool her. And remember, I can always tell her I was discriminated against . . . That one always gets 'em . . .

BOBBY. You'll have to get up in the morning . . .

THEO. And I won't like it—but you can't win 'em all . . . I'll get up, like the good guy I am—leave the house, walk across 126th till I hit Fifth Avenue, make a right to 125th, back across to Lenox, make another right on Seventh, then another right on 126th, and by that time, she should be downtown, slaving away for the man.

BOBBY. That sounds more like work than getting a job . . . After all that, then what?

THEO. Back to bed—maybe get on the phone and call up one of my little girls . . .

BOBBY (*His father has finished with his hair. He hops down out of the chair*). I thought you said you wanted to do something with them pictures. You just jiving—you ain't no painter!

THEO (*heads for the back room*). I see you've got to be convinced . . . (THEO *rushes into the back room and unwraps his bundle on the old desk, takes out a painting, and hurriedly returns to the outer area of the shop. He holds the painting up before the eyes of* BOBBY. *It is an abstract conglomeration of many colors. Surprisingly, the painting is well done, and de-*

notes a sense of style. MR. PARKER *is at the other end of the shop, sweeping the floor.*) Now tell me what you see . . .

BOBBY. Nothing . . .

THEO. You've got to see something—even an idiot has impressions.

BOBBY. I ain't no idiot . . .

THEO. All right—sub-idiot.

BOBBY. Now look, you better stop throwing them words "fool" and "idiot" at me any time you feel like it. I'm gonna be one more "fool," and then my fist is gonna land right upside your head!

THEO. Take it easy now—look, Bobby, you must see something . . . I tell you what: try to see something . . .

BOBBY. Try?

THEO. Yeah, close your eyes and really try . . .

BOBBY (*closing his eyes*). Okay, I'm trying, but I don't know how I'm gon see anything with my eyes closed.

THEO. Well open them!

BOBBY. They opened . . .

THEO. Now tell me what you see . . .

BOBBY. I see paint . . .

THEO. I know you see paint, stupid!

BOBBY (*slaps him ferociously across the face*). Now I told you to stop it!

THEO. That hurts!

BOBBY. You ain't begun to hurt yet, if you keep calling me out of my name.

THEO. Can I call you *Robert* or *Bob*?

BOBBY. Just call me Bobby—that's what I'm used to . . .

THEO. *Bobby,* tell me about the paint you see . . .

BOBBY. There's red, yellow, and—

THEO. *Colors?*

BOBBY. That's right—colors . . .

THEO. Do the colors remind you of anything or anybody?

BOBBY. Russians and cowards!

THEO. Oh no! You will never understand!

BOBBY. All I know is that a picture is supposed to be pretty, but I'm sorry, that picture is ugly!

THEO. You're hopeless . . . You understand this, don't you, Pop? (*Moving towards his father to exhibit the painting.*)

MR. PARKER. (*ignoring him in not looking at the painting*). Don't ask me—I don't know nothing about no painting.

THEO. You were an artist once . . .

MR. PARKER. That was a different kind . . .

THEO. Didn't you ever go out on the stage with a new thing inside of you? One of them nights when you just didn't want to do that ol' "Uncle Tom" soft shoe routine. You knew you had you gave it a little bite here, a little acid there, and still with all of that, they laughed at you anyway. Didn't that ever happen to you?

MR. PARKER. More than once . . .

THEO. Well, it's the same way with me . . . I want you and Bobby to look at this painting and see what's behind it. Not just colors that are pretty or ugly, but life!

MR. PARKER. Then you better stop beating around the bush about it, and stop trying to make me think to see . . . I got eyes —let me see first, let me have no doubts about what I'm seeing, Then I'll tell you what I'm thinking about.

BOBBY. Me too . . .

THEO. You! (*Pause*) Maybe you got something . . .

MR. PARKER. I think you're BS'n boy . . . You been something every year since you quit school . . . First you was going to be a writer, then a airplane pilot, then a office big shot. Now it's a painter. As smart a boy as you is, you should stick to one thing, and maybe you'll be it. But who do you think you're fooling—it all boils down to one thing—you don't want to work —but I'll tell you something, Theo—time done run out on you . . . Adele's not playing, so you just might as well put them pictures away.

THEO. Aw no, Pop, I believe in these paintings. I put a lot of my time, and myself, into this.

MR. PARKER. Don't tell it to me—tell it to Adele . . .

THEO. Who the hell is Adele . . . you're my father, you're the man of the house . . .

MR. PARKER. True, and that's what I intend to be, but until I get a job, I'm gon play it cool . . .

THEO. You're going to let her push you out into the streets to hussle up a job. You're an old man, Pop. You ain't used to working—it might kill you . . .

MR. PARKER. Yeah, but what kind of leg do I have to stand on if she tells me to get out?

THEO. She's bluffing!

MR. PARKER. The last fellow I knew who was in this kind of fix told me exactly what you just said. Well, the last time I saw him, he was standing on the corner of Eighth Avenue and 125th Street, at four o'clock in the morning—twenty degree weather! In nothing but his drawers! Mumbling to himself, "I could've sworn she was bluffing!"

THEO. Let me put it to you this way. If none of us come up with anything in that two-week deadline she gave us . . . None of us, you hear me?

MR. PARKER. I hear you, and that's about all . . .

THEO. Don't you get the point? That's three of us—you, me, and Bobby. What she gon do? Throw the three of us out? I tell you, Pop, she ain't gon do that!

MR. PARKER. If you want to take that chance, that's your business, but don't try to make me take it with you. Anyway, it ain't right, she has to work for three grown rusty men—it just ain't right . . .

THEO. Mama did it for you . . .

MR. PARKER. That was different . . . She was my wife . . . She knew things about me you will never know. We oughtn' talk about her at all . . .

THEO. I'm sorry Pop, but ever since Mama's funeral, I've

been thinking. Mama was the hardest working person I have ever known, and it killed her! Is that what I'm supposed to do? No, that's not it—I know that's not it . . . So, I went to talk to some people—some people right here in Harlem. I told them about this big idea of mine—

MR. PARKER. You are loaded with ideas, boy—*bad ideas!*

THEO. WHY DON'T YOU LISTEN TO WHAT I HAVE TO SAY?

MR. PARKER (*pause*). Let me see those paintings.

(THEO *gives him the one painting he has been holding in his hand and moves into the back room to get the others. He rushes back out with two other paintings and holds them up before* MR. PARKER'S *eyes.*)

THEO. How am I doing?

MR. PARKER. (*scanning*). Bobby was right, they're ugly . . .

THEO (*moves back into the back room to put the paintings away*). I haven't seen many pretty things in my life, Pop.

MR. PARKER (*talking to him from out in the shop*). Whatever it was you had in mind when you painted these colors, it was all your own—you weren't lying!

THEO (*stands in the doorway of the back room*). Naw, I wasn't lying—*this is something I really want to do*—I can feel it worrying me when I don't think I know what I'm doing—when I think, maybe I wasn't cut out to be anything but what I am. I need my own time to find that out—I swear to God I do, Pop . . .

MR. PARKER. You're a smart boy—in a strange sort of way though. I call it uneducated smart, and that's the best kinda smart there is. That's the way I am. I think I'm gon let you help me with the writing of my book of old time stories.

THEO (*turns into the back room, drops to his knees, and opens up a trap door on the floor*). When you get ready for me to help you, I'll be right here, but first I got something here I want you to taste . . . (*Takes out a jug from under the floor, rises, moves out into the shop, holding it up in his right hand.*)

MR. PARKER. What is it?

THEO. Whiskey—corn whiskey . . . You want some?

(BOBBY *fetches three glasses and places them on the table.*)

MR. PARKER. Well I'll try a little bit of it out. But we better not let Adele see it . . .

THEO (*sits at the table*). You cold let that girl put a scare in you Pop—and I remember you when you wouldn't take no stuff off Mama, Adele or nobody. You used to get so mean and bad, you'd get scared of yourself . . .

MR. PARKER. God is the only person I fear . . . (*Sits.*)

THEO (*starts to unscrew the top*). You're all alike!

MR. PARKER. Who're you talking about?

THEO. You, the way Mama was—ask you a question—any question you can't answer, and you throw that Bible stuff at us.

MR. PARKER. I don't get you . . .

THEO (*having trouble unscrewing the cork*). For instance, let me ask you about the black man's oppression; and you'll tell me about some small nation in the East rising one day to rule the world . . . Ask you about pain and dying; and you say, God wills it . . . Fear?—and you'll tell me about Daniel, and how Daniel wasn't scared of them lions . . . Am I right or wrong?

MR. PARKER. It's in the book and you can't dispute it.

THEO (*finally opens the jug*). You wanta bet? If that nation in the East ever do rise, I don't think I'm gon be around that long to see it, and if by some chance I am, how can I be sure they won't be worse than the jokers we got already . . . Nobody, but nobody wills me to pain and dying—not if I can do something about it—that goes for John, Peter, Mary, J. C., the whole bunch of 'em! And as for ol' Daniel— Sure, Daniel didn't care nothing about them lions—*but them lions didn't give a damn about him, either! They tore him up!*

MR. PARKER (*rises from the table indignantly*). That's an ungodly, unholy lie! (*Takes his Bible from the shelf*) And I'll prove it!

THEO. What lie?

MR. PARKER (*moving to the table thumbing through his Bible*). You and those bastard ideas of yours . . . Here, here it is! (*Reading from the Bible*)

> And when he came near unto the den to Daniel, he cried with a pained voice; the King spoke and said to Daniel: "O Daniel, servant of the living God, is thy God, Whom thou servest continually, able to deliver thee from the lions?" Then said Daniel unto the King: "O King, live forever! My God hath sent His angels, and hath shut the lions' mouths, and they have not hurt me; forasmuch as before Him innocency was found in me, and also before thee, O King, have I done no hurt." Then was the King exceeding glad, and commanded that they should take Daniel up out of the den. So Daniel was taken up out of the den, and no manner of hurt was found upon him, because he trusted in his God!

(*Slams the book closed, triumphantly.*)

THEO. Hollywood, Pop, Hollywood!

MR. PARKER. Damn you! How I ever brought somethin' like you into this world, I will never know! You are no damn good! Sin! That's who your belief is! Sin and corruption! With you, it's nothing but women! Whiskey! Women! Whiskey! (*While he is carrying on in this ranting fashion,* THEO *pours out a glass of his corn and slides the glass just under* MR. PARKER's *hand at the table. Reaches for the glass*) Whisk—(*Takes a taste*) Where did you get this from!?

THEO (*slapping* BOBBY's *hand*). I knew you'd get the message, Pop—I just knew it!

MR. PARKER. This is great corn, boy!

BOBBY. And Theo makes it like he was born to make it!

MR. PARKER. Where did you learn to make corn like this?

THEO. Don't you remember?—you taught me.

MR. PARKER. By George, I did . . . Why, you weren't no morn' nine years old . . .

THEO. Eight—let's have another one . . . (*He pours another round for the three of them.*) Drink up . . . Here's to ol' Daniel . . . You got to admit one thing—he had a whole lot of heart!

MR. PARKER. (*drinks up and puts his hand out again*). Another one, please . . .

THEO (*pouring*). Anything you say, Pop! *You're the boss of this place!*

MR. PARKER (*drinks up*). Now that's the truth if you ever spoke it . . . (*Puts his glass out again*) Whew! This is good! (*Getting tipsy now.*)

THEO (*pouring*). About this idea I had, Pop . . . Well, it's got something to do with this corn . . .

MR. PARKER (*drinks up*). Yeah! (*Puts his glass out again.*)

THEO. Well, I tested some of it out the other day, and I was told this corn liquor here could start a revolution—that is, if I wanted to start one. I let a preacher taste some, and he asked me to make him a whole keg for his communion next month.

MR. PARKER (*drinks up*). God dammit! (*Throws his glass on the floor.*)

BOBBY. What's wrong, Pop?

MR. PARKER. I miss her, boy, I tell you, I miss her!

BOBBY. Pop—Pop, don't, don't you cry like that—don't you cry.

MR. PARKER. Was it really God's will?

THEO. Don't you believe that—don't you ever believe that!

MR. PARKER. But I think, boy—I think hard!

THEO. That's all right . . . We think hard too. We got it from you, ain't that right, Bobby?

BOBBY. Yeah . . .

MR. PARKER (*pause*). You know something? That woman was the first woman I ever kissed . . . Your Mama . . .

BOBBY. How old were you?

MR. PARKER. Twenty . . .

BOBBY. Aw come on, Pop!

MR. PARKER. May God wipe me away from this earth . . .

THEO. Twenty years old—damn, you must've been in bad shape!

MR. PARKER. I'll tell you about it . . .

THEO. I knew it! Here he goes with another one of his famous stories!

MR. PARKER. I can always go on upstairs, you know . . .

THEO. All right, let us hear it . . .

MR. PARKER. Well, I was working in this circus in Tampa, Florida—your mother's home town. You remember Bob Shepard—well, we had this little dance routine of ours we used to do a sample of outside the tent. One day, we was out there doing one of our numbers, when right in the middle of the number, I spied this fine, foxy looking thing, blinking her eyes at me. Course ol' Bob kept telling me it was him she was looking at, but I knew it was *me*—cause if there was one thing that was my specialty, it was a fine-looking woman.

THEO. Twenty years, and *your specialty?*

MR. PARKER. Yeah, being that—

THEO.—that you had never had a woman for all them terrible years, naturally, it was on your mind all the time . . .

MR. PARKER. That's right . . .

THEO.—and it being on your mind so much, you sorta became a specialist on women.

MR. PARKER. Right again . . .

THEO (*laughs*). I don't know, but I guess you got a point there! (*Continues to laugh.*)

MR. PARKER. You want to hear this or not!

BOBBY. You go on, Pop . . .

MR. PARKER. Well, while I was standing on the back of the platform, I motions to her with my hand to kinda move around to the side of the stand, so I could talk to 'er. She strolled round to the side, stood there for a while, and you know what? Ol' Bob wouldn't let me get a word in edgewise. But you know what she told him; she said, "Mister, you talk like a fool!" (*Laughs.*)

BOBBY. That was Mama . . .

MR. PARKER. So, I asked her if she would like to meet me after the circus closed down, and I would take her for a walk. When I got off that night, sure enough, she was waiting for me. We walked up to the main section of town, off to the side of the road, cause we had a hard rain that day, and the road was full of muddy little ponds. I got to talking to her and telling her funny little stories, and she would laugh—boy I'm telling you, that woman could laugh!

THEO. That was your technique, huh? Keep 'em laughing . . .

MR. PARKER. Believe it or not, it worked—cause she let me kiss her. I kissed her under this big ol' pecan tree. She could kiss too. When that woman kissed me, somethin' grabbed me so hard, and shook me so, I fell flat on my back into a big puddle of water! *And that woman killed herself laughing!* (*pause*) I married her two weeks later . . .

THEO. And then you started making up for lost time. I'm glad you did, Pop—cause if you hadn't, I wouldn't be here today.

MR. PARKER. If I know you, you'd have made some kind of arrangement.

BOBBY. What happened after that?

MR. PARKER. We just lived and had fun—and children too, that part you know about. We lived bad and we lived good—and then my legs got wobbly, and my feet got heavy, and nothing seemed to change any more. I lost my feeling, and everything just stayed as it was. (*Pause*) I only wish I had been as good a haircutter as I was a dancer. Maybe she wouldn't have had to work so hard. She might be living today.

THEO. Forget it Pop—it's all in the gone by . . . Come on, you need another drink . . . (*Pouring.*)

MR. PARKER (*taking the drink*). Get me talking about them old days—it hurts, I tell you it—

THEO. Pop, you have got to stop thinking about those things. We've got work to do!

MR. PARKER. You said you had an idea . . .

THEO. Yes—you see, Pop, this idea has to do with Harlem. It has to do with the preservation of Harlem. That's what it's all about. So, I went to see this leader, and I spoke to him about it. He thought it was great and said he would pay me to use it!

MR. PARKER. Who the hell wants to preserve this dump? Tear it down is what I say!

THEO. But this is a different kind of preserving . . . Preserve it for black men—that's my idea—preserve it for men like you, me and Bobby.

MR. PARKER. That sounds good . . .

THEO. Well, I told this leader, I would never promise to do anything until I had spoken to my father. So, I said, after I had straightened out everything with you, I would make arrangements for the two of you to meet.

MR. PARKER. Meet him for what?

THEO. For making money! For business! *This man knows how to put people in business!*

MR. PARKER. All right, I'll meet this man, what his name—

THEO. But you're gonna have to have a showdown with Adele, and put her in her place, once and for all . . .

MR. PARKER. I don't know how I'm gon do that now . . .

THEO. This man can't be dealing with no men who let women rule them. Pop, you've got to show that girl a thing or two, or we cannot call ourselves men!

MR. PARKER. And if I don't—what do we call us?

THEO. What do they call men who wear pink and silk bloomers?

MR. PARKER. All right! If Adele don't like it that's too bad! That's one thing I ain't never been accused of!

THEO. Now, that's the way I like to hear my old man talk! Take a drink, Pop! (THEO *starts popping his fingers and moving dancingly about the floor.*)

We're gonna show 'em now

We're gonna show 'em how

All over

This ol' Harlem Town!

(THEO *and* BOBBY *start making rhythmic scat sounds with their lips as they move about dancing on the floor.*) Come on, Pop—show us how you used to cut one of them things!

BOBBY (*trying his hand at the dance*). This is the way he did it!

THEO. Nawwww, that's not it—he did it like this! (*Makes an attempt.*)

MR. PARKER. No, no! Neither one of you got it! Speed that riff up a little bit . . . (*The two boys speed up the riff a bit, singing, stomping their feet, and clapping their hands. Humped over, looking on the floor with pointed concentration*) Faster! (*They speed it up more.*)

THEO. Come on now, Pop—let 'er loose!

MR. PARKER. Give me time . . .

BOBBY. Let that man have some time!

(MR. PARKER *breaks into his dance.*)

THEO. Come on Pop, take it with you!

BOBBY. Work, Pop!

THEO. Downtown!

(MR. PARKER *does a coasting "camel walk."*)

BOBBY. Now bring it on back uptown!

(*He really breaks loose into a rapid series of complicated dance steps.*)

THEO. Yeah!

BOBBY. That's what I'm talking about!

(ADELE *enters and quickly moves out into the shop.* BOBBY, *in one motion, grabs the broom and starts sweeping;* THEO, *in one motion, picks up the waste basket and is heading for the door.* MR. PARKER *reaches for his razor and starts sharpening on his throne's belt.*)

ADELE. Fellows! (*They all stop in their motions.*) You can come upstairs now—dinner is served!

CURTAIN

ACT I

Scene 2

Two weeks later . . . late afternoon.
BOBBY *is seated in the barber's throne, eating away on a sandwich.* THEO *enters from the front of the shop.*

THEO. At it again, dammit!

BOBBY. Hi . . .

THEO. This is a miserable world we live in . . .

BOBBY. Uh huh . . .

THEO. Don't you think so?

BOBBY. Naw . . .

THEO (*snatching the sandwich out of his mouth*). Because you eat too damn much!

BOBBY. Why did you do that?

THEO (*handing the sandwich back to him*). Because I can never talk to you . . . I can never talk to you like brother to brother—cause you always got a mouth full of peanut butter and jelly!

BOBBY. I'm hungry! And let me tell you something—don't you *ever* snatch any food from my mouth again.

THEO. You'll hit me—that's because you're violent . . . You don't care nothing about your brother—that's why you're always hitting me. One of these days, I'm gon hit back.

BOBBY. The day you swing your hand on me, you'll draw back a nub!

THEO. You see! That's exactly what I mean. Now when Blue gets here tonight I don't want you talking like that or else you gon blow the whole deal.

BOBBY. I know how to act, and I don't need no lessons from you.

THEO. Good—cause I got a job for you.

BOBBY. A job! (*Jumps out of the chair.*)

THEO. Don't get knocked out—it ain't no real job. I just want

you to jump over to Smith's on 125th, and pick me up a porta-
ble typewriter.

BOBBY. Typewriter—for what?

THEO. Don't ask questions, just go and get it . . .

BOBBY. Them typewriters cost a lotta money . . .

THEO. You ain't gon use money . . .

BOBBY. You mean—

THEO. I mean you walk in there and take one . . .

BOBBY. Naw, you don't mean I walk into nowhere and take
nothing!

THEO. Now, Bobby—

BOBBY. No!

THEO. Aw, come on baby Bobby, you the one been bragging
about how good you are, and how you can walk into any store
and *buy* anything you wanted, provided it was not too heavy
to carry out.

BOBBY. I ain't gon do it!

THEO. You know what day it is?

BOBBY. Thursday . . .

THEO. That's right, Thursday, October 10th . . .

BOBBY. What's that suppose to mean; thieves' convention at
the furniture stores on 125th?

THEO. You know? For a brother of mine, you sure don't have
much faith in me . . . *It's Pop's birthday!*

BOBBY. I didn't know he was still having them . . .

THEO. Oh yes, and you wanta know who remembered it before we did? Adele, and she's planning on busting into this
shop tonight with a birthday cake to surprise him—all she gon
have is a cake and a box of cigars—but with a typewriter, we'll
be giving him something different!

BOBBY. Nope . . .

THEO. Okay, I'll go get it myself . . .

BOBBY. That I'd like to see . . . TYPEWRITER! (*Laughs.*)

THEO. Have all the fun you want . . .

BOBBY. What's he gon type?

THEO. Them lies he's always telling—like the one about how he met Momma. Pop can tell some of the greatest lies you ever heard of . . . You heard him say he was writing them down.

BOBBY. Pop don't know nothing about writing—specially no typewriting!

THEO (*takes out his father's notebook*). Oh no—take a look at this . . . (*Hands the notebook to his brother*) All he has to do is put it down on paper the way he tells it. Who knows, somebody might get interested in it, and we can make ourselves some money, and besides, I kinda think he would get a real charge out of you thinking about him that way—don't you.

BOBBY. Well, ain't no use in lettin' you go over there with your old clumsy fingers . . .

THEO. Good boy, baby Bobby . . . (MR. PARKER *enters the shop from the front entrance.*) Hey, Pop!

MR. PARKER. Hi son . . .

THEO. Did you get that thing straighten out with Adele, yet?

MR. PARKER. What?

THEO. *Adele?*

MR. PARKER. Oh yeah, I'm gon do that as soon as I get time . . .

THEO. Where you been all day?

MR. PARKER. Downtown, seeing about some jobs . . .

THEO. You sure don't care much about yourself . . .

MR. PARKER. I can agree with you, because looking for a job can really hurt a man . . .

THEO. Didn't I tell you . . .

MR. PARKER. I was interviewed five times today, and I could've shot every last one of them interviewers—the white ones, and the colored ones too. I don't know if I can take any more of this.

THEO. Yeah, looking for a job can be very low grading to a man, even more so after you get one. Anyway, I'm glad you got back here on time or you would've missed your appointment.

MR. PARKER. What appointment?

THEO. Now don't tell me you don't remember! The man, the

man that's suppose to come here and tell you how life in Harlem can be profitable.

MR. PARKER. Oh, that . . .

THEO. Oh, that my foot! Today is the day we're suppose to come up with those jobs, and you ain't said one word to Adele about it—not one single word! All you do is waste your time, looking for work! Now that don't make no sense at all, Pop, and you know it . . .

MR. PARKER. Look, son—let me go upstairs now and tell her about all the disappointments I suffered today—that'll soften her up a bit, and then I'll come on back down here to meet your man. I promise, you won't have to worry about me going downtown anymore—not after what I went through today, and I certainly ain't giving up my shop, for nobody!

THEO. Now that's the way to talk!

(MR. PARKER *moves through the back room and on up the stairway. A jet black-complexioned young man, dressed in all black, wearing large dark sun glasses, and holding a gold-top cane in his right hand, enters. He is carrying a large salesman's valise in his left hand. He stops just inside the door.*) Blue baby! (*Extending his hand for a shake.*)

BLUE. Am I late?

THEO. No, my father just walked into the door—he's upstairs now, but he'll be right back down in two minutes . . . Let me take your things . . . (*Relieves* BLUE *of his cane and valise*) Sit down man and I'll serve you a drink . . . (*Moves into the back room and places* BLUE's *things on the bed.*)

BLUE. Hey, Bobby, how's the stores been treating you? (*Sits.*)

BOBBY. I'm planning on retiring next year . . . (*Laughs.*)

THEO (*Returning with his jug and three glasses. Moves to the table and starts pouring*). I was thinking, Blue—I don't think we oughta tell Pop about our "Piano Brigade" . . . That's the one thing he will not buy. Let's just keep that to ourselves, and we can play it where he will never never know.

BLUE. You know your father . . . (*Takes a drink.*)

BOBBY (*taking his drink*). What's the "Piano Brigade"?

THEO. Blue here has some of the best thieves in this part of town, and we plan to work on those stores over on 125th until they run the insurance companies out of business . . .

BOBBY. You mean breaking into people's stores at night, and taking their stuff?

THEO. That's right, but not the way you do it. We'll be organized, and on top of it, we'll be revolutionary.

BOBBY. If the police catch you, he ain't gon care what you is, and if Pop ever finds out, the police gon seem like church girls! (*Moves hurriedly out of the front door.*)

THEO. You just remember that the only crime is the one you get caught at!

BLUE. How's your sister, Theo?

THEO. You mean Adele?

BLUE. You got a sister named Mary or something?

THEO. What's this business with Adele?

BLUE. I want to know how are you going to get along with her, selling bootleg whiskey in this place?

THEO. This is not her place—it's my father's, and once he puts his okay on the deal, that's it . . . What kind of house do you think we're living in, where we gon let some woman tell us what to do . . . Come here, let me show you something . . . (*Moves into the back room as* BLUE *follows*) How you like it? Ain't it something?

BLUE (*standing in the doorway*). It's a back room . . .

THEO. Yeah, I know, but I have some great plans for reshaping it by knocking this wall down, and putting—

BLUE. Like I said, it's a back room—all I wanta know is will it do the job . . . It's a good room and you'll do great with that good-tasting corn liquor of yours. You're going to be so busy here, you're going to grow to hate this place—you might not have any time for your love life, Theopolis!

THEO. (*laughing*). Don't you worry about that—I can manage my sex life!

BLUE. Sex? Who's talking about sex? You surprise me, Theo . . . Everyone's been telling me about how you got so much heart, how you so deep. I sit and talk to you about life, and you don't know the difference between sex and love.

THEO. Is it that important?

BLUE. Yes it is ol' buddy if you want to hang out with me, and you do want to hang out with me, don't you?

THEO. That depends . . .

BLUE. It depends on you knowing that sex's got nothing to do with anything but you and some woman laying up in some funky bed, pumping and sweating your life away all for one glad moment—you hear that, *one moment*!

THEO. I'll take that moment!

BLUE. With every woman you've had?

THEO. One out of a hundred!

BLUE (*laughing*). One out of a hundred! All that sweat! All that pumping and grinding for the sake of one little dead minute out of a hundred hours!

(MR. PARKER *enters the shop from upstairs briskly, but stops in his tracks upon seeing* BLUE. *He stares bewilderedly at the man.*)

THEO. Pop, you know who this is?

MR. PARKER (*moves near the young man, bends, straining his eyes to get a good look*). I can't see him . . .

THEO. This is Blue!

MR. PARKER. Blue who?

THEO. The man I was telling you about . . . *Mr. Blue Haven.*

MR. PARKER. Oh yeah . . . (*Extends his hand for a shake*) Glad to make your acquaintance, Mr Haven . . .

BLUE (*shaking* MR. PARKER's *hand*). Same to you, Mr. Parker . . .

MR. PARKER. I'm sorry to keep you waiting, but my daughter and me, we had to talk over some important matters . . .

THEO. You sure you don't know who Blue Haven is, Pop?

MR. PARKER. I'm sorry, but I truly don't know you, Mr.

Haven . . . If you're a celebrity, you must accept my apology. You see, since I got out of the business, I don't read *Variety* anymore.

THEO. I'm not talking about a celebrity.

MR. PARKER. Oh, no?

THEO. He's the leader!

MR. PARKER. OH!

THEO. Right here in Harlem . . .

MR. PARKER. Where else he gon be but in Harlem—we got more leaders within ten square blocks of this barbershop than they got liars in City Hall—that's why you dressed up that way, huh boy? So they can pick you out of a crowded room!

THEO. Pop, this is serious!

MR. PARKER. All right, go on. There are some things I don't catch on to right away, Mr. Blue . . .

THEO. Get to this. I got to thinking the other day when Adele busted in here shoving everybody around—I was thinking about this barbershop, and I said to myself: Pop's gon lose this shop if he don't start making himself some money.

MR. PARKER. Now tell me something I don't know . . .

THEO. Here, I go . . . What would you say, if I were to tell you, that Blue here can make it possible for you to have a thriving business going on, right here in this shop, for twenty-four hours a day?

MR. PARKER. What is he? Some kind of hair-grower!

THEO. Even if you don't cut but one head of hair a week!

MR. PARKER. Do I look like a fool to you?

THEO (*holds up his jug*). Selling this!

MR. PARKER (*pause*). Well, well, well. I knew it was something like that. I didn't exactly know what it was, but I knew it was something, and I don't want to hear it!

THEO. Pop, you've always been a man to listen . . . Even when you didn't agree, even when I was wrong, you listened! You are charitable that way, that's the kind of man you are! You—

MR. PARKER. I'm listening!

THEO (*pause*). Tell him who you are, Blue . . .

BLUE. I am the Prime Minister of the Harlem De-Colonization Association.

MR. PARKER (*pause*). Some kind of organization?

BLUE. Yes . . .

MR. PARKER (*as an aside, almost under his breath*). They got all kinds of committees in Harlem. What was that name again, "De"?

THEO. De-colo-ni-zation! Which means that Harlem is owned and operated by "*Mr. You Know Who.*" Come on here in the back, and we will show you something. (MR. PARKER *follows the young men into the back room where they get busy immediately, pinning charts on the wall.*) Take a look at these charts if you think we're fooling.

MR. PARKER (*reading from the center chart*). The Harlem De-Colonization Association, with future perspectives for Bedford Stuyvesant. (*Turns to* BLUE) All right, so you got an organization. What do you do? I've never heard of you.

BLUE. The only reason you've never heard of us is because we don't believe in picketing, demonstrating, rioting, and all that stuff. We're different . . . We're nonviolent. I wouldn't ask you to do anything that was violent. You might get yourself hurt that way. I have a sworn affidavit, signed personally by myself, that none of my members will ever get hurt. We stand firm as nonviolents. Of course, that don't mean we're passive. To the contrary—we believe in direct action. We are doers, enterprisers, thinkers, and most important of all, we're businessmen! Our aim is to drive "Mr. You Know Who" out of Harlem.

MR. PARKER. Who's this "Mr. You Know Who"?

THEO. Damn, Pop! *The white man!*

MR. PARKER. OH, himmm!

BLUE. We like to use that name for our members, in order to get away from the bad feelings we have whenever we use the word "white." We want our members to always be objective.

And in this way, we'll drive forward, and before we get through, there won't be a single "Mr. You Know Who" left in this part of town. We're going to capture the imagination of the people of Harlem. That's never been done before, you know.

MR. PARKER. Now tell me how.

BLUE (*standing before the charts with his cane pointed on the wall*). You see this here . . . This is what we call a "Brigade." And you see this yellow circle here?

MR. PARKER. Uh huh . . .

BLUE. That's what we call the "Circle Brigade."

MR. PARKER. What's that for?

BLUE. That is part of my dream to create here in Harlem a symbolic life force in the heart of the people . . .

MR. PARKER. I see . . .

BLUE. Pin up that target, Theo . . .

(THEO *takes a large sheet of paper from* BLUE's *bag and pins it on the wall. It is a dart target with the face of a beefy-faced Southern-looking white man right in the bull's-eye area of the target.*)

MR. PARKER. Why that's that ol' dirty sheriff from that little town in Mississippi!

BLUE (*taking one of the darts from* THEO). That's right—we got a face on a target for every need. We got governors, mayors, backwoods crackers, city crackers, Southern crackers, and Northern crackers. We got all kinds of faces on these targets, that any good Harlemite would be willing to buy one for the sake of slinging one of these darts right in this bastard's throat!

(BLUE *throws the dart and it punctures face on the board.*)

MR. PARKER. Let me try it one time . . . (*He takes dart from board, moves back, and slings it into the target's face.*) Got him! (*A big laugh*).

BLUE. It's like I said, Mr. Parker, the idea is to capture the imagination of the people of Harlem!

MR. PARKER. You got more? Let me see more!

BLUE. Now over here where you see this red circle. That's

Theo and his corn liquor. This corn liquor of Theo's can make an everlasting contribution to this life force I've been talking about. I've tested this whiskey out in every neighborhood in Harlem, and everybody claimed it was the best they ever tasted this side of Washington, D. C. We plan to supply every after-hour joint in this area.

THEO. You see, Pop, this can only be unless the barbershop is opened night and day, so the people can come and go as they please, to pick up their play for the day, to get a bottle of corn, and to take one of the targets home to the kiddies. They can walk in just as if they were getting a haircut. In fact, I told Blue that we can give a haircut as a bonus for anyone who buys two quarts at a time, and later on we can give out "Triple S Stamps" for gifts. (*Pause.*)

MR. PARKER. What am I suppose to say now?

THEO. You're suppose to be daring. You're suppose to wake up to the times, Pop . . . These are urgent days—a man has to stand up and be counted!

MR. PARKER. The police might have some counting of their own to do . . .

THEO. Do you think I would bring you into something that was going to get us in trouble? Blue has an organization! Just like "Mr. You Know Who." He's got members on the police force! In the city government, the state government, and we're working on the White House!

MR. PARKER. Boy, there is no end to you. You're just like that old man in that song about a river. You just go on and on and on!

BLUE. Mr. Parker, if you have any reservations concerning the legitimacy of my association, I'd be only too happy to have you come to my summer home, and I'll let you in on everything —especially our protective system against being caught doing this thing.

THEO. You hear that, Pop, *he's got a summer home!*

MR. PARKER. Aw shut up boy! Let me think! (*Pause*) So you

want to use my place as a headquarters for Theo's corn, and them targets?

BLUE. Servicing the area of 125th to 145th, from East to West rivers.

MR. PARKER (*pause*). I'm sorry fellows, but I can't do it . . .

THEO. Why, Pop?

MR. PARKER. It's not right . . .

THEO. Not right! What are you talking about? Is it right, that all that's out there for me is to go downtown and push one of them carts? I have done that, and I ain't gon do it no more! You hear me, Pop? No more!

MR. PARKER. That still don't make it right . . .

THEO. I don't buy it! I'm going into this thing with Blue, with or without you!

MR. PARKER. Go on, I don't care! You quit school, I couldn't stop you from that! I asked you to get a job, you wouldn't work! You have never paid any attention to any of my advice, and I don't expect you to start heeding me now!

THEO. Pop, please—it'll work, I know it'll work . . . Give me this one chance, and I swear to do something with my life! Please!

MR. PARKER. Stop begging, Theo! (*To* BLUE) Why?

BLUE. I don't get you . . .

MR. PARKER. Why have you gone to so much pain to dream up this cockeyed ridiculous plan of yours?

BLUE. It is not ridiculous! It works! It grooves! It moves! It soothes the soul! It upends! It transcends! It deliberates! It copulates!

MR. PARKER. Hold it! Hold it! I believe you!

BLUE. Mr. Parker, I was born and raised about six blocks from here, and before I was ten, I had the feeling I had been living for a hundred years. I got so old and tired, I didn't know how to cry. Now you just think about that— a ten-year-old boy who couldn't cry. But about two years ago, I woke up one morning, bawling and wailing like a baby—what a reverse that was—and I've been crying like a man that was out of his mind ever since! (*Reaches into his pocket, pulls out a stack of bills, and places it on the table*) I'm ready to put you in business, *man!*

(MR. PARKER *takes the money from the table and sifts through the stack.*)

THEO. That's to get us started—and if we can make a dent into "Mr. You Know Who's" going-ons in Harlem, nobody's gon think of us as crooks. We'll be heroes from 110th Street to Sugar Hill. And just think, Pop, you won't have to worry about jobs and all that. You'll have so much time for you and Mr. Jenkins to play checkers, your arms will drop off. You'll be able to sit as long as you want, and tell enough stories and lies to fit between the covers of a five-hundred-page book. That's right! Remember you said you wanted to write all them stories down! Now you'll have the time for it! You can dress up the way you used to in the old days—and the girls . . . Remember how you used to be so tough with the girls before you got married? All that can come back to you, Pop! And some of that you never had. It's so easy! All you have to do is call Adele down those stairs, and let her know that you're going into business, and if she don't like it, she can move out, because you're not going to let her drive you down, you've got too much at stake, you're a man, and—

MR. PARKER. All right! All right! (*Pause*) I'll do it under one condition . . .

BLUE. Yes . . .

MR. PARKER. That is if my buddy Jenkins wanta buy into this deal, you'll let him . . .

BLUE. Theo . . . ?

THEO. Why not . . .

MR. PARKER (*extending his hand to* BLUE). Then you got yourself some partners, Mr. Haven!

BLUE. Welcome into the Association, Mr. Parker . . .

MR. PARKER. Welcome into my barbershop!

THEO (*jumps up into the air*). Yeah!

BLUE (*checks his watch, and immediately starts gathering his materials and putting them into his large valise*). Well I have to check out now, but I'll stop over tomorrow and we'll set the whole thing up just as you want it, Mr. Parker . . . See you later Theo . . . (*Starts out the door.*)

MR. PARKER (*To* BLUE *as he is moving out of the door*). You should stick around awhile and watch my polish!

THEO. Pop, don't you think it would be better if you would let me give the word to Adele?

MR. PARKER. No. If I'm going to run a crooked house, *I'm* going to run it, and that goes for you as well as her.

THEO. But Pop, sometimes she kinda gets by you.

MR. PARKER. Boy, I have never done anything like this in my life, but since I have made up my mind to do it, you have nothing to say! Not a word! (*Moves to the base of the stairs in the back room*) Well, here goes nothing . . . ADELE! (*Moves back out into the shop.*)

BOBBY (*stopping just inside the door*). Hi . . .

MR. PARKER. Hi son, what you got there?

BOBBY. Uh, uh—fish!

MR. PARKER. Well, you better get them in the refrigerator before they stink on you . . .

BOBBY. Refrigerator?

MR. PARKER. Where else you gon put them?

BOBBY. That's right, Pa—you sure is right . . . (*Heads for the back room.*

The lights suddenly go out, and then come back up. ADELE *is standing in the shop with a birthday cake in her hands, smiling gleefully.*)

ADELE. Happy birthday, Daddy!

MR. PARKER. What is this?

ADELE. Surprise!

MR. PARKER. Now hold on!

ADELE. What's wrong, Daddy?

MR. PARKER. Well, it's—it's . . . (*Pause*) Nothing . . .

ADELE (*placing the cake on the table and handing him a knife*). Here . . .

MR. PARKER (*takes the knife*). I, er . . . This just knocks me out . . . I swear, it just completely knocks me out! (*Cutting the cake.*)

ADELE. Something else for you! (*Hands him a gift-wrapped package.*)

MR. PARKER (*takes the package*). Now what—(*Unwraps the package*) Cigars! The same brand I used to smoke when I was on the stage! Look at this fellows!

THEO. Me an' Bobby got something for you too, Pop . . .

MR. PARKER. What's going on here?

THEO. Give it to him, Bobby . . .

BOBBY (*hands him the package wrapped in newspaper wrappings*). Here, Pop . . .

MR. PARKER. The fish! (*Hurriedly unwraps the package*) Well, I'll be damn, a typewriter!

THEO. That's right . . .

MR. PARKER (*laughing*). Now what am I going to do with a typewriter? Son, I don't know nothing about typing!

THEO. You know what you told me about writing down your stories. You can write them down, three times as quick!

MR. PARKER. But I don't know how to type!

THEO. With the money we're gonna be having, I can hire a somebody to teach you!

ADELE. What money you're going to have?

THEO. We're going into business, baby—right here in this barbershop!

MR. PARKER (*tapping the boy on the shoulder*). Theo . . .

THEO (*paying no attention to his father*). We're going to sell bootleg whiskey!

ADELE. You're what?

MR. PARKER. Theo . . .

THEO. You heard me, and if you don't like it, you can pack your bags and leave . . .

ADELE. Leave? I pay the rent here!

THEO. No more! I pay it now!

MR. PARKER. Shut up, Theo!

THEO. We're going to show you something, girl, we'll—

MR. PARKER. *I said shut up!*

ADELE. Is he speaking the truth?

MR. PARKER. Yes he is . . .

ADELE. You're going to turn this shop into a bootleg joint?

MR. PARKER. I'll turn it into anything I want to!

ADELE. Not while I'm still here!

MR. PARKER. The lease on this house has my signature, not yours!

ADELE. And I pay for it!

MR. PARKER. And that's what I'm goin' to put a stop to—you pay no more!

ADELE. I'm not going to let you do this!

MR. PARKER. You got no choice, Adele—you hear me—you don't have a single thing to say!

ADELE (*turns on* THEO). You put him up to this!

MR. PARKER. Nobody puts me up to anything I don't want to do! These two boys have made it up in their minds that they're not going to work for nobody but themselves, and the thought in my mind is, *why should they?* I did like you said, I went downtown, and it's been a long time since I did that, but you're down there every day, and you oughta know by now that I'm too old a man to ever dream I could overcome the dirt and filth they got waiting for me down there. I'm surprised at you, that you would have so little care in you to shove me into the middle of that mob.

ADELE. You can talk about caring? What about Mama? *She was old!* She *died* working for you! Did you ever stop to think about that? In fact, DID YOU EVER LOVE HER? NO!

MR. PARKER. That's a lie!

ADELE. I hope that one day you'll be able to do one good thing to drive that doubt out of my mind . . . *But this is not it!* You've let this hoodlum sell you his twisted dream of getting through life without caring that there are other people about him—who have feelings—who hurt the same as he does. Don't let this boy ruin you, Daddy—don't let him do it!

THEO (*into her face*). Start packing, baby!

ADELE (*strikes him across the face*). Don't you talk like that to me!

(THEO *draws his hand back in retaliation.*)

MR. PARKER. Drop your hand, boy! (THEO *does not respond to his father's command. He still has his hand held up as if to strike.*) *Drop your god damn hand!*

THEO (*backing away from his father*). She hit me!

MR. PARKER. I don't care if she had broken your jaw—if you ever draw your hand back to hit this girl again—*as long as you live!*—you better not be in my hand's reach when you do—*I'll split your back in two!* (*To* ADELE) We're going into business, Adele. I have come to that conclusion, and I have come to it on my own. I am going to stop worrying once and for all whether I live naked in the cold or whether I die like an animal, unless I can live the best way I know how to. I am getting old and I oughta have some fun. I'm going to get me some money, and I am going to spend it! I'm going to get drunk! I'm going to dance some more! *I am getting old! I am going to fall in love one more time before I die!* So get to that, girl, and if it's too much for you to take, I wouldn't hold it against you if you walked away from here this very minute . . . (*He moves through the back room.*)

ADELE (*moves swiftly to the door leading to the back room*). I am not leaving . . . I am not moving one step . . . *Happy birthday!*

MR. PARKER (*stops in his tracks and turns sharply*). That's another thing! I fooled all of you! *Today is not my birthday!*

(*Turns, moves through the room and up the stairs to the apartment.*)

ADELE. It's not going to work! You're going to cut your throat! You hear that? You're going to rip yourself into little pieces! (*Turns on* THEO) Now, boy, the world's going to spin itself all around just for you—is that what it's going to do? (THEO *does not respond to her.*) I am talking to you!

THEO (*pause*). It might . . . Me and Bobby—we're men . . . If we lived the way you wanted us to, we wouldn't have nothing but big fat veins popping out of our heads.

ADELE. Are you sure that won't happen anyway? That this whole damn house won't crumble down into your face one day?

THEO. No, I am not sure!

ADELE. Then you think about that every time a cop walks through that door—every time a stranger steps into this back room, and you can't be so sure that you can trust him—you think about your father sitting alone in a jail man's cell one day . . .

THEO. What else am I going to do? You tell me when and where I can go to spin the world round before it gets too late— like Mama living fifty whole years just to die on a 126th Street! *You tell me of a place to go where there are no old crippled vaudeville men!*

ADELE. THERE IS NO SUCH PLACE! (*Turns and moves slowly for the entrance upstairs*) but the one you make for yourself—even where you are sick—where you are alone in some cold dark place—*where everything in you wants to erupt into joy!*—and there is no joy—there is nothing but the cold boundaries of trying to keep alive so that you don't lose the most precious thing that's yours, and that is your wonder, boy—your everlasting gift to WONDER!

THEO. I wonder all the time, Adele—I wonder how you ever got to be such a damn fool . . .

CURTAIN

ACT II

Scene 1

Two months later . . . It is about 9:00 P.M. *in the evening.
As the curtain rises, the lights come up on the back room
where* THEO *is busy at the desk going over a set of books with
a pen in his hand. He puts the pen down hurriedly and rushes
to the latest addition to the room, a stove, where there are two
huge pots steaming with his recipe of corn liquor. He moves
away from the stove and looks on an uncompleted painting of
his, resting on a canvas near the stairs. He moves back to the
desk and continues to work on the books.*

* BOBBY *descends the stairs and moves right past* THEO *out into
the outer part of the shop, carrying a target rolled up in his
hand and two darts. He is wearing a fancy sport shirt, new
trousers, new keen-toed shoes, and a stingy-brimmed, diddy-bop
hat. He pins the target up on the wall of the shop. The face
at the center of the target is that of a well-known American
racist.*

  BOBBY (*moves away from the target, aims a dart, and throws
it*). That's for Pop! Hunh! (*Throws another dart*) And that's
for me! Hunh! (*He moves to the target to pull the darts out.
The doorbell rings.*)

  THEO (*calling out to* BOBBY *from the back room*). Lock that
door!

  BOBBY. Lock it yourself!

  THEO (*with definite, hurried steps, he moves out of the back
room for the front door*). I'm not selling another bottle, target
or anything til' I get some help! (*Locks the door to the per-
sistence of the ringing*) We're closed!

  BOBBY. I don't think Blue is gonna like you turning away
customers.

  THEO. You can tell Blue I don't like standing over that stove
all day—that I don't like him promising me helpers that don't

ever show up. There are a lot of things I don't go for, like Pop taking off and not showing up for two days. I don't like having to make whiskey—to sell it, keeping books, and peddling those damn targets! *And I don't like you standing around here all day not lifting a finger to help me!*

BOBBY. (*sits in the throne, takes out a cigar and lights it up*). I don't hear you . . .

THEO. I know what your bag is—you're a stealer . . .

BOBBY (*jumps down out of the throne*). I don't wanta hear nothing! You do what you wanta do, and leave me alone!

THEO. What am I suppose to be, a work mule or something?

BOBBY. You're the one that's so smart—you can't answer your own stupid questions?

THEO. You done let Blue turn you against me, huh?

BOBBY. You ask the questions, and you gon answer them—but for now, stop blowing your breath in my face!

THEO. (*moves away from* BOBBY *and steps into the back room and looks on his painting*). At the rate I'm going, I will never finish this painting!

(ADELE *steps down immediately from the stairs and looks on the painting with amazement. She is dressed in a very smart outfit.*)

ADELE. What is this?

THEO (*moves to the stove and proceeds to stir his mixture with a long ladle.*) Somebody I know!

ADELE (*she turns the easel, making the painting visible downstage*). This, you call somebody? (*The painting is an abstraction of something or other, but it is definitely not representative of a human person.*)

THEO. Yeah, Johnny!

ADELE. Johnny?

THEO. Johnny All American—everybody knows Johnny All American but you . . .

ADELE (*moves from the painting*). It's terrible!

THEO. Don't you ever have anything good to say?

ADELE. I'm honest . . .

THEO. Honest? You're just hot because Pop decided to do something my way for a change . . .

ADELE. That's a joke, when you haven't seen him in two whole days. Or do you know where he has gone to practically every night since you opened up this little store?

THEO. He's out having a little sport for himself. What's wrong with that? He hasn't had any fun in a long time . . .

ADELE. Is fun all you can think of? When *my* father doesn't show up for two days, I worry . . .

THEO. Don't—when Blue comes tonight with that money, he'll be here!

ADELE. I hope so . . . (*Starts out.*)

THEO. Where are you going?

ADELE (*stops and turns abruptly*). I'm going out! Do you mind?

THEO. That's all you ever do!

ADELE. Yes, you're right . . .

THEO. What are you doing, girl? You got a man or something out there on that Avenue?

ADELE. What I have or don't have is none of your damn business! (*Moves out of the door sharply.*)

THEO (*stands in the back room doorway with a long, deep look in his eyes*). I'm beginning to have a thought about that girl—a thought I don't particularly want to think about . . . (*He closes the door behind him. Blackout on the back room. MR. PARKER steps into the shop, all dapper, dressed in a light beige suit, black shirt, brown tie, tan and white shoes, large dark sunglasses, holding a gold-top cane in one hand and a book in the other. BOBBY is staring on him with bewildered eyes.*)

BOBBY. What's that you got on?

MR. PARKER. What does it look like?

BOBBY. Nothing . . .

MR. PARKER. You call this nothing!

BOBBY. Nothing—I mean, I didn't mean nothing when I asked you that question . . .

MR. PARKER. Where's Theo?

BOBBY. In the back, working . . .

MR. PARKER. Good! Shows he's got his mind stretched out for good and great things . . .

BOBBY. He's been stretching his mind out to find out where you been . . .

MR. PARKER. Where I been is none of his business—Blue is the man to think about—it's pay day, and I wanta know where the hell is he! (*Checks his watch, taps* BOBBY *on the hip, indicating that he should step down from the throne.*)

BOBBY (*hopping down from the chair.*) Whatcha reading?

MR. PARKER. A book I picked up yesterday. I figured since I'm in business, I might as well read a businessman's book. (*Sits in the chair.*)

BOBBY. Let me see it . . . (*Takes the book in his hand*) *A Thief's Journal* by Jean Gin-net . . . (*Fingering through the book*) Is it a good story?

MR. PARKER. So far . . .

BOBBY (*hands it back to him*). What's it all about?

MR. PARKER. A Frenchman who was a thief . . .

BOBBY. Steal things?

MR. PARKER. Uh huh . . .

BOBBY. Where did he get all that time to write a book?

MR. PARKER. Oh, he had the time all right, cause he spent most of it in jail . . .

BOBBY. Some thief!

MR. PARKER. The trouble with this bird is that he became a thief, and then he became a thinker.

BOBBY. No shucking?

MR. PARKER. No shucking—but it is my logicalism that you've got to become a thinker, and then you become a crook! Or else, why is it when you read up on some of these politicians' backgrounds, you find they all went to one of them big law colleges—that's where you get your start!

BOBBY. Well, I be damn!

MR. PARKER. You see, son, stealing done got educational as well as political . . . You have to study it out, get yourself a plan the way me and Blue did, and then you get into operation. If this fellow had been thinking before he started stealing, he wouldn't have been a failure . . . (*Jumps down out of the chair and moves briskly for the door*) Now where is Blue! He said he would be here nine-thirty on the nose! (*Opens the door*) Hey, Jenkins! What's up?

MR. JENKINS. That Blue fellow show up yet?

MR. PARKER. No, he didn't and I'm gon call him down about that too—

MR. JENKINS. It don't matter—I just want whatever money I got coming, and then I'm getting out of this racket . . .

MR. PARKER. This is not a racket, it's a committee!

MR. JENKINS. This committee is no committee—it ain't nothing but a racket, and I'm getting out of it!

MR. PARKER. You put your money into this thing, man—it ain't good business to walk out on an investment like that . . .

MR. JENKINS. I can, and that's what I'm doing before I find myself in jail!

MR. PARKER. There ain't nothing for you to be scared of, Jenkins—Blue guaranteed me against ever being caught by the police. Now that's all right by me, but I've got some plans of my own. Tonight, I'm gon force him to make me one of the leaders in this group, and if he don't watch out, I just might take the whole operation over from him—I'll make you my right-hand man, and not only will you be getting more money, and I just won't guarantee you against getting caught, but I'll guarantee you against being scared!

MR. JENKINS. There's nothing you can say to make me change my mind. I shouldn't've let you talk me into this mess from the start. I'm getting out, and that's it . . . (*Starts for the door*)

And if he gets back before I do, you hold my money for me!
(*Exits.*)

MR. PARKER. Suit yourself, but you're cutting your own throat
—this little setup is the biggest thing to hit this neighborhood
since the day I started dancing! (*Goes to the mirror to primp*)
Fool . . .

BOBBY. Going somewhere again?

MR. PARKER. Got myself a little date to get to, if Blue ever
gets here with our money—*and he better get here with our
money!*

BOBBY. You been dating a lot lately—nighttime dates, and
day ones too, and Theo's not happy about it. He says you don't
stay here long enough to cut Yul Brynner's head . . .

MR. PARKER. He can complain all he wants to—I'm the boss
here, and he better not forget it . . . He's the one that's got
some explaining to do—don't talk to nobody no more—don't
go nowhere, looking like he's mad all the time. I've also noticed
that he don't get along with you anymore . . .

BOBBY. Well, Pop, that's another story . . .

MR. PARKER. Come on boy, there's something on his mind,
and you know what it is . . .

BOBBY. Nothing, except he wants to tell what to do all the
time—but I've got some ideas of my own. I ain't no dumbbell
—I just don't talk as much as he do . . . If I did, the people
that I talk to would know as much as I do. I just want him to
go his way, and I'll go mine . . .

MR. PARKER. There's more to it than that, and I wanta know
what it is.

BOBBY. There's nothing . . .

MR. PARKER. Come on now, boy . . .

BOBBY. That's all, Pop!

MR. PARKER (*grabs him by the collar*). It's not and you better
say something!

BOBBY (*pause*). He—he found out Blue killed a man one
time . . .

MR. PARKER. Where did he hear this?

BOBBY. Somebody on the Avenue told him—said Blue killed this man for saying something about his woman, and this woman got a child by Blue, but Blue never married her, and this man started signifying about it . . . Blue hit him, the man reached for a gun in his pocket, Blue took the gun from him, and the man started running, but by that time, Blue had fire in his eyes, and he shot the man three times.

MR. PARKER. Well . . .

BOBBY. Blue got only two years for it!

MR. PARKER. Two years, huh? That's another thing I'm gon throw in his face tonight, if he tries to get smart with me. Ain't that something! Going around bumping people off, and getting away with it too! What do he think he is, white or something! (*Checks his watch*) I'm getting tired of this! (*Moves and snatches the back room door open to the surprise of* THEO *sitting at the desk*) Where's that friend of yours? I don't have to wait around this barbershop all night for him. It's been two months now, and I want my money! When I say be here at nine-thirty, I mean be here!

THEO (*rising from the chair at the desk*). Where have you been, Pop?

MR. PARKER. That's none of your business! Now where is that man with my money?

THEO. Money is not your problem—you've been spending it all over town!

MR. PARKER. What do you know?

THEO. It's in the books and the books don't lie!

MR. PARKER. So what—I borrowed a little from the box . . .

THEO. You call seven hundred dollars a little?

MR. PARKER. Never mind what I do! It's been two months now, and he ain't shown me a dime!

THEO. What are you doing with all that money, Pop?

MR. PARKER. I don't have to answer to you! I'm the boss here! And another thing, there's a lot about Blue and this association I want to know about! I want a position! I don't have to sit around here every month or so, waiting for somebody to bring me *my* money.

THEO. Why don't you think about us once in a while? I didn't go into this thing just for myself—I wasn't out to prove how wrong Adele was . . . I wanted to make up for all them years we laid around here, letting Mama break into pieces! (*Pause*) And Pop, do you know about that girl?

MR. PARKER. What about her?

THEO. She's out of this house every night, and you know how strict she is about saving money—well let me tell you something—half of her savings are gone . . .

MR. PARKER. What?

THEO. And I am not talking about the money—*I'm talking about what's happening to her!*

MR. PARKER. I didn't know all of this was going on . . .

THEO. If you stayed in the shop more, you'd know what's going on.

MR. PARKER. That's too bad—I have things to do. I don't worry about where you're going when you leave here . . .

THEO. I don't go anywhere and you know it . . . If I did, we wouldn't do an hour's business. *But we have been doing great business!* And you wanta know why? They love it! *Everybody* loves the way ol' Theo brews corn! Every after-hours joint is burning with it! And for us to do that kind of business, I've had to sweat myself down in this hole for something like sixteen hours a day for two *whole* months!

MR. PARKER. What do you want from me? I don't know how to boil that stuff!

THEO. You can get Blue to move his stuff out and rent another place! A cop walked in that door this afternoon while I had three customers in here, and I had to put one of them in that chair, and cut his hair!

MR. PARKER. How did you make out?

THEO. What do you think?

MR. PARKER. All right, I'll talk to him—

THEO. And make him guarantee me three helpers.

MR. PARKER. You'll get that too . . . But you've got to admit one thing, though, you've always been a lazy boy. I didn't expect you to jump up and all of a sudden act like John Henry!

THEO. I have never been lazy—I just didn't wanta break my back for the man!

MR. PARKER (*puts his arm around his son's shoulders*). I can't blame you for that. I know because I've done it. I did it when they didn't pay me a single dime!

BOBBY. When was that, Pop?

MR. PARKER. When I was on the chain gang!

THEO (*breaks way from him*). Now you know you ain't never been on no chain gang!

MR. PARKER (*holds up two fingers*). Two months, that's all it was—just two months . . .

THEO. Two months, my foot!

MR. PARKER. I swear to heaven I was—It was in nineteen-o-something, I was living in Jersey City, New Jersey . . .

THEO. Here we go with another story!

MR. PARKER (*snaps his fingers*). And I'm gon put this one down! Get the pencil and paper out, Theo!

THEO (*takes a pencil and pad from the shelf and moves for the throne*). Now where did you say this place was? (*Sits in the chair.*)

MR. PARKER. Jersey City . . .

THEO (*writing*). In "19 'o' something" the man said . . .

MR. PARKER. That was just before I started working as a vaudeville man, and there was this ol' cousin of mine we used to call "Dub," and he had this job driving a trailer truck from Jersey City to Jacksonville, Florida. One day he asked me to come along with him for company—I weren't doing nothing at the time, and—

THEO. Say that again . . .

MR. PARKER. I said I weren't doing nothing at the time!

THEO. As usual . . .

MR. PARKER. I didn't say that! What you trying to do, make out like I didn't wanta work? I was unemployed! I was oppressed! So, I went along with him . . .

THEO. Go on . . .

MR. PARKER. Anyway, we drove along, everything was fine til' we hit Macon, Georgia. We weren't doing a thing, but before we knew it, this cracker police stopped us, claiming we'd ran through a red light. He was yelling and holling, and boyyy did I get mad—I was ready to get a hold of that cracker, and work on his head, until—

THEO. I know, but what happened?

MR. PARKER. Oh, they put us on the chain gang, and the chain gang they put us on was a chain gang and a half! I busted some rocks John Wayne couldn't've busted. I was a rock-busting fool! (*Gives a demonstration as to how he swung the hammer*) I would do it like this! I would hit the rock, and the hammer would bounce—bounce so hard it would take my hand up in the air with it, but I'd grab it with my other hand, and bring it down like this, "Hunh!" (*He gets carried away by the rhythm of his story, and he starts twisting his whole body to the swing of it.*) It would get so good to me, I'd say, "Hunh! Yeah! Hunh!" I'd say, "Oooooooo weeee!" I'm wide open now! (*Swinging and twisting*) Yeah baby, I say, "Hunh!" Sooner or later, that rock would crack! Old "Dub" one day ran into a rock that was hard as Theo's head. He couldn't bust that rock for nothing. He pumped and swung, but that rock would not move. So, finally he said to the captain, "I'm sorry, Cap, but a elephant couldn't break this rock." Cap didn't wanna hear nothing—he said, "Well 'Dub,' I wanna tell you something—your lunch and your supper is in the middle of that rock." On the next swing of the hammer, "Dub" busted that rock into a thousand pieces! (*Laughs*) I'm telling you, them crackers is mean—don't let nobody tell you about no communists, Chinese or anything—there ain't nothing on this earth meaner and dirtier than an American-born cracker! We used to sleep in them long squad tents on the ground, and we was all hooked up to this one big long chain—the guards had orders to shoot at random in the dark if ever one of them chains would rattle. You couldn't even turn over in your sleep!

THEO. A man can't help but turn over in his sleep!

MR. PARKER. Not on this chain gang you didn't. You turn over on this chain gang in your sleep, and your behind was shot! But if you had to; you would have to wake up, announce that you was turning over, and then you go back to sleep!

THEO. What?

MR. PARKER. Just like this: Number four turning over! But that made all the other chains on the other convicts rattle, and they had to turn over and say: Number five turning over! Number six! Number seven turning over!

THEO. Why don't you stop it!

MR. PARKER. I ain't lying!

THEO. Is that all?

MR. PARKER. Yeah, and I'm gon get Adele to type that up for me on my typewriter! (*Goes to the window*) Now where the hell is that Blue Haven? (*He sees* MR. JENKINS *coming and he opens up the door.* MR. JENKINS *enters.*) I see you're back—well, he didn't show up yet, but if you've got a moment, I'll beat you a game one time . . . (*Takes out the checkerboard.*)

BOBBY. Tear him up, Pop!

(MR. PARKER *is at the table setting up the board.*)

MR. JENKINS (*joining him*). It's hopeless—I been playing your father for three solid years, and he has yet to beat me one solid game!

MR. PARKER. Yeah, but his luck done come to past!

MR. JENKINS. My luck ain't come to past, cause my luck is skill . . . (*Spells the word out*) S-K-I-L-L . . .

MR. PARKER. And I say if you call your playing any kind of skill, I say you're lying like a thief . . .

MR. JENKINS. You better be careful how you call me a liar, Parker . . .

MR. PARKER. I say you're lucky, you say you ain't, and I say you're lying . . .

MR. JENKINS. That's calling me a liar!

MR. PARKER. I said you was lying—I didn't say you were a liar.

MR. JENKINS. You did!

MR. PARKER. Now when did I say that?

MR. JENKINS. You said, cause I said I got the greatest skill, you said I was lying . . . Now tell me you didn't say that . . .

MR. PARKER. I did . . .

MR. JENKINS. That's calling me a liar!

MR. PARKER. Spell it . . .

MR. JENKINS (*spelling*). L-I-A-R . . .

MR. PARKER. Now spell lying . . .

MR. JENKINS (*spelling*). L-Y-I-N-G . . .

MR. PARKER. You see the difference?

MR. JENKINS. There ain't no difference!

MR. PARKER (*shakes up the can*). Come on now Jenkins, let's play the game . . . Take one . . . (MR. JENKINS *pulls a man*) You see there, you get the first move . . .

MR. JENKINS. You take me for a fool, and just for that, I ain't gon let you get a king . . .

MR. PARKER. Put your money where your lips is . . . I say, I'm gon win this game!

MR. JENKINS. I don't want your money—I'm just gon beat you!

MR. PARKER. I got twenty dollars here to make a liar out of you! (*Slams down a twenty-dollar bill on the table.*)

MR. JENKINS. You see, you see, he said it!

MR. PARKER. Said what?

MR. JENKINS. You called me a liar!

MR. PARKER. Sit down, Jenkins! (*Pause*) Now you doing all the bragging about how I never beat you, but I'm valiant enough to say that from here on in, you can't win air, and I got twenty dollars up on the table to back it up.

MR. JENKINS (*pause*). Oh well, he ain't satisfied with me beating him all the time for sport—he wants me to take his money too . . .

MR. PARKER. But that's the difference . . .

MR. JENKINS. What kind of difference?

MR. PARKER. We're playing for money, and I don't think you can play under that kind of pressure. You do have twenty dollars, don't you? (*Looks back at* THEO *and* BOBBY, *breaking out with a big laugh.*)

MR. JENKINS. I don't know what you're laughing about—I always keep some money on me.

MR. PARKER. Put it on the table where I can see it.

MR. JENKINS. You don't trust me?

MR. PARKER. I trust you all right, but to see it gives me inspiration!

MR. JENKINS (*puts twenty dollars on the table*). You get a little money in your pocket, and you get carried away.

MR. PARKER. Your move . . .

MR. JENKINS. Start you off over here in this corner.

MR. PARKER. Give you that little ol' fellow there . . .

MR. JENKINS. I'll take him . . .

MR. PARKER. I'll take him, so you can take that . . .

MR. JENKINS (*thinks for a while*). I'll jump him . . .

MR. PARKER. And I'll take these three . . . Boom! Boom! Boom! (*Jumping* MR. JENKINS' *men and laughing loud. There are a series of grunts and groans as they exchange men. The game is now in definite favor of* MR. PARKER. MR. JENKINS *is pondering over his situation. Relishing* MR. JENKINS' *predicament*) Study long, you study wrong . . . (*Pause*) I'm afraid that's you, ol' buddy . . . (*Pause*) I knew it, I knew it all the time— I used to ask myself, I used to say: I wonder how ol' Jenks would play if he really had some pressure on him? You remember how the Dodgers used to raise hell every year until they met the Yankees in the World Series, and how under all that pressure they used to crack up? (*Laughs*) That pressure got him!

MR. JENKINS. Hush up man, I'm thinking!

MR. PARKER. I don't know what you thinking about—cause the rooster done came and wrote, skiddy biddy!

MR. JENKINS (*finally makes a move*). There . . .

MR. PARKER (*singsong*). That's all . . . That's all . . . (*Makes another jump*) Boom! Just like you say, Bobby, "tear him up!" (*Rears his head back in laughter.*)

MR. JENKINS (*makes a move*). It's your move . . .

MR. PARKER (*brings his head back down, and the laughing trails off sickly upon the realization that the game is now in his opponent's favor*). Well, I see . . . I guess that kinda changes the color of things . . . Let me see . . .

MR. JENKINS (*getting revenge*). Why don't you laugh some more . . . I like the way you laugh, Parker . . .

MR. PARKER. Shut up Jenkins, I'm thinking!

MR. JENKINS. I don't know what you could be thinking about . . . (*Rises, moves away from the table fanning his hand*) When I get up from the table that's it! (*Laughs heavily.* MR. PARKER *sorrily makes his move. Rushing back to the table*) Uh huh! Lights out! (*Still laughing and making his move*) Game time and you know it! Take your jump! (MR. PARKER *is forced to take his jump;* MR. JENKINS *takes his last three men*) I told you about laughing and bragging in my game! Boom! Boom! Boom!

MR. PARKER (*rising abruptly from the table*). Dammit! (*Rushes into the back room.*)

MR. JENKINS. Where you going, ain't we gon play some more?

MR. PARKER. I don't wanta play you no more, you too lucky!

MR. JENKINS. Aw come on, Parker . . . I don't want your money, I just want to play!

MR. PARKER. You won it, you keep it—I can afford it! But one of these days, you're going to leave that voodoo root of yours home, and that's gonna be the day . . . You hear me, you sonofabitch!

THEO. Pop!

MR. PARKER. I don't want to hear nothing from you!

MR. JENKINS (*realizing that his friend is honestly upset over the affair*). It's only a game . . .

(MR. PARKER *is standing in the center of the back room, with his back towards them.* MR. JENKINS *steps out into the center of the outer area, and addresses his remarks to* MR. PARKER'S *back.*) and it don't have nothing to do with luck . . . But you keep trying, Parker, and one of these days you're going to beat me—and when you do, it won't have nothing to do with luck— it just might be the unluckiest and worst day of your life. You'll be champion checker player in all this world. Meanwhile, I'm the champ, *and you're gonna have to live with it!*

MR. PARKER (*smiling, moves out toward him with his hand extended*). Jenkins! All right, Champ! (*They shake.*) But I'm going to beat you! I'm going to whip your behind until it turns white!

BOBBY. That's gon be some strong whipping! (*There is a tap at the door.*) That must be Blue . . . (*Goes to the door and opens it.*)

MR. PARKER. About time . . . (*Reaches for his coat on the rack and puts it on.* BLUE *enters.*) Hey boy, where have you been?

BLUE (*moving in carrying a regular attaché bag*). You'll have to forgive me, Mr. Parker, but I got stuck with an emergency council meeting . . .

MR. PARKER. What kind of council?

BLUE. *The council of the Association*—I see you're sporting a new piece of cloth there, "Mr. P" . . .

MR. PARKER. Just a little something I picked up the other day . . .

BLUE. The next time you want to dress up, you come to me, and I'll get you the best for the least cost . . .

MR. PARKER. You can do that?

BLUE. That's right . . . Blue Haven, mastermind, evil genius, racketeer, hijacker, bootlegger, pirate on the high seas of the Harlem River, hipper like a long-tongued fox, crouched in the alleys and hallways for the great seige upon all the young cherries of the world. A house possessor of young black-brown-high yellow girls of classic beauty, strong-long-short agile legs, smooth healthy bodies with breasts so full—with so much life in 'em to cause a hundred-year-old buzzard to have visions of living forever!

MR. PARKER. Where is this house, Blue? (THEO *and* BOBBY *burst out laughing.* BLUE *just smiles surreptitiously.*) Cut it! There's too much that's funny when I'm talking, and I want you to put a stop to it! (*Pause*) Where's the money, Blue?

BLUE. You'll get your money, but first I want to see those books. (THEY *move into the back room.* BLUE *sits at the desk, pulling out pencil, pad, and a group of papers.*) Well, look at this, that corn whiskey of yours is flying, Theo!

THEO. I've tried . . .

BLUE (*closing one book and opening up another one*). And I see the targets are doing well . . .

MR. PARKER. Come on man, give me my money!

BLUE. Take it easy, Mr. Parker . . . (*He takes a white envelope from his inside pocket and passes it on to* MR. PARKER.) Here's your money . . .

MR. PARKER. Now this is what I like to see! (*Starts counting the money.*)

BLUE (*passes a group of bills on to* MR. JENKINS). And you too, Mr. Jenkins . . .

MR. JENKINS. Thank you young man, and from here on in, you can count me out of your operation . . .

BLUE. What's the trouble?

MR. JENKINS. No trouble at all—I just want to be out of it . . .

BLUE. People and headaches—that's all I ever get from all the *Mr. Jenkinses* in this world!

MR. PARKER. Why don't you be quiet sometime, boy . . .

BLUE (*pause*). I got a call the other day from one of them committees here in Harlem . . .

THEO. What did they want?

BLUE. They wanted to know what we did—they said they had *heard* of us, but they never see us—meaning, they never see us picketing, demonstrating, and demanding something all the time . . .

THEO. So . . . ?

BLUE. They want us to demonstrate with them next Saturday, and I have decided to set up a demonstrating committee, with you in charge, Mr. Parker . . .

MR. PARKER. You what!

BLUE. You'd be looking good!

MR. PARKER (*cynical laughter*). You hear that! *I'd be looking good!* Count me out! When I demonstrate, it's for real!

BLUE. You demonstrate in front of any store out on that street, and you'll have a good sound reason for being there!

MR. PARKER. Aren't we doing enough? Two stores already done put up "going out of business" signs . . .

BLUE. That's what we started this whole thing for—to drive the man back to where he came from, and that's what we're doing.

MR. PARKER. Well then you tell me—you tell me what we're doing that's so hot, that would cause a liquor store, a clothing store, and a radio store to just all of a sudden close down like that. Unless we've been raiding them at night or something like that . . .

(BOBBY *moves out of the shop and up the back room stairs.*)

BLUE. It's the psychological thing that's doing it, man!

MR. PARKER. Psychological? Boy, you ain't telling me everything, and anyway, I wanna know who made this decision about picketing . . .

BLUE. The council!

MR. PARKER. Who is on this council?

BLUE. You know we don't throw names around like that!

MR. PARKER. I don't get all the mystery, Blue. This is my house, and you know everything about it from top to bottom. I got my whole family in this racket!

BLUE. You're getting a good share of the money—ain't that enough?

MR. PARKER. Not when I'm dealing with you in the dark . . .

BLUE. You're asking for something, now what is it?

MR. PARKER. You been promising my boy some help for two months now, and he's still waiting . . . Now I want you to give him that help starting tomorrow . . . and from here on in, I want to know everything that's to be known about this "de-colonization committee"—how it works, who's in it, who's running it, *and I want to be on that council you was talking about!*

BLUE. That can't be, Mr. Parker!

MR. PARKER. Then I can't cooperate with you anymore!

BLUE. What does that mean?

MR. PARKER. It means we can call our little deal off, and you can take your equipment out of here . . .

BLUE. Just like that?

MR. PARKER (*starts getting his cane, coat, etc.*). Just any ol' way you want it . . . I take too many risks in this place, not to know where I stand . . . (*Starts out*) Good night!

BLUE. Mr. Parker . . .

MR. PARKER (*stops and turns*). All right, let me hear it and let me hear it quick!

BLUE. There is an opening on our council—it's a—

MR. PARKER. Just tell me what position is it!

BLUE. President . . .

MR. PARKER. President?

BLUE. The highest office on our council . . .

MR. PARKER. Boy, you're gonna have to get up real early to get by an old fox like me. A few minutes ago you offered me nothing, and now you say I can be president—that should even sound strange to *you!*

BLUE. There's nothing strange—a few minutes ago you weren't

ready to throw me out of your place, but now *I've got no other choice!*

MR. PARKER (*pointing his finger at him and laughing*). That's true! You don't! . . . All right, I'll give you a break—I accept! But I want it in writing by tomorrow night! (*Puts on his coat, sunglasses, etc.*) Come, Jenkins, let's get out of here! (*Starts out with* MR. JENKINS.)

THEO. Hey Pop, you're going out there with all that money in your pocket . . .

MR. PARKER. I'm a grown man, I can take care of myself . . .

THEO. But what about our part of it . . .

MR. PARKER. You'll get it when I get back . . .

THEO. But Pop—

MR. PARKER. Look son, he held me up—I'm late already—good night, Theo! (*He bolts out of the door with* MR. JENKINS *following.*)

THEO (*rushes to the door*). Pop, you better be careful! I'll be waiting for you! I don't care if it's dawn!

BLUE. You're becoming a worrier, Theo! (*Pause*) But that's the nature of all things . . . I'm forever soothing and pacifying someone—sometimes, even myself. Now you don't think that that president stuff is going to mean anything, do you? He'll know less, and I'll have more control over him . . . And over you too . . .

THEO. What do you mean by that?

BLUE. I mean that I know he's been spending money out of the box, and I'm not being told about it . . .

THEO. Why should I? I trust your intelligence . . .

BLUE. But whether I know or not, I don't want it to happen again!

THEO. Then hire yourself a bookkeeper!

BLUE. What about Adele? That was a thought in my mind, but I put that away real quick—seems she's took to the Avenue —and with the good-time company she's keeping, I'd probably have more trouble with her than I'm having with you . . .

THEO. She's got nothing to do with anything . . .

BLUE. But she does—when a girl like your sister takes to the Avenue, it means that she's got some trouble in her, and that trouble can break us up!

THEO. What do you want me to do? Knock her over her head?

BLUE. You told me you were going to get her out of here!

THEO. You want her out—you talk to the old man about that—

BLUE. Look, man—we're into something . . . To be honest with you, I didn't really think this thing was going to work—but Theo, *it is working!* I've got three places, just like this one, and another one is on the way—a man has to care about what he does—don't you want to get out of this place?

THEO. Yes, but lately, I've been getting the feeling that I'm gonna have to hurt somebody to do that—I've been working like a dog here every day, trying to get out of here—and if you were to ask me where would I go, if I did, I couldn't answer you, because everybody around me is breaking down!

BLUE. I see . . .

THEO. For instance—you think the old man was asking you those questions about stores closing down as a joke or something?

BLUE. He asked because he's in the dark!

THEO. He was playing with you! And when my father holds something inside of him, and plays with a man, he's getting meaner and more dangerous by the minute . . .

BLUE. Then that's something else you better get straight—now it's your time to soothe and pacify!

THEO. Why should I, when you've been sending my brother out every night with that band of thieves of yours . . .

BLUE. He wanted to go—he said he needed the money, and he's a better man than anybody I got . . .

THEO. And I told you, I didn't want that!

BLUE. Well, let's face it, baby! Bobby's been prancing around stores and stealing all of his life!

THEO. I don't care if he was born at midnight in Gimbel's basement, I want a stop put to it!

BLUE. I have enough trouble as it is, man . . . Bobby loves to steal, and I think that's something to bow down to—your old man is smart, and I respect him, but they're both black, and they're in trouble just like you and me! So, don't ride so hard, Theo! Get off the talk! the walk! the balk! the stalk! cause the monkey is dead and in his grave, no more signifying will he crave, on his tombstone, these words are writ, he died as he lived, with his signifying shit!

THEO. Blue, that kind of talk don't sell to me—not with all that I feel tonight . . .

(BOBBY *descends the stairs and moves out into the shop.*)

BLUE. Your brother is getting scared, Bobby . . . (*Moves to* THEO *and places his hand on his face*) He's cold too . . . (*Moves away from him*) I'm scared too, and as for my hands, they stay cold all the time—not to mention the rest of me . . . (*Moves to the room in the back, opens up one of the books, and starts running his fingers across one of the pages*) I went up to the hill the other day to see my little boy . . . I took the little fellow out for a ride, and as we were riding along the streets, he asked me where all the people were coming from. I said, from work, going home, going to the store, and coming back from the store . . . (*Closes the book and turns towards* THEO) Then we went out to watch the river, and he asked me about the water, the ships, the weeds—everything . . . That kid asked me so many questions, I got dizzy—I wanted to hit him to shut him up. He was just a little dark boy, discovering for the first time that there are things in the world, like stones and trees. (*He starts putting his papers away in his attaché bag.*) It got late and dark, so I took him home, and watched him fall asleep. Then I grabbed his mother, and put her into bed, and I laid there for a while, listening to her call me all kinds of dirty motherfuckers . . . (*Closes the bag and puts it down on the desk, and moves for the rack to get his coat*) and after she got that out of her system, I put my hands on her, and before long, our arms were locked at each others' shoulders, and then my thighs moved down between her thighs . . . and then my honeycomb rolled with her sweetbread until the both of us were screaming as if the last piece of love was dying forever. (*Moves back into the back room and picks up his attaché bag from the desk*) After that, we just laid there, talking soft. I would tell her she was the loveliest bitch that ever lived, and all of a sudden, she was no longer calling me a dirty motherfucker, she was calling me a sweet motherfucker! It got quiet, I sat up on the edge of the bed, with my head hanging long and deep, trying to push myself out of the room, and back into it at one and the same time. She looked up at me, and I got that same question all over again—will you marry me? Will you be the father of your son? I tried to move away from her, but she dug her fingernails into my shoulders—I struck her once, twice, and again, and again—with this hand! And her face was a bloody mess! I put my clothes on and I walked out into the streets, trembling because I knew, for the last time, I was gonna have to go back and save that little boy from being a bastard all the days of his life. So, now I have a tender little boy to walk in the park every Sunday, who may one day blow my head off—and an abiding wife, who on a given evening may get herself caught in the bed of some other man, and I could be sealed in a dungeon until dead! I was found lying in a well of blood on the day I was born! I have been kind! I have kissed babies for the simple reason they were babies! I'm going to get married, and that gets me to shaking all over! The last time I trembled this way, *I killed a man!* I can't ever let that happen again. Yes, I'm scared too, Theo—but my head is not hanging! (*Starts to leave*) I'm leaving it up to you for now—but if your father gets too sporty—you get sporty with him, and don't let him spend all that money in one city . . . (Exits. THEO *moves into the back room and sits on the bed.* BOBBY *moves to the door and stands there for a while.*)

THEO. Bobby, I want you to stay away from those store raids . . .

BOBBY. Not as long as I can get myself some extra money.

THEO. Extra money or no, I don't want you doing it!

BOBBY. You don't tell me what to do!

THEO. What are you, some kind of idiot?

BOBBY (*strikes him across the face*). Every time you call me that, you get hit! You didn't say nothing to me before, when I was stealing every other day, and I was giving you half of everything I stole! You didn't think nothing that day you sent me for that typewriter!

THEO. No, I didn't, stupid! Idiot! Fool! (BOBBY *draws back to hit him.*) Hit me! Go on, hit me!

BOBBY. (*pause*). I don't want to hit you . . . You don't hit back, unless it's a woman . . .

THEO. I don't know what you're going to do from here on in—because I'm telling Pop it's time to call the whole thing off with Blue . . .

BOBBY. That won't stop me, and you know it!

THEO. What is it Bobby? We used to be so close, and I—

BOBBY. You know what they called me when we was so tight? Faggot. They said you was slapping me on my naked behind.

THEO. You didn't go for that!

BOBBY. Hell no, I didn't . . . Anybody said something like that to me, got stomped in the ground!

THEO. Bobby, don't get too far away from me!

BOBBY. What do you want me to do? Stick around you all the time? *I'm tired of you!*

THEO. You can get hurt!

BOBBY. Nobody's gonna put their hands on me! (*Pause*) I stick by you, and I don't know what to do! I steal, and that puts clothes on my back, and money in my pockets! *That's something to do!* But I sit up here with you all day, just thinking about the next word I'm gonna say . . . *I'm not stupid! I sit here all day thinking about what I'm going to say to you.*

But all I can think about is knowing that that is not enough! I stuck by you, and I hoped for you, because whatever you became, I was gonna become . . . I thought about that too, and that ain't shit! I don't want to talk like that to you, Theo— I swear to that, Theo—I swear to that! I don't want to hurt nobody! (*Pause*) Can we let it be what Pop always say—can we throw it away—can we throw it into the river, Theo?

THEO. Yeah—let's do that . . . (*He hears approaching sounds.*) Shhhh! (*Rising from the bed quickly*) That's Pop, with somebody!

(*They dash out into the outer area of the shop.* THEO *quickly turns the lights out, and they hide in the far right corner of the shop, against the wall, next to the back room.*)

MR. PARKER (*stepping down into the room*). Come on girl!

(*A very beautiful, well-dressed young* GIRL *in her early twenties steps down into the room behind him.*)

GIRL (*looking about the place*). So this is where you do all your business . . .

MR. PARKER. You like it—ever been in a place like this before?

GIRL. Now what would I be doing in a place like this?

MR. PARKER (*opens the door to the shop and takes a look about in the dark*). I'll fix us a drink . . . (*Heads for the refrigerator*) Sit down, sweetheart . . . (*The* GIRL *sits on the bed as* MR. PARKER *opens the refrigerator and takes out a jug of corn.*) I'm going to give you a special drink, made from my own hands.

GIRL. That should be exciting . . .

MR. PARKER. Here . . . (*Hands her the drink.*)

GIRL (*taking the drink*). Thank you . . .

MR. PARKER (*sits next to her on the bed*). Toujours L'amour!

GIRL. Same to you! (*She drinks.*) Hmmmmmm . . . its delicious!

MR. PARKER. I told you, didn't I . . . I only make that for the family here . . . Private stock—never let a drop of it out of the house . . . (*Kisses her on the cheek.*)

GIRL. Did you give any thought to what I said to you last night?

MR. PARKER. I certainly did, but I'll have to wait a little while before we can go ahead . . .

GIRL. You said you loved me . . .

MR. PARKER. Like a flower—like singing a song in the rain . . . (*Kisses her on the cheek.*)

GIRL. Sometimes, you make me feel as if you don't trust me, but I thought that love and trust went together.

MR. PARKER. I'm not so sure about that . . . My son, Theo— I'm wild about him, but I wouldn't trust him no farther than I could throw him.

GIRL. I'm not your son! (*Pause*) Well, what can I say if you don't trust me?

MR. PARKER. I didn't say that at all, honey . . . What I said, was that I still don't know if I can get married right now. My wife ain't been dead a year yet, I just can't up and get married, like that. It would break the children's hearts.

GIRL. But where does that leave me? I'm a woman, and I've got feelings . . . I'm alive. It's not every day I fall in love with someone, and as for marriage, I've never given it a thought, for anyone! Now you think about that!

MR. PARKER (*starts to fondle her thighs*). I think all the time, sweetheart . . .

GIRL (*breaks away from him*). No!

MR. PARKER. What's wrong?

GIRL. You've got to say you'll marry me!

MR. PARKER. All right, I'll say it . . .

GIRL. And you've got to mean it!

MR. PARKER (*pause*). I mean it—I'll take you down to the courthouse on Monday . . .

GIRL. I don't want to push you into anything, Russell, but all men ever want to do is put you into bed.

MR. PARKER. You don't say! I'm not like that . . . I'm a man of many worlds, many things, and I've been taking care of you, and I'm gon continue to take care of you . . . (*Takes out the envelope from his pocket and exhibits a stack of bills*) You see this . . . I'm gon take you downtown tomorrow, and let you spend til' the store runs out. (*Peels off a few hundred*) Here's some pocket money for you . . .

GIRL (*taking the money quickly and putting it away*). Russell, you're always giving me money, and you've got to stop it!

MR. PARKER. Now, I don't want to hear you talking about money to me, baby. I've got plenty of it! (*Rises quickly, moves to the desk, and takes out his notebook*) You've got to understand—I'm the most different man you ever met . . . I've been around this world—I danced before the King and Queen of England . . . I've seen and heard a whole lot of things in my lifetime. And you know what—I'm putting it all down on paper. My story!

GIRL. Your story?

MR. PARKER. Here it is, right here . . . (*Sits back down next to her on the bed and opens up the notebook.*)

GIRL. You write too?

MR. PARKER. I certainly do . . .

GIRL (*opens up the book*). All this you wrote . . . A whole page!

MR. PARKER. Every word of it, and I been thinking about writing a poem about you . . .

GIRL. What? Write a poem about me?

MR. PARKER. I'm gon do it tonight before I go to sleep.

GIRL. You're so kind to me, Russell . . . I guess that's why I'm so impatient . . . I just can't wait to get all of you for myself. I do love you, Russell . . . (*He embraces and kisses her.*) You hold a woman so much like a man . . .

MR. PARKER (*kissing her on the neck and reaching for the tip of her dress at the knees*). Uh huh . . .

GIRL (*breaks away from him*). No, Russell, not here!

MR. PARKER. Why not, we're on a bed!

GIRL. Just because there's a bed wherever we go don't mean that we have to jump into it.

MR. PARKER. I have heard of people doing it on the floor—that's not my style, but if the floor is all right by you, I'm willing to go along with the program, so long as we—

GIRL. You don't understand, Russell!

(*Blackout on back room, and spots come up on* BOBBY *and* THEO *in the outer part of the shop.*)

BOBBY. What's going on in there?

THEO. Didn't you hear them?

BOBBY. Let's peep!

THEO. We can't do that! If he catches us here, he'll kill us. (*Pause*) Come on, let's ease our way out of the door before the action starts.

(*Spots off* BOBBY *and* THEO. *Lights come up full on the back room.*)

GIRL. You've got to start treating me the same as if I was your wife!

MR. PARKER. That's exactly what I'm trying to do!

GIRL. You keep yelling at me, I'm going to cry!

MR. PARKER. All right, whatever you do, don't cry . . . I tell you what, let's just lie down for a while and talk . . . I ain't gon try nothing . . .

GIRL. Russell . . .

MR. PARKER. May the Lord smack me down this minute into hell . . . I swear I won't do nothing.

GIRL. What are the three biggest lies men tell to women, Russell?

MR. PARKER. I ain't just any man—you already said that yourself!

GIRL. Okay, Russell, we'll lie down but you've got to keep your word. If I'm the girl you want to marry, you've got to learn to keep your word. (*Sits on the bed.*)

MR. PARKER (*jumps on the bed and lands on his back*). Ahhhhh—that feels good! (*Pause*) Baby, you are as cute as a button, the way you say things, when you ain't too sure of yourself . . .

GIRL (*still sitting, looking down on him*). Am I?

MR. PARKER (*stroking her back*). Yeah, and you're soft like a kitten . . . (*Pulls her by the shoulders*) Come here . . . (*He pulls her down to the bed, takes her in his arms, and kisses her. Immediately, he is again reaching for the tip of her dress.*)

GIRL (*struggling*). Russell, you said you wouldn't do anything!

MR. PARKER. I ain't! I just want to get a little closer to you!

GIRL. Russell, not here!

MR. PARKER. Just let me feel it a little bit!

GIRL. You swore to God, Russell!

MR. PARKER. I ain't gon do nothing! (*A big noise lets out in the shop. One of the boys has knocked down the clothes rack. MR. PARKER rises quickly, goes to the door, opens it, and turns the lights on. There are BOBBY and THEO, on their knees, crawling frantically to get to the door leading to the street.*) What are you doing here?

(BOBBY *jumps up and dashes out of the front door.*)

THEO (*rising slowly*). Er—er . . .

MR. PARKER. Er, what?

THEO. We, we were just trying to er—it was so dark in here, we were trying to feel our way to the door, and we didn't want to disturb you . . .

MR. PARKER. Disturb what?

THEO. Well, you was er, you was er—

MR. PARKER. You waser! You waser! I have been having a private talk with a good friend of mine . . . Now get out of here!

(*The* GIRL, *still on the bed, rises sharply as* ADELE *staggers down from the stairs. She leans on the wall at the base of the stairs. She is obviously drunk.*)

ADELE. Who are you?

(*The* GIRL *does not answer, and rushes out of the room into the outer part of the shop, closing the door behind her.*)

MR. PARKER. Where are you going?

GIRL. I'm going home!

MR. PARKER. Hold it now, honey . . .

GIRL. If you want me, I'll be home . . . I never should have come to this barbershop in the first place!

MR. PARKER. I'll be right over there as soon as I get things straight here. Will you be waiting for me?

GIRL. Yes, but don't you keep me waiting for you all night . . .

MR. PARKER (*kisses her on the cheek*). You run along now, I'll be right over there . . . (*The* GIRL *exits out of the front door. To* THEO) I thought I told you to move!

THEO. I'm not going anywhere until I get my money . . .

MR. PARKER. You'll get your part tomorrow, I told you that!

THEO. I want it now, before you give it all to that girl! . . . Cut that broad loose, Pop!

MR. PARKER (*turns back toward* THEO *sharply*). What did you say?

THEO. Give me my money . . . I worked hard for that money! *You are my father!* I don't have to be treated like this! (*Tears are welling in his eyes.*)

MR. PARKER. You heard me—*what did you say?*

THEO. I said, cut her loose! That bitch is a hustler!

MR. PARKER (*strikes him across the face with the back of his hand*). *Bite your tongue!*

THEO (*pause*). Just be careful, Pop . . . please be careful . . .

MR. PARKER. If there's anybody I got to be careful of, it's you! You lying, selfish sonofabitch! You think I don't know about you and Blue running that gang of thieves?

THEO. You know why I didn't tell you?

MR. PARKER. I don't give a damn about those stories! But you sent your own brother out there!

THEO. I didn't do that!

MR. PARKER. If Bobby gets hurt on them streets out there, I'm gonna kill you, boy! I'm gonna kill you!

THEO. You're not worried about Bobby! All you can think

about is the money you're rolling in! The clothes! And that stupid outfit you've got on—and now you're the great lover!

(ADELE *staggers to the doorway leading out into the shop.*)

ADELE. He loves the way she walks, he loves the way she talks. *He is the apple in her orchard grove; He is her master!* He is a fool . . .

MR. PARKER. Adele . . . (*Goes to her and puts his arm around her shoulders.*)

ADELE. Take your hands off me!

THEO. Did you think that everything would stop and stand still while you were being reborn again?

MR. PARKER. What do you want from me? Call this whole thing off? This was your idea, not mine! I've got myself something, and I'm not going to throw it away for nobody!

THEO. But can't you see what's happening here?

MR. PARKER. If she wants to be a drunken wench out in that street—let her do it! But I'm not going to take the blame for it! That's not me out there throwing myself in the arms of a bunch of rattlesnakes! And as for you . . . (*Goes into his pocket*) If you want this money, you can take it from me—I can throw every dollar of it into the ocean if I want to! *I'm burning!* I'm going to marry that girl! She is not a whore! She is a woman! And I'm going to marry her! And if you don't like it, you can kiss my ass! (*Bolts out of the door and into the streets.*)

ADELE (*staggers to the door hurriedly and stops there*). You're going to kill yourself, old man! You're nothing but a stupid old man that's about to die!

THEO (*goes to her and puts his arm around her*). What are you doing to yourself?

ADELE (*breaks away from him, mocks*). "I'm black—I've been violated by my environment," so anything goes! Isn't that the damnable excuse we always give?

THEO. I see a boy dying in the streets from an overload of cocaine—I don't pity him, I don't put him down, and I don't feel guilty because I'm too chicken shit to go near him. He's gon die anyway—this whole place was built for him to die in, but I'm not going to die, Adele—I'll do anything to keep alive, even if I have to live in this hole forever!

ADELE. If you wanta live, Theo, and if you think you've got anything to spread across that canvas, then you should take that brush and stroke that canvas until your hands bleed, until you get so tired you want to cry.

THEO. It's not that simple!

ADELE. Nothing is!

THEO. Why don't you leave me alone, woman!

ADELE. If I did, all of you would be on the streets tomorrow!

THEO. And don't hand me all that business about sacrificing your life away for the house—taking care of everybody. You stayed here because you had no other place to go. You got scared too soon and too young, and you're still shaking in your bones, baby!

ADELE (*pause*). Yes, that's true, and I suppose I did know the difference between what was happening to me here, and what could have happened any place—that somehow, Mother would have died whether I was with her or not, that life was just as dangerous on a countryside in California as it was here, because what I did was to merely wait for her to die, and still she took too long for that, and when life did pass on for her—*I wanted to celebrate*! I thought then I was going to build a huge bright palace only suited for the living, but all I could feel was the trouble of having someone to die in order that I might finally wake up and live—I began to know what was nailing Father against all these walls, and I wanted to rip him loose—I thought it would be my duty to free all of us, but who the hell ever told every black woman she was some kind of damn saviour! (*Pause*) That can cause your body to grow cold until pain becomes a pleasure—till you have no sense for the sweetness of water, because you're already drenched in it—till you live everyday as if it was a desperate task or duty—Sure, this place was built for us to die in, but if we're not very, very careful, Theo—that can actually happen . . . (*Pause.*)

THEO (*rushes into the back room*). Dammit! (*Takes out the targets and starts tearing them up.*) Get away from me, Blue! Get away man! Get out of here! (*Takes out some of his bottles. There is a loud banging on the front door.*) Get out of there! We're closed! Forever! (*The banging persists with a voice calling out to* THEO.)

ADELE (*rushes to the door and peeps from behind the shade*). It's Mr. Jenkins . . . (*She opens the door and allows him to enter.* MR. JENKINS *enters.*)

ADELE. Something wrong, Mr. Jenkins . . . ? (*He does not respond.*) Mr. Jenkins, I asked if there was something wrong. (*He still does not respond.*)

THEO. God dammit man, what's wrong with you?

MR. JENKINS (*pause*). I . . . (*Looks long at her, then turns his back to walk away*) No . . .

ADELE (*grabs him by the arm and spins him around*). Mr. Jenkins!

MR. JENKINS (*searching for a word to begin what he has to say*). They . . . I was having a drink at Lou's, and they broke into this store, right next door—three of 'em . . . Two got caught, and the other one ran . . . They shot him two times!

ADELE. Oh no . . . (*Moves away from him briskly and stops at the door to the back room with her back on them.*)

THEO. What is it, Mr. Jenkins?

MR. JENKINS. Your brother Bobby is dead . . .

THEO (*pause*). It's a crime, Mr. Jenkins . . . It's a crime—that's all it is . . .

MR. JENKINS. If there's something I can do to—

THEO. There is nothing, Mr. Jenkins . . .

MR. JENKINS. Good night, Theo . . . Good night, Adele . . . (*He moves out of the front door.*)

THEO (*looks in on* ADELE, *still with her back to him in the back room doorway, with her head buried in her hands*). Let's go see him, and then we'll try to find the old man . . .

CURTAIN

ACT II

Scene 2

About two hours later, in the shop.

MR. PARKER *and* MR. JENKINS *enter the front part of the shop.* MR. PARKER *is drunk, and* MR. JENKINS *is assisting him to move on his feet. He finally seats him on the barber's throne.*

MR. PARKER. Thank you, Jenkins—you are the greatest friend a man can have. They don't make 'em like you anymore. You are one of the last of the great friends, Jenkins . . . Pardon me— Mr. Jenkins. No more will I ever call you Jenks or Jenkins . . . From now on, it's Mr. Jenkins!

MR. JENKINS. Thank you, but when I ran into Theo and Adele tonight, they said they had something important to say to you, and I think you oughta see them . . .

MR. PARKER. I know what they want . . . They wanta tell me what an old fool I am . . .

MR. JENKINS. I don't think that's it, and you should go on upstairs and—

MR. PARKER. Never! Upstairs is for the people upstairs!

MR. JENKINS. Russell, I—

MR. PARKER. I am downstairs people! You ever hear of downstairs people?

MR. JENKINS (*pause*). No . . .

MR. PARKER. Well, they're the people to watch in this world . . .

MR. JENKINS. If you say so . . .

MR. PARKER. *Put your money on 'em!*

MR. JENKINS. Come on, Mr. Parker, why don't you at least lie down in the back room . . .

MR. PARKER. Oh no—you don't think I'd have you come all the way over here just for me to go to bed, do you? I wouldn't do a thing like that to you, Jenkins—I'm sorry—"Mr. Jenkins" . . .

MR. JENKINS. Well, for one thing, I could use some sleep myself.

MR. PARKER. Just stay with me for a little while, Mr. Jenkins . . .

MR. JENKINS. For a little while . . .

MR. PARKER. Why did that girl lock me out? She said she would be waiting for me but she locked me out. Why did she do a thing like that? I give her everything—money, clothes, pay her rent—I even love her!

MR. JENKINS. Please, Mr. Parker, you have got to get yourself some sleep.

MR. PARKER. Tell me something, Mr. Jenkins—since you are my friend—why do you think she locked me out?

MR. JENKINS. I don't know what to tell you . . .

MR. PARKER. I am an old man and all I've got is a few dollars in my pocket—ain't that it?

MR. JENKINS. I don't know, Parker!

MR. PARKER. Come on man, the truth!

MR. JENKINS (*pause*). Well that's the way it is with these young girls . . .

MR. PARKER. How would you know?

MR. JENKINS (*pause*). I had a young girl myself about a year ago—that was enough for me, and now I've got to—(*Starts for the door.*)

MR. PARKER (*stumbles down from the chair and blocks him at the door*). You never told me about that . . .

MR. JENKINS. Let me out of here, Parker—please let me out of here!

MR. PARKER. Something happened to you, man, I need to know!

MR. JENKINS. It's not that important!

MR. PARKER. I am your friend—you talk to a friend about things like that . . .

MR. JENKINS. I was ashamed!

MR. PARKER. Before me? Russell B. Parker?

MR. JENKINS. I just didn't want to talk about it! It happened so fast, I wanted to forget it!

MR. PARKER (*pause*). Please stay and tell me what happened, Mr. Jenkins . . . (*He moves away from him, takes up a jug of whiskey from the table, and moves back to him, pouring a drink.*)

MR. JENKINS (*takes the glass of whiskey from him*). She left me, but what hurted me was that she didn't leave me for another man, she left me for *another woman* . . .

MR. PARKER. Took your love and your materials, and left you for *another woman*?

MR. JENKINS. Yes . . .

MR. PARKER. That's a dirty way to lose a woman . . .

MR. JENKINS (*puts his glass out for another drink*). I didn't tell anybody about it . . . I just wanted to forget it as quick as *I could.*

MR. PARKER (*pours him a big drink*). I can't blame you for that—It ain't every day a man loses his *woman* to a *woman.*

MR. JENKINS (*drinks up*). Good night, Parker . . .

MR. PARKER (*immediately taking the glass from his hand and pouring him another large drink*). You think a man was in that room with my girl?

MR. JENKINS (*taking the glass back into his hand with his patience just about gone*). YES!

MR. PARKER. God dammit! God dammit!

MR. JENKINS. Russell . . .

MR. PARKER. I don't believe it! When I love 'em, they stay loved!

MR. JENKINS. Nobody's got that much love, man!

MR. PARKER (*pause*). No, no . . . You're wrong . . . My wife—my dear Doris—had more love in her than life should've allowed . . . A hundred men couldn't have taken all that love . . .

MR. JENKINS. We're not talking about Doris, Russell—We're talking about these young girls—either they're not built to take what we can give them, or we're just old men with nothing much to give them anyway . . .

MR. PARKER. Aw forget it! (*Moves into the back room, and takes out a bottle from the refrigerator*) It just can't be! (*Pours a drink for himself and passes the bottle on to his friend*) A long time before my wife died, I stopped loving her, and for a long time, I spent all of my days and nights feeling sick about it, because not a day passed I didn't look out of that window to see some woman I wanted to at least try to love . . . I tried to push the feeling back . . . I had it in me! Why can't I live and love until the day I die?

MR. JENKINS (*pours himself a drink*). When you live as long as we have, you begin to think that everything is possible. I mean, that's all we've got, Parker. You go downtown, looking and believing you can get a job as an elevator operator in one of those high buildings, and when they send you to the basement with a broom, you still don't believe it, because when you go to work, you wear a better suit of clothes than the man who runs the place. You change over into overalls, but you don't give a damn about them overalls. You go home in your suit, you conquer the saloons, the pool halls, the numbers, and the checker games. You lie like all hell. You smile at them young girls, and tell them you're the supervisor of the place where you work—you dine 'em, dance 'em, and you take 'em to bed—you're a moon messiah, a desert God! But everything you do is nothing more than what you do from *memory*!

MR. PARKER (*after a moment of complete silence, standing before* MR. JENKINS *with his hands in his pockets, does a little dance*). All from memory? (*Stops.*)

MR. JENKINS. All . . .

MR. PARKER. Dammit! You die in your heart not to forget!

MR. JENKINS. You stumble about like an old black cow!

MR. PARKER (*does another little dance*). You fall down one day! (*Deliberately lets himself fall to the floor.*)

MR. JENKINS. And you never get up again!

MR. PARKER (*lying on the floor in a relaxed position, singing*).
> I have had my fun!
> If I don't get well no more!
> I have had my fun!
> If I—

Get up old bastard! Get up! (*Rises to his feet*) Get up and fall back down again . . . Come on, Mr. Jenkins, let's play a game of checkers!

MR. JENKINS. Man, why don't you go to bed!

MR. PARKER (*starts setting up the board*). Playing checkers Mr. Jenkins is all right—you have nothing to remember but how you beat me all the time . . .

MR. JENKINS. *I want to get out of this damn place!*

MR. PARKER (*pause*). Why do you curse my home, Mr. Jenkins?

MR. JENKINS (*pause*). I apologize for that . . .

MR. PARKER. Come on, have a game of checkers with your good friend . . .

MR. JENKINS (*moves to the table*). All right, one game and then I'm going home.

MR. PARKER. One game. (*He shakes up the can, and* MR. JENKINS *takes a man. They start their exchange of moves and jumps.*)

MR. PARKER (*pause*). I said a lot of dirty things to my children tonight. The kind of things you have to live a long time to overcome.

MR. JENKINS. I know what you mean—That's why I'm glad none of mine are living anywhere close to me.

MR. PARKER. Theo is a good boy, and a smart one too, but he lets people push him around. I guess that's because he's always trying to con somebody out of something—you know the kind, can't see for looking . . . And Bobby? You should've seen him . . . take off from here, when I caught him and Theo peeping on me tonight . . . (*Laughs*) Bobby wouldn't hurt a flea . . . A lot of people think that boy is dumb, but just let somebody try to trick or fool him if they dare! (*Pause*) Got a story for you . . .

MR. JENKINS. No stories tonight, Parker . . .

MR. PARKER. Call me Mr. Parker . . .

MR. JENKINS. Mr. Parker . . .

(*The last move is made. The game is over, and* MR. PARKER *is, at long last, the victor.*)

MR. PARKER (*rises from the table*). Call me champ!

(THEO *and* ADELE *enter from the front entrance.* THEO *remains at the door, and* ADELE *moves down the aisle of the shop and stops just at the doorway of the back room.*)

MR. PARKER (*laughing*). You're beat! I beat you! I beat you! (MR. JENKINS *starts out, but* MR. PARKER *throws his arms around his waist and holds him from the rear.*) You fall down, and you never get up! (*Laughing*) Fall down, old man! Fall down! (*He releases* MR. JENKINS.) You hear that, children, I beat him! I beat him! (*He realizes that they are not responding to him. He looks about, groping, then reaches into his inside coat pocket, and pulls out the money.*) Here, Theo—here's your money . . . (*Goes to him*) . . . Take it, it's yours—go out and try to get happy, boy. (THEO *does not move, nor does he speak.* MR. PARKER *then turns to* ADELE; *her face is almost a blank.*) Why don't somebody say something? (*With still no reaction from them, he moves for the back room.*) I know, you have some trouble with me . . . (*He takes his notebook from the old desk in the back room, moves back out into the shop, and stands before* ADELE.) You have a woman—you love her—you stop loving her, and sooner or later, she ups and dies, and you sit around behaving like you was a killer. I didn't have no more in me. *I just didn't have no more in me!* (*pause*) I know you don't believe I *ever* loved her, but it's here in this book . . . Read it . . . (*She does not respond, but he turns sharply to* THEO.) You wanta read something, boy? (THEO *just stands there with his hands in his pockets.* MR. PARKER *moves to the throne and sits. He hands the notebook out to* MR. JENKINS.) Please say something to me children! (*Almost in a whisper*) I just didn't have no more in me . . . (*He moves down out of the chair and addresses his remarks to* MR. JENKINS.) I got sour the day my legs got so trembly sore on the stage of the Strand Theatre—I couldn't even move out to take a proper bow. That was a long hard day for me, and it took me three weeks to talk to my Doris about it. And you know something? She didn't say a word —she just went out and got a job—she did it as if it was her duty. And as for me, I didn't know what I was supposed to do—I just couldn't run downtown to meet the man the way she did—not after all those years of shuffling round like I was a dumb clown, with my feet hurting and aching the way they did, having my head patted as if I was some little pet animal, back of the bus, front of the train, yassah, nosuh, grinning when I was bleeding to death! After all of that I was going to ask for more by throwing myself into the low drag of some dusty old factory in Brooklyn? Sure, I felt sick for having to depend so much on my wife, and my daughter here—but if I had done the right thing—just think about that now, the right thing!—it would have blinded my eyes forever, ruptured my heart, and broken every bone in my soul. All I could do was to stay here in this shop with you, my good friend, and we played a game. I just couldn't move! An old man pays his dues, and a time comes when all he can do is to act out the ceremony of a game, and hope to lie down easily one day, and die quietly . . . That's all we could afford, Mr. Jenkins . . . And you, boy . . . (*Turns to* THEO) you and Blue with your ideas of overcoming the evil of white men—to an old man like me, it was nothing more than an ounce of time to end my dragging about this shop—it sent me sailing out into those streets to live a time—and I did live myself a time. I did it amongst a bunch of murderers, all kinds of 'em—where at times it gets so bad, til' it seems that the only thing that's left for you is to go out there and kill somebody before they kill you. To eat out your own gizzards, just so's you don't get to become a killer. *That's all that's out there!* And if at my age, I was stupid enough to think that I could have stepped out of here and won that little girl, loved her, and moved through the rest of my days without killing anybody, *that was a victory!* (*He moves to the center of the floor, stands silently for awhile, and then does a little dance.*) Be a dancer—any kind of dancer you wanta be—but whatever you do, dance it! (*Tries out a difficult step, but can't quite make it*) Uh uhhh! Can't make that one no more . . . (*Continues to dance*) Be a singer—sing any song you wanta sing —but sing! (*Stops in his tracks*) *And you've got enough trouble to take you to the graveyard! But think of all that life you had before they buried you!* (*He breaks into a frantic dance, attempting steps that are crossing him up. He stumbles about until he falls.* THEO, MR. JENKINS, *and* ADELE *rush to pick him up from the floor.*) I'm okay—I'm okay . . . (*He rises from the floor quickly on his own. They stop in their tracks.*) I'm tired, I'm going to bed, and by the time tomorrow comes around, children, let's see if we can't throw it all into the river. (*Moves into the back room, singing*)

> I have had my fun
> If I don't get well no more
> I have had my fun
> If I don't get well no more

(*Stops in the center of the room, turns looking over* ADELE's *shoulder through the door out into the shop*) Jenkins, you said the day I beat you playing checkers, you said it could be the unluckiest day of my life . . . But after all that's happened today—I'm straight—I feel just great! (*Moves sharply to the stairs, stops and turns*) Say, where's Bobby?

CURTAIN

Goin' a Buffalo

A Tragifantasy

ED BULLINS

Sometimes . . .
I'd like to be
a Stranger in town . . .
Sort'a mysterious.
Strange tales would be
told about me . . .
And they would be
FANTASTIC!

MARTIN P. ABRAMSON

Cast of Characters

CURT: *29 years old.*
RICH: *28 years old.*
PANDORA: *22 years old. Curt's wife.*
ART: *23 years old.*
MAMMA TOO TIGHT: *20 years old.*

SHAKY: *36 years old. Mamma Too Tight's man.*
PIANO PLAYER.
BASS PLAYER.
DRUMMER.
BARTENDER.
DEENY.
BOUNCER.
CUSTOMERS.
SHOWGIRL.
VOICE.

Synopsis of Scenes
    ACT ONE: *Evening.*
    ACT TWO: *Later that evening.*
    ACT THREE: *Three days later.*
    The action of the play takes place in Curt's apartment and at the Strip Club.

ACT I

Scene I

This play is about some black people: CURT, PANDORA, ART, RICH, *and* SHAKY, *though* MAMMA TOO TIGHT *is white. The remainder of the cast is interracial, but two of the musicians are black and if* DENNY, *the* BOUNCER *and one of the* CUSTOMERS *are white, there might be added tensions. But it is left to the director's imagination to match the colors to the portrayals.*

Time: Early 1960's, late evening in January.

Scene: A court apartment in Los Angeles in the West Adams district. The room is done in white—white ceiling, white walls, white overly elaborate furniture—but a red wall-to-wall carpet covers the floor. A wall bed is raised. Upstairs, two doorless entrances stand on each side of the head of the bed. The right entrance is to the kitchen; the backstage area that represents the kitchen is shielded by a filmy curtain, and the actors' dim silhou-

ettes are seen when the area is lighted. The left entrance will be raised and off stage right at the head of a short flight of stairs and a platform which leads into the combination bathroom–dressing-room–closet. When the actors are within this area, their shadows will be cast upon the wall fronting the stairs. And when the bed is lowered a scarlet spread is shown.

Within the interior of the front room the light is a mixture of red, blues, and violet, with crimson shadows bordering the edges of the stage to create the illusion of a world afire, with this pocket of atmosphere an oasis.

A telefunken, turned very low, plays the local jazz station, and CURT *and* RICH *lean over a chess board.* CURT *squats upon a stool, and, facing him across the coffee table and chess board,* RICH, *a stocky, brooding man, studies his next move, seated on the edge of the couch. Each has an empty beer bottle and a glass close at hand.*

CURT. I just about have you up tight, Rich.

RICH (*annoyed*). Awww . . . Curt, man . . . don't try and hustle me!

CURT (*looks at him*). Did I say somethin' to upset you, man? (RICH *shakes his head and curses to himself.*

A shadow appears at head of stairs and pauses as if the figure is listening for conversation. Then PANDORA *enters—a beautiful black girl wearing tight white pants, a crimson blouse, and black boots—and slowly descends the stairs while looking at the men. She crosses behind them and walks toward the kitchen.* RICH *looks a second at her behind, but drops his gaze when* CURT *begins tapping the chess board with a finger nail.* CURT *gives no discernible attention to* PANDORA. *She enters the kitchen; a light goes on.*)

CURT (*staring at Rich*). This game's somethin' else . . . man.

RICH (*studies board, looks up at* CURT, *and concentrates upon the board again. Mutters to himself*). Ain't this somethin' else though . . . (*Looking up*) You almost got my ass, man.

CURT (*mocking*). I have got your ass, Rich.

RICH (*half-hearted*). Awww . . . man . . . why don't you go fuck yourself? (*He places hand upon a piece.*)

CURT (*warning and placing hand upon one of his pieces*). Wouldn't do that if I were you, good buddy.

RICH (*frowns and takes hand from board. He shakes head and mumbles, then curses his own caution*). Sheeet! (*He makes move.*) Let's see what you're goin' ta do with that, man!

CURT (*deliberately*). Checkmate!

RICH (*half rising*). What you say, Curt?

CURT (*toneless*). Checkmate, man.

(CURT *looks toward the rear of the apartment; the faucet has been turned on, and in the kitchen* PANDORA *leisurely crosses the entrance doorway*).

CURT. WE'RE READY FOR ANOTHER ONE, PAN-DORA!

PANDORA (*off*). Already?

CURT. That's what I said, baby!

PANDORA (*crosses doorway again*). Okay.

RICH (*mumbles and studies chessboard*). Well . . . I'll be god-damned.

(*Faucet sound goes off.*)

PANDORA (*off*). You don't need fresh glasses, da ya?

(*Sound of refrigerator opening.*)

CURT (*surely*). NO, PANDORA, JUST THE BEER!

PANDORA (*raising voice*). Okay . . . Okay . . . wait a fuckin' minute, will ya? Be right there!

(*Rattles of bottles.*)

CURT (*glowering toward the kitchen, then staring at* RICH *who sits stoop-shouldered*). How 'bout another one, Rich?

(RICH *reaches into pocket and brings out a small roll and pulls off two bills and places them beside* CURT's *glass. He mutters to himself*).

RICH. I wonder why in the fuck I didn't see that?

PANDORA (*with a cross expression, enters carrying two bottles *of Miller's Highlife).* Just because you're pissed off at the world don't take it out on me! What'ta hell ya think ya got 'round here, maid service? (CURT *stands to meet her; she slows. Whining).* Awww . . . Curt . . . *(A knock comes from backstage; relieved, she looks at* CURT.) I wonder who would be knocking at the kitchen door, honey?

CURT *(reaches down, palms and pockets the money).* There's only one way to be sure, sugar. *(Sits down, looks at* RICH) You clean, man?

RICH *(nods).* Yeah . . . Curt.

CURT *(nods to* PANDORA *as the knock sounds again).* Just watch your mouth, pretty baby . . . it's goin' ta get you in trouble one of these days, ya know. (PANDORA *places bottles on the edge of the table and briskly goes to open back door.)*

PANDORA. Maybe it's little Mamma already.

CURT *(mostly to himself).* She wouldn't come around to the back door for nobody. *(Disregards the noise of the kitchen door's lock snapping back and the rattle of the night chain being fixed in its hasp)* I have the black men this time, right, Rich?

RICH *(reaching for the beer).* Yeah.

ART *(off).* Hello, is Curt home? My name's Art. I ran into Curt this afternoon and he told me to drop by.

PANDORA *(off).* Just a minute . . . I'll see. *(The sound of the door closing is heard, and* PANDORA *returns to the main room.)* Curt . . . Curt?

CURT *(setting up his chess pieces; in a bored voice).* Yeah, baby?

PANDORA. There's a guy named Art out here who says you told him to drop around.

CURT *(not looking at her but down at the board).* Invite him in, baby.

(PANDORA *exits.)*

RICH. Is this the guy?

CURT (*nods, in low voice*). Never a dull moment . . . right, Rich?

RICH (*sarcastic*). Yeah. We're really in ta somethin', man.

(*The music changes during the remainder of this scene. "Delilah" and "Parisian Thoroughfare" as recorded by Max Roach and Clifford Brown play. These will be the themes for the scenes between* ART *and* PANDORA, *except when other music is necessary to stress altering moods. If Act I extends long enough, "Sketches in Spain" by Miles Davis is to be played also, but "Delilah" should be replayed during* PANDORA's *box scene.*)

PANDORA (*off*). Just a minute.

(*noise of the lock and chain.*)

ART. Good evening.

(*She leads him into the living room.* RICH *has poured beer for* CURT *and himself; he stands and saunters to the radio as if to change stations, but turns after* ART *has passed behind him and sizes up the stranger from the rear.*)

CURT (*stands*). Hey, good buddy! You found the place okay, huh?

ART (*pleased by greeting*). Yeah, it wasn't so hard to find but I guess I came around to the wrong door.

CURT (*with a wave*). Awww . . . that's okay. One's good as the other. It's better to come in that way if you're walkin' from Washington Boulevard. You live somewhere 'round there, don't ya?

ART (*hesitant*). Well . . . I did.

CURT (*gesturing*). Here, I want you to meet my wife and a buddy of mine. (*Introducing* PANDORA) This is my wife, Pandora . . . and . . .

PANDORA (*smiles brightly*). We already met, kinda. He told me his name at the door.

CURT (*ignoring* PANDORA). . . . and this is Rich.

RICH (*remains in same spot.* ART *turns and* RICH *gives him a casual salute*). What's happen'n, brother?

CURT (*to* PANDORA *and* RICH). This is a guy I met in jail. (*Introduces* ART) Art Garrison. (*Shows* ART *a seat on the couch, downstage from Rich.*) Yeah, Art was one of the best young cons on Tier Three . . . (*To Pandora*) Get my boy here a drink, baby.

PANDORA (*starts for kitchen*). You drink beer, Art?

ART. Sure . . . that sounds great.

PANDORA (*over her shoulder*). We got some scotch, if you want it.

ART. No, thanks.

(RICH *sits, makes opening move, not looking at* ART.)

CURT (*to* RICH). Yeah, if it wasn't for Art here I wouldn't be sittin' here.

RICH (*bored*). Yeah?

CURT. This is the kid who banged Scooter aside the jaw during the riot last summer in the joint.

RICH (*sounding more enthused*). Yeah . . . you were doin' a stretch down at county jail when that happened, weren't you?

CURT. Yeah, man. I was there bigger den shit. (*Takes seat*) Yeah, that paddy mathafukker, Scooter, was comin' down on me with an ice pick, man . . . we had all been rumblin' up and down the cell block and I slipped on somethin' wet . . . I think it was Cory's blood 'cause Miles and his boys had stomped the mathafukker so good . . .

(*During the telling of the incident,* PANDORA *stands framed in the kitchen doorway, watching the men.*)

CURT. And I went to look up and all I could see was that gray-eyed mathafukkin' Scooter comin' at me with that ice pick of his . . . He reached down and grabbed my shirt front and drew back his arm and WHAMMO . . . (*Indicating* ART) just like a bat out'ta hell my boy here had scored on the sucker's jaw.

ART (*pleased*). Well . . . I couldn't let that white sonna bitch do you in, man.

RICH (*dryly*). What was the beef about, man?

CURT. Well you know Miles goes for the Muslims though he

ain't one hisself. Now the Muslims were in a hassle at the joint with the guards and the big people on top because of their religious beliefs, dig?

RICH (*interested*). What do you mean?

CURT. Well the guards didn't want them havin' their meetin's 'cause they said they were organizing' and plottin'. And the Muslims wanted some of the chow changed 'cause they don't eat the same kind'a food we do.

RICH. Yeah!

CURT. So while this was all goin' on, Cory . . . a young, wise nigger who thinks he's in ta somethin' . . . well he started agitatin' and signifyin' bout who the Muslims think they was. And what made it so rank was a lot of the ofays, ya know, Charles, the white man, start in sayin' things they had held back before, so Miles and some of the boys got together one day and caught that little jive-sucker Cory outside his cell block and stomped him so bad the deck was greasy wit' his blood, man. That's when the shit started really goin' down, right there, man. Bumpy, Cory's cousin come runnin' up, man, and that big nigger kicked Miles square in the nuts and laid out two of his boys before the rest of them got themselves together. By that time some of the whiteys come runnin' up and a few more of Miles's boys. Yeah, the whole shit started right there where Cory lay almost done in . . .

RICH. Yeah . . . I heard a couple of cats got stabbed, man.

CURT. Yeah, man, it was pretty scary for a while, mostly black cons against white ones except for the studs who just tried to stay out of the shit and the Uncle Toms . . . those Toms we were really out to cool.

RICH (*heated*). Yeah, you should have done those mathafukkers in!

CURT. Even the guards wouldn't come into the cell block and break it up at first . . . a whole lot of shit went down that day. (*Looking at* ART) I owe my boy here a lot for that day.

ART (*embarrassed*). Yeah, man, I would have liked to have stayed out of it but I couldn't.

CURT. Yeah, Art, I us'ta wonder about that . . . (*A two-beat pause*) How could you just go about your business and stay in the middle all the time in that place when so much crap was goin' down?

ART. I just stayed out of everything, that's all.

CURT. But didn't you care about anything, man? Didn't you feel anything when that shit was happen'n to you?

ART. Yeah, I cared but I just didn't let it bother me too much. I just froze up on everything that tried to get in and not too much touched me.

PANDORA (*from doorway*). Talk about somebody bein' cold!

CURT (*having noticed her in doorway for first time, stares at* ART). But you don't know how I appreciate what you did, man. It wasn't your fight, man. You weren't takin' sides. You were one of the quiet guys waitin' for trial who just kept his mouth shut and minded his own business.

ART. I never do try and take sides in stir, just serve my time and forget about it, that's all.

(PANDORA *has moved out of the doorway.*)

CURT. Well, I'm glad you did that time, man, and if there's anything I can ever . . .

RICH (*interrupting*). What were you in for, Art?

(CURT *takes a drink of his beer, lights a cigarette and blows smoke across the table above the two men's heads.* PANDORA *drops something made of glass in the kitchen and curses.*)

ART. Well . . . I was waiting for trial . . . attempted murder.

RICH. That's a tough one to have on your rap sheet.

ART. Yeah, it doesn't do your record or you any good, especially when it ain't for money.

CURT (*finally makes answering chess move*). It was over a broad, wasn't it?

ART (*lights a cigarette, offers* RICH *a light but is refused*). Yeah. I guess girls are my main weakness.

RICH (*with unlit cigarette dangling from his lips, makes move*). How much time did you do?

ART. Waited on my trial for nine months at county when the husband of the girl dropped the charges and left town.

CURT (*replies to move*). That's who you shot, the girl's husband?

ART (*his eyes following game*). Yeah.

RICH (*moves quickly*). You pretty good with a gun?

ART (*caught up in game*). I can usually hold one without it blowing my foot off.

RICH (*sharply*). Any simple ass can do that! I asked you are you any good with one!

(*The three men are fixed in tableau for a three-beat interval:* ART *strains forward from his seat and is about to speak.*)

CURT (*to* RICH *as he makes his move*). This move's goin' ta show ya to stop fuckin' with Curt the Kid, good buddy.

(*Noise of refrigerator opening and slamming, and* PANDORA *enters with a bottle and a glass. She pours beer for* ART *and sets the glass down beside him as the men all look at the chessboard.*)

PANDORA (*in a light mood*). Sorry I took so long, Art. I just dropped the supper. (*To Curt*) Honey, the beans are all messed up. Little Mamma won't have anything to eat 'cept eggs.

CURT (*not looking at her*). Didn't want no fuckin' beans anyhow! And I know Mamma Too Tight don't want any either . . . what kind'a shit is that . . . givin' that broad beans on her first night on the streets?

PANDORA (*defensively*). That's all we got, honey . . . You know we won't have any spendin' money until Deeny pays me.

RICH. Why don't you have a seat, Pan?

PANDORA. I gotta finish cleanin' the kitchen . . . I don't want no roaches 'round here. Last place we had we had to split 'cause the roaches took it over. The little mathafukkers got mo' of the food than Curt or me. Soon as I bring in a little money to get some food with . . . (CURT *looks at her sharply but she is turned toward* RICH *and* ART.) there's mo' of them little mathafukkers there than your eyes could see. And I put too much time in fixin' this pad up nice the way it is to have them little mathafukkers move in on me and try to take it over.

CURT. You better finish up, sweetcake, so I can take you to work. (*The term sweetcake is used with derision and seldom with affection.* PANDORA *picks up* CURT's *empty bottles and exits.*)

CURT. Your move, Richie.

RICH. Are you sure, man?

CURT. Just ask Art, he's been watchin' the game.

ART. Well, I ain't in it, man.

RICH. That's right, you ain't in it.

CURT (*watching* ART's *face*). Yeah, it's your move, Richie, babe.

RICH (*to* ART). That was pretty nice of that girl's ole man to let you off, Art.

ART. Nawh . . . he wanted his ole lady to leave the state with him so he had to drop the charges against me to let her off the hook too.

RICH. She was in it too, huh?

ART. She shot him with me.

CURT. You play this game, Art?

ART. Yeah, some. But I haven't had much practice lately.

CURT. Well, this one's about over.

RICH (*snorts*). Sheeet!

CURT. Maybe you'd like ta play the winner.

RICH (*grimacing before making hesitant move*). Where ya livin' now, Art?

ART. I just got locked out of my room.

RICH. Yeah, Curt said you wanted to make some money.

ART (*intensely*). I have to, man. I'm really on my ass.

CURT. Check!

RICH (*makes move*). Not yet, sucker.

ART. I gotta get out of this town.

RICH. You got a car, ain't ya?

CURT (*moves*). Not long now, Rich.

ART. Yeah, that's about all I got. A car and a suitcase. I've also gotten more jail time in this town than in my whole life, and I've been halfway round the world and all over this country.

RICH (*moves and acts angry*). Yeah, L.A.'s no fuckin' good, man. If I was off parole now I would get the first thing on wheels out of here. How bout you, Curt? If you weren't out on bail wouldn't you make it?

(CURT *doesn't answer. Stage left, a knock sounds and* PANDORA *comes out of the kitchen striding toward the entrance which serves as the front door to the apartment.*)

PANDORA. That must be little Mamma.

CURT. Sure hope it is . . . I would really like to see that little broad.

PANDORA (*peers through window*). Yeah, there's that chick. (*Calling outside in jocular way*) Hey, broad, what they doin' lettin' you out'ta jail? (*An indistinct shout and a laugh comes from outside.*)

CURT (*to Rich*). Checkmate, man!

(*Lights lower to blacken the stage.*)

ACT I

Scene II

When the lights go up MAMMA TOO TIGHT *and* SHAKY *sit upon the lowered bed. Faintly reflecting a glow, the bedspread gives them the appearance of sitting upon smoldering coals.* MAMMA TOO TIGHT, *a small, voluptuous girl, is dressed well. Her shift complements her creamy complexion and full-blown build.* SHAKY *is nondescript but dresses in expensive casual clothes.*

CURT, RICH, *and* ART *sit in the same area, stage right, facing*

the bed, forming the lower lip of a half-moon, and PANDORA
*has changed to a black cocktail dress and sits upon the stairs to
the bathroom. She faces front with a bit of red ruffled slip peek-
ing beneath and around her black stockinged legs.*

*They all eat chicken from cardboard containers and reach
for beers and cigarettes. The light in the kitchen is off, and the
radio plays.*

ART. Thanks again, Curt . . . if you hadn't invited me to eat
I don't know what I'd do . . . probably had to drive downtown
on what little gas I got and eat at one of those Rescue Missions.

MAMMA TOO TIGHT (*nudging* SHAKY *in the ribs*). Well, I'll be
damned . . . Ole Curt done saved himself a soul . . .

SHAKY (*slow and languid*). Easy, baby, you gonna make me
spill my beer.

MAMMA TOO TIGHT. What you know 'bout eatin' at Rescue
Missions, boy?

PANDORA (*interjecting*). You better stop callin' that guy ah
boy, Mamma . . . ha ha . . . girl . . . you got mo' gall.

RICH (*drinking beer*). Yeah, Mamma, how fuckin' big do boys
grow where you come from?

CURT (*with food in mouth*). Forget about it, Art, glad to have
ya. One more don't mean a thing.

PANDORA. Listen to that, Mamma Too Tight . . . (*Mocking*)
"One mo' mouf don't mean a thing." . . . We eat beans all week
and when you and Curt's friends come in we play big shit! . . .
And call out for food and beer.

(CURT, SHAKY, *and* ART *stop eating.* CURT *stares at* PANDORA
and ART *holds his plate like it is hot and he is trying not to
drop it on the floor.* SHAKY *eyes* MAMMA TOO TIGHT *and gives a
mean scowl.* MAMMA *has seen the look on* CURT'S *face before.*
RICH *goes on enjoying his meal.*)

MAMMA (*in a jolly tone, to* PANDORA). Girl, you don't have ta
tell me a thing . . . these here men think that money can be
just picked up off'a them pavements out there like chewin'

gum paper . . . until they got ta get out there for themselves. (*She swings off the bed and shows flashes of lingerie.*) Like this pretty boy here with the fuzz on his face. (*She approaches* ART *and stands so her hips form a prominent profile to* CURT's *line of vision.*) He ain't even eatin' no mo' . . . and Curt's not either, honey. What I tell ya? These men are somethin' else. So weak from plottin' what we should be doin' to bring some money in that they can't eat themselves. (*Puts her plate on coffee table*) I knows that Curt is a big strong man . . . he's always lettin' Pan know. (*Strong dialect*) So he don't need no help from us frail ass women but maybe ole fuzzy wuzzy face here needs some help. (*Her audience is in better humor once more. To Art*) You wants Mamma Too Tight to feeds him some food, baby boy?

SHAKY. Cut out the Magnolia act. Everything wears thin, *Queenie!*

MAMMA (*sudden anger*). Don't you call me no fuckin' Queenie!

SHAKY (*sarcastic*). Anything you say, baby.

(PANDORA *guffaws at* SHAKY's *tone.*)

PANDORA (*mimicking Mamma's drawl*). But ain't dat yo name, hooneee?

(MAMMA *ignores* SHAKY *and* PANDORA, *picks drumstick from plate and offers it to* ART *who frowns, and pulls it away and puts it to her mouth imitating a mother feeding a reluctant child. Finally,* ART *smiles at her as* SHAKY *speaks.*)

SHAKY. Why don' chou lighten up, woman!

MAMMA. Lighten up? . . . Damn . . . man . . . I ain't here ten minutes before I see your face and you tell *me* to lighten up! I been with you since I hit the streets at noon and you still checkin' up on me . . . don't worry, man . . . I'm goin' ta get right ta work.

SHAKY (*slow and languid*). I know that, baby.

MAMMA (*to* PANDORA). Girl you should of seen Shaky . . . ha ha ha . . . almost swept me off my feet, girl. Said he loved me and really missed me so much the last ninety days that he almost went out of his mind . . . ha ha . . . (*Coyly*) I was so embarrassed and impressed, girl, I liked to have blushed and nearly peed on myself like a sixteen-year-old girl. (*Change of voice*) But the ole sonna bitch didn't fool me none with that shit . . . The only thing he missed was that good steady money!

CURT (*picqued*). Why don't you check yourself, Mamma!

MAMMA (*waving* CURT's *threat off and returning to the edge of the bed*). But, girl, he sho threw some lovin' on me . . . hee heee . . . sheeet, I should go away again after this afternoon. (PANDORA *laughs throughout.*) Ummm . . . chile . . . I nearly thought I was on that honeymoon I never had.

PANDORA. You should after that routine, baby.

MAMMA. And then when the sun start goin' down and things got really gettin' romantic, girl . . . this mathafukker says . . .

(*Lights lower; spot on bed.* SHAKY *speaks the line.*)

SHAKY. I want you to bring in a yard tonight, baby.

(MAMMA *resumes speech. Bed spot off; colored spot on* MAMMA.)

MAMMA. You what, man?

(*Colored spot off; bed spot on.*)

SHAKY. A hundred stone cold dollars, baby. Tonight, baby!

(*Spot off; lights go up.*)

MAMMA (*to* PANDORA). And girl, do you know what I said?

PANDORA. Yeah, I know what you said.

MAMMA. That's right, baby, I said to Shaky, "How do you want them daddy . . . in fives or tens?"

(*Laughter halts the speeches; the glasses are filled and fingers cleaned of chicken grease and cigarettes lit.*)

CURT (*to* SHAKY). Don't let Mamma try and fool you . . . she wanted to see you so bad . . . everytime Pan us'ta go visit her she would say to Pan, "How's that ole dirty Shaky doin?"

MAMMA. Yeah, I'd ask . . . cause I'd be wonderin' why ain't the mathafukker down here.

SHAKY. Now, let's not go into that again, baby.

CURT. Yeah, Mamma . . . you know what's happen'n behind that. You know why Shaky didn't come down . . . you never can tell when they might have a warrant out on him or somethin' and keep him too. You remember what happened at court, don't cha?

MAMMA. Yeah, I remember. How can I forget? The judge said for Shaky to leave the court cause every time I'm on trial he's in the back row hangin' round and that last ole woman judge said she knew who Shaky was an' she'd like to put him behind bars instead of me . . . but comin' down to visit me in jail is different, Curt!

SHAKY (*pleading*). Now, baby . . .

CURT. Listen, Mamma . . . how old are you?

MAMMA. Twenty.

CURT. That means you're a big girl now, a woman who should be able to understand things, right?

MAMMA. Yeah, but . . .

CURT (*cutting*). Right! Now listen, baby . . . and listen hard . . . now how many times you been busted?

MAMMA. Thirty-three times . . . but I only fell this once for more than ten days and that was because I got that new fuckin' woman judge. I got the best record in town of any broad on the block I know. Pandora's rap sheet is worse than mine and I was on the block two years before she was.

CURT. Exactly, baby. Now if you didn't have an old man like Shaky out there workin' for you, you'd be out of business and servin' some big time . . . right? Wouldn't that be a drag to be servin' some grand theft time behind givin' up a little body! Pan ain't been snatched since before we were married . . . ain't that right, Pandora? See there? Now let me tell you, baby, and listen hard. (*Intensely*) A self-respectin' man won't let his ole lady stay in jail. If he can't get the bail for her or the juice to pay off somebody downtown like Shaky done you to have your time cut to one third . . . (*Disgust*) he's a punk! And any broad that even looks at the jive-sucker should get her funky ass run into the ground like a piece of scum!

MAMMA (*on defensive*). I know all that, Curt, but I got so lonely down there. Nothin' down there but broads and most of them are butches.

PANDORA. Mamma . . . don't even talk about it. Makes cold chills run up my back just thinkin' bout it.

CURT. Yeah, we know it was hard, baby, but you can't afford to lose your old man by his gettin' busted behind a jail visit. That would be a stone trick, Mamma. Nothin' but a hummer . . . Right?

MAMMA. Awww . . . Curt, you try and make it sound so smooth.

PANDORA. He can really make it do that, girl.

RICH (*finishes drinking the last of his beer*). Hey, Shaky, I want you to take a walk with me, okay?

SHAKY (*standing slowly and visibly rocking*). Yeah, man. (*To Mamma*) I'll see you back at the house, baby. Watch yourself.

MAMMA. I'll probably be in early, Shaky. Unless I catch somethin' good.

(RICH *and* SHAKY *exit by the front door.* PANDORA *accompanies them and checks the outside before they step out.*)

MAMMA. Sheeet, Pandora, I thought Shaky was the Chicken Delight man when he knocked. I wasn't here ten minutes before he was knockin' on the door to see if I had my ride to the club. Didn't even think about feedin' me. (*Soulful*) Just give me some good lovin' ta show me where it's at.

PANDORA. These men are somethin' else, girl . . . 'spect a girl to go out'ta here on an empty stomach and turn all kinds of tricks . . . but Curt and me did have some beans for you, girl, but I dropped them.

MAMMA. Well, I'm glad you did.

CURT (*packing away chessboard*). I told her you didn't want no beans, Mamma.

MAMMA. I got too many beans in the joint.

PANDORA (*peeved*). Well that's what I had for you, chick.

MAMMA (*to* ART). Hey, pretty baby, why you so quiet?

ART. Oh, I ain't got much to say, I guess.

CURT. This is my boy Art, Mamma. I introduced you when you came in.

MAMMA (*sultry*). I know his name . . . ha ha . . . I just want to know his game, dat's all. Hey, fuzz face, what's yo game? Is you kinda fuzzy wuzzy 'round the edges?

ART. I'm sorry . . . I don't know . . .

CURT. Awww . . . he's okay, Mamma . . . he was in the joint with me. He's just quiet, that's all. Reads too much . . . somethin' you should do more of.

PANDORA. Why should she? Ain't heard of nobody gettin' no money readin'.

MAMMA (*to* ART). Now I know your name, fuzzy boy, now you say my name.

ART (*surprise*). Your name?

MAMMA. Yeah. Say MAMA TOO TIGHT!

ART. I know your name.

MAMMA. But I want you to say it.

ART. I don't have to with you broadcasting it all over the place ever since you been here.

MAMMA (*cross*). You must think you're wise, man.

ART (*in low, even voice*). I am, you big-mouthed bitch and I want you to stop jivin' with me.

(PANDORA *giggles.* CURT *looks on enjoying the surprise showing on* MAMMA'S *face.*)

MAMMA. Well . . . 'scuse me, tiger. (*Walks over to* ART *and sits beside him.*) Aww . . . forget it. I always act this way, ask Pan and Curt. 'Specially when I'm ah little bit loaded . . . Hey, Pandora, your friend here ain't got no sense of humor.

PANDORA. Nawh . . . he's too much like Curt. Serious. That's why they probably get along so good, girl . . . they probably made for each other.

(*The girls laugh.*)

CURT. C'mon, Pan . . . it's almost time for you to go to work. Deeny will be callin' nex' thing and that's one mathafukker I don't even want to see much less talk to. Go on and get the stuff.

(PANDORA *exits through the bathroom door.*)

MAMMA (*to* ART). You want to know why they call me Mamma Too Tight, pretty baby?

CURT. If Shaky ever heard you callin' my boy that he'd break your arm, Mamma.

MAMMA. Yeah, he might. But Shaky ain't where nothin's shakin' at the moment. . . . Just out givin' Rich a fix . . .

CURT. Both of you bitches talk too much!

MAMMA (*to* ART). You know what, fuzz wuzz? I sho wish I had a lil fuzzy wuzzy like you up there some of those cold nights in the joint. (*She gets up and walks to stand before the men. She plays it strictly for laughs, swinging her hips to the radio music, and singsongs in a hearty, brazen voice like one of the old-time red hot mamma's. Singing*) Why do they call me what they call me, baby. When what they call me is my name.

ART (*dryly*). I have suspicions but I'm not positive.

MAMMA (*ridiculing, but friendly*). You have suspicions as every little fuzzy wuzzy does but let me tell you . . . because my real name is Queenie Mack! Queenie Bell Mack! Ain't that some shit? No self-respectin' whore in the world can go 'round with a name like that unless she's in Mississippi . . . sheeet . . . Queenie!

ART. So you named yourself Mamma Too . . .

MAMMA (*cutting*). No! It just happened. I don't know how. I just woke up one day with my name that way . . . And I like it that way . . . it's me! (*Turning toward* ART) Don't you think it fits, honey?

ART. I think it really does.

MAMMA. Damn right it does. It makes me feel so alive. That's why I'm glad to be out . . .

CURT (*yelling*). Hey, Pandora!

MAMMA. Man, but it's so good to be high again. It's so good to be free.

(PANDORA *enters from the bathroom and descends the stairs and places a cardboard box on the table as the lights blacken briefly and the music rises.*)

ACT I

Scene III

As the lights go up and the music lowers, the scene has shifted. CURT *and* PANDORA *sit upon the couch, across from* ART, *and* MAMMA TOO TIGHT *has taken the stool* CURT *was seated on. Uncovered, the box waits in the center of the table.* CURT *is licking a brown cigarette as the theme plays.*

CURT. Yeah. We want to make some money, Art, so we can get out of this hole. (*Lights the cigarette and inhales fiercely. Drops head. Two-beat pause. In strained voice, holding smoke back*) We're makin' it to Buffalo, man. You hip to Buffalo?

ART. No, I don't think so . . .

CURT (*takes another drag*). It's a good little hustlin' town, I hear. I got a case comin' up here for passin' some bad paper, ya know, forgin' payroll checks . . . and when I get the money to make restitution and give the people downtown some juice, ya know, man, pay them off, I'm makin' it East. But I need some grand theft dough.

ART. But won't you get some time with your record?

CURT. Nawh. Probably not. You see, I'm a good thief. I take money by my wits . . . ya know, with a pen or by talkin' some sucker out of it. It's only seldom that I'm forced to really take any money by force. If I make full restitution for these checks and fix my lawyer up and the other people downtown, I'll get probation. They'll reduce it to a misdemeanor and breakin' probation for somethin' like that ain't nothin' . . . besides, Buffalo's a long way away, man.

PANDORA (*receiving cigarette from* CURT). It's supposed to be a good little town. A different scene entirely. I'm due for a good scene for a change.

CURT. Yeah, but we have to get that juice money first, baby. We gotta get us some long money.

MAMMA. Any place is better than L.A. but I heard that Buffalo is really boss.

PANDORA (*languid*). It sho is, baby.

MAMMA. I wonder if I could get Shaky to go?

CURT. Sure you could, Mamma. He can get connections to deal his stuff there just like here. That's the idea. When we make our hit and split out of here we're gon'a take as many as we can with us. You know, set up a kinda organization.

PANDORA (*passing cigarette to* MAMMA). They really got respect for cats from the coast back there.

ART (*getting caught up in the mood*). Yeah, they really do . . . when I . . .

PANDORA (*cutting speech*). With me workin' on the side and with Curt dealin' we'd be on our feet in no time.

CURT. We want to be on our feet when we get there, baby.

ART. And that's where I come in, right?

CURT. Right, good buddy.

MAMMA (*handing cigarette to* ART). Here, baby.

ART (*waving it away*). So what's on your mind, Curt?

MAMMA (*extending cigarette*). I said here, baby, I just don't like to hold this thing and see all this bread go up in ashes.

ART. I don't want any.

(*A three-beat stop, all caught in tableau staring at* ART, *then* PANDORA *snickers and breaks into a tittering laugh, looking at* CURT.)

PANDORA (*ridicule*). You and your friends, Curt . . . I thought . . .

CURT (*heated*). Shut up, bitch . . . you talk too much!

PANDORA (*rising anger*). Why shouldn't I when you bring some square-all little . . . (CURT *slaps her; she jumps to her feet and spins to claw him but* CURT *lunges forward and slaps her again, causing her to trip backwards across the edge of the coffee table. From the floor, removing one of her shoes)* God-damn you Curt . . . (*She begins to crawl to her knees and* CURT *moves around the table after her. Then* ART *steps between them and pushes* CURT *backward on the couch. Surprise is upon* CURT'S *face and* MAMMA TOO TIGHT *seems frozen in place.)*

CURT. *What the fuck's goin' on, man?*

ART (*low*). Don't hit her any more, Curt.

CURT (*incredulous*). What? . . . Man, are you payin' this woman's bills . . . have you got any papers on her?

PANDORA (*to* CURT). *Are you payin' my bills, mathafukker?*

CURT (*rising to attack* PANDORA; ART *blocks his way*). I've told you to keep your mouth . . . (*To Art when he won't let him pass*) Now listen, Art, you're like a brother to me but you don't know what's goin' down, man.

ART. Why don't we all sit down and try and relax, Curt? Why don't you do it for me, huh? As a favor. I'm sorry for buttin' into your business between you and your ole lady but somethin' just happens to me, man, when I see a guy hit a girl.

(*After a minute,* CURT *is soothed and sits upon the couch again, glaring at* PANDORA *who holds her shoe like a weapon.*)

MAMMA (*partially recovered*). Oh, man, I just hit the streets and this is what I run into . . .

CURT (*intense, to* ART). What are you doin', man? Squarin' out on me? Man, I've went a long way . . .

ART (*leaning forward*). Well, look, Curt . . . I can split . . .

(CURT *stands and looks down on* ART. *Changing expression,* PANDORA *makes a move for the box but* CURT *waves her hand away.*)

CURT. No, I don't think you better try that, Art. (*Pause*). Tell me, Art. Why don't you want to smoke any marijuana?

ART. Why don't . . . I don't understand why you should ask me that.

CURT. Is your playin' hero for Pandora a game to cover up somethin', man?

(MAMMA *is clutching herself as if she has returned to the womb.*)

MAMMA. Oh . . . shit shit shit . . . shit . . . just today . . . just today they cut me loose . . . just today.

PANDORA (*no longer angry, placing hand on* CURT'S *arm*). Easy, baby, I think he's okay.

CURT. You would!

ART. Now, look, man, I don't put down anybody for doin' what they want but just don't hassle me!

PANDORA (*hostile, to* ART). Cool it, baby, you're in some deep trouble now.

MAMMA. Oh, goddamn . . . why can't I just be plain ass Queenie Bell Mack?

CURT (*low*). What's happen'n, brother?

ART. I just don't get high . . . that's all . . .

MAMMA (*nearly screaming*). Neither does J. Edgar Hoover, sucker, but he don't come in here pretend'n to be no friend!

PANDORA (*enraged, fearful of losing control, to* MAMMA). Shut up, bitch! This is Curt and our place. We got mo' to lose than just our ass. Just shut on up!

(MAMMA *looks almost like a small girl with wide, moist eyes.*)

CURT. For the last time, Art, tell me somethin'.

ART. I just don't . . .

(PANDORA *stands and moves in front of* CURT. *The coffee table separates them from* ART, *but she leans over.*)

PANDORA (*to* CURT, *behind her*). He's all right, honey. If he were a cop he'd be smokin' stuff right along with us . . . you know that . . .

ART (*bewildered*). A cop! . . .

PANDORA (*sarcastic*). He's just a little square around the edges, Curt . . . (*Silence, then to* ART) But why, honey?

ART (*shrugging sheepishly*). I had a bad experience once behind pot, that's all.

(MAMMA *cackles until* CURT *stops her.*)

MAMMA. He had a bad experience . . . hee hee hee . . . ha ha ha . . . He had . . .

CURT (*menace*). Pan has already told you to check yourself, woman, he's still my friend.

PANDORA. What was it all about, man . . . can you tell us about it?

ART. I'd rather not . . .

CURT (*cutting*). We know you'd rather not but . . .

PANDORA (*cutting*). Now look, Art, you're not givin' us much of a break . . . we don't want to act like this but we got a lot of the future riding on what happens in the nex' few days. Why don't you tell us?

ART. I would but it don't seem that much . . .

CURT (*not so threatening*). But it is, Art!

PANDORA. C'mon, trust me. Can't you say anything? We've gone more than half- . . .

CURT. Stop rankin' him, will ya!

PANDORA. I'm only doin' it for you!

(*Silence as* CURT *and* PANDORA *stare at each other.*)

ART. Yeah, I'll talk about it . . . (CURT *sits.* PANDORA *moves around the table closer to* ART. *The cigarette has been dropped by* MAMMA *beside the box. "Delilah" plays.*) You see . . . it was about three years ago. I shipped out on a freighter . . . ya know, one of those scows that fly the Panamanian or Liberian flag but don't really belong to any country . . .

MAMMA (*in small girl's voice*). Ain't they Americans?

ART. Well, in a way. They belong to American corporations and the businessmen don't want to pay high taxes on 'em. They're pretty ratty. (PANDORA *makes a seat on the floor between the men.*) Well I went on a four-month cruise, ya know, to ports around the West Indies and then to North Africa.

MAMMA. Wow . . . that sounds gassy . . . I wish . . .

PANDORA (*cutting*). Mamma!

ART. Well I been blowin' weed since I was about twelve . . .

MAMMA (*ridicule*). Ha ha ha . . . since he was twelve . . .

(PANDORA *and* CURT *frown at her and she huddles in her seat and looks cold.*)

ART. . . . and everything was cool. I smoked it when I ran into it and never thought about it much unless someone turned me on. But in Tangier it was about as easy to get as a bottle of beer. Man, I had a ball all the while I was over there and before I left I bought a big bag. (*Showing with his hands*) This big for about five bucks. All the way back on my night watches I just smoked grass and just thought of what the guys on my corner back home would say when I would pull out a joint or two and just give it to them. Prices back East are about triple what they are here, so you can guess what it was worth . . . And all the broads I would make . . . you know how it goes . . . take a broad up to your room and smoke a little weed and if you have anything goin' for you at all, man, that's it.

PANDORA (*disgust*). Yeah, there's a lot of stupid broads in this world.

ART (*sensing the reduced tension*). And I could still sell some when my money got low and come out beautiful. I was really feeling good about that grass, Curt. Well this tub docks in Philly about 1:00 A.M. and I have to leave ship and when I get to the station I find that my train don't leave until two the next afternoon. I got my pay and my belongings, so I stash most of my bags in a locker at the station, the bag of weed is in one but I have about half a dozen joints on me. Now I know Philly a little. I know where there's an after-hour joint so I grab a cab and go over there. The place is jumpin' . . . they're havin' a fish fry, and I start in drinkin' and talkin' to girls but none of them are listen'n 'cept for seven bucks for them and three for the management for rentin' one of the upstairs rooms, and I ain't buyin' no cock . . . not in the States . . .

PANDORA. Well, I'm glad of that. I can take squares but not tricks, baby.

CURT (*to* PANDORA). You still runnin' your mouth, ain't you?

ART. So I start talkin' with some guy and he tells me of a place he knows 'cross town that's better than this one. He looks okay to me. A blood. Dressed real sharp with a little goatee and everything. I had been talkin' to him about bein' out to sea and since he don't try and con me into a crap game and is buyin' one drink for every one of mine, I don't give a damn where we go cause I got the whole night to kill.

MAMMA. Oh wow . . . I know this is the bad part . . .

PANDORA. Listen, Mamma.

MAMMA (*turning her face away*). I don't like to hear bad things.

ART. So we drinkin' bottles of beer and drivin' up Broad Street in Philly in his old wreck of a Buick and I think how it would be nice to turn on and get really loaded before we get where we're goin'. So I reach for my pocket but it's wintertime and I got on a pea jacket and sweaters and I have trouble gettin' to my pocket. And while I was lookin' I start in laughin'.

CURT. Laughin'?

ART. Yeah. I start wonderin' what would happen if this was a cop I was with and the idea was just too much. So funny. So I started in laughin'. And the guy asks me what I was laughin' at and I said I was just laughin' about him bein' a cop. And he said that he was and how did I know. (*Two-beat pause*) I don't know how I got out of that car or away from him. But soon after I was pukin' my guts up, and I threw those joints into a sewer and they wouldn't go down 'cause snow and ice was cloggin' it up. And I was stompin' on 'em so they would go down and gettin' sick and after a while my feet were all covered with ice and snow and puke and marijuana . . . Ya know . . . I had nearly twenty bucks worth of dope frozen to the soles of my shoes.

MAMMA (*seriously*). Awww . . . no, man . . . I can't stand any more.

PANDORA (*giggling*). That's the best trip I've been on this week, Art.

ART. Nawh, really . . . baby. And the bag . . . I left it in a locker. Not the one I used but another empty one.

MAMMA. Those janitors must'a naturally been happy the next day.

ART. Yeah, they must have been but I couldn't even think of the stuff for a long time without wanting to heave up my guts.

CURT. That must'a been pretty scary, man.

(PANDORA *has reached over and gotten the cigarette and relit it.*)

PANDORA (*offering it to* ART). Now it's time to get back on the horse, cowboy.

ART (*placing hand on stomach*). I don't think I can.

MAMMA. You'll never think about that time in Philly again after the first drag, baby.

CURT. C'mon, man, you're already one of us. Do you think I'd bring you in if I thought you'd be a square?

PANDORA. Don't say that, Curt. He's not. Somethin' like what happened to him can mess up your mind about things. (*She stands over him and puffs on the cigarette. Staring at him*) Now don't think about anything . . . just look into my eyes. (*She inhales once more and gives the cigarette to* ART.) Now, here, put it in your mouth.

ART (*takes it and puts to lips*). I can do it all right but I just don't want to.

PANDORA (*staring*). Look into my eyes and inhale. Don't think about it being in your hand. (ART *inhales and looks at her.*) All the way down now and hold it.

MAMMA. Don't ever say you don't believe in witches, boy.

CURT. Cool it, Mamma!

PANDORA. Now one more drag, Art.

(ART *takes another puff and hands the reefer to* CURT. ART *has a great grin on his face.*)

ART. So that's what's in Pandora's box.

(*Lights change.*)

PANDORA (*fantasy*). Among other things, Art. Among other

things. But those have been lies you've been told about bad things comin' out of Pandora's box.

MAMMA. Most people think that a girl's box is in other places.

PANDORA. Nothin' can be found bad in there either. People only bring evil there with them. They only look for evil there. The sick . . .

ART. What do you mean by sick?

PANDORA. The come freaks, that's who. The queers who buy sex from a woman.

MAMMA (*bitterly*). Yeah, they say we're wrong but they're the queers . . . payin' for another person's body.

CURT (*in euphoria, musing*). Art, my man, we're goin'a Buffalo . . . goin' one day real soon.

PANDORA (*repulsion*). Some of them are real nice-lookin' cats. Not old with fat greasy bellies. Real nice-lookin' studs. (*Bitterly*) Those are the real queers you have ta watch. They want ta hurt women.

MAMMA. You hip ta that, baby? Those muscle cats, you know, muscle queens . . . always wantin' ta freak out on ya.

ART. And that's all that comes out of Pandora's box?

(CURT *pulls a nickel-plated revolver out of the box.*)

CURT. No. Right now this is the most important thing. There's always something new in there. (*Handing gun to* ART) Feel it, brother.

(ART *takes the gun. He is caught up in the music and with his new friends.*)

ART. It's a good one.

MAMMA. Look how it shines.

(*Lights change.*)

ART (*dreamlike*). Yeah . . . like Pandora's eyes.

(*Lights change.*)

PANDORA (*fantasy*). Nothin' bad comes out of me or from my box, baby. Nothin' bad. You can believe that. It's all in what you bring to us.

(*Lights change.*)

MAMMA. That's wha's happen'n, baby.

CURT. It's yours now, Art, as much yours as mine. Can you handle it, brother?

ART (*looking at Pandora and taking a new reefer*). If that's my job, brother.

(*The cigarette has been replaced by a new one and others are in the hands of the group;* PANDORA *drags in deeply.*)

PANDORA. Buffalo's goin'a be a gas.

(*The phone rings from the dressing room and* CURT *goes to answer. His shadow can be seen upon the wall at the top of the stairs.*)

CURT (*off*). Yeah, Deeny . . . yeah yeah yeah . . . yeah, man, . . . yeah.

MAMMA. Who ever heard of a telephone in the toilet?

PANDORA. It's in the dressing room next to the bathroom, Mamma.

MAMMA. Sho is strange . . . Hey, are you goin'a Buffalo too, fuzz wuzz?

ART. It looks that way.

PANDORA (*smiling*). I think I'll like that, Art. I think that'll be nice.

(*A knock sounds at the front door.* CURT's *shadow hangs up the phone and retreats farther into the area.*)

CURT (*off*). Pandora! Move! Goddamn it! Get a move on!

(ART *stands as* PANDORA *jumps to her feet. He has a cross expression as he looks toward the dressing room entrance.*)

ART (*to* PANDORA). Can I help you?

(PANDORA *shakes her head.*)

ART. Is there anything I can do?

PANDORA. No, I don't think anybody can do anything, especially you. (*She places the gun and the marijuana in the box and hurries up the stairs. The knock comes again.*)

MAMMA (*still seated, toward door*). Just a minute!

(ART *watches* PANDORA *enter dressing room.*)

MAMMA. You want to get the door, Art?

ART. I learned once never to open another man's door.

(PANDORA *and* CURT, *in coats, come from the dressing room;* PANDORA *has her costumes in her arms.* MAMMA TOO TIGHT *gets up and walks downstage.*)

CURT. That fuckin' Deeny wants you to rehearse some new music before your act, Pan.

PANDORA. Sonna bitch! Always late payin' somebody and always wantin' you to work your ass off.

CURT. Is your car parked far, Art?

ART. Not too far.

MAMMA (*looking out window*). It's only Rich.

CURT. Good. He can stay here and watch the phone while we're at the club. First, we'll stop and get you some gas, Art, and then you can take us to the Strip Club.

PANDORA. Is your car big enough to get us all to the Strip Club on Western, Art?

ART. It'll even get us as far as Buffalo, Pandora.

(*They exit.* RICH *enters, turns in doorway and is seen talking to someone outside. Then he shuts door, saunters gracefully across the room, and turns the radio off. Lights dim out as he sprawls upon the couch.*)

CURTAIN

ACT II

The curtain opens showing the Strip Club, or rather the suggested representation of a cheap night club in the Wilshire area of Los Angeles, featuring "Bronze" stripteasers. But the effect should be directed toward the illusions of time, place, and matter. Reality is questionable here. The set should be painted in lavish phony hues except for the bare brown floor. Seeing the set the female audience should respond with: "gorgeous, lovely, marvelous, delightful," and similar banalities. The men should wonder if the habitat of whores is not indeed the same as the region of their creatures of private myth, dream, and fantasy.

A rotating color wheel, in front of the major lights, should turn constantly throughout this scene, giving an entire spectrum of altering colored shadows. Additional colored lights and spots should be used to stress mood changes and the violence of the ending scene.

A musician plays randomly at the piano. He is tall, wearing a dark suit with an open-necked dark shirt. The bartender, wiry with his head shaven clean, sweeps the floor and empties ash trays. A few customers sit and watch the musician, and, later, the group, as the show hasn't begun.

The voice which is heard at the close of this act can be that of a customer.

Two other musicians enter and climb upon the stage.

PIANO PLAYER (*joking, to* BASS PLAYER *seated at piano*). Hey, man, they lookin' for bass players all up and down the street but you cats are all bangin' out chords on out-of-tune pianos.

BASS PLAYER. What's happen'n, man? Say . . . listen to this . . . (*He plays a couple of frames.*) What about that, man . . . huh?

PIANO PLAYER. Man, like I said . . . you're a damn good bass man . . .

BASS PLAYER (*getting up*). What you say about somebody lookin' for bass men? . . . Man! Turn me on. I wouldn't be here in this trap if I knew where one of those gigs were.

DRUMMER (*seated, working up a beat*). Yeah, man, they need you like they need me.

PIANO (*wryly*). How's it feel to keep gettin' replaced by a juke box?

(BASS PLAYER *begins working with* DRUMMER. PIANO PLAYER *strikes a few chords, then lights a cigarette.*)

BASS. Hey, where's Stew and Ronny? I want to practice those new charts before Pandora gets in.

PIANO (*blowing smoke out*). They quit.

BASS (*halting*). What?

DRUMMER. Deeny wouldn't pay them this afternoon and pushed the new charts on them. They didn't want to learn new scores, not getting paid the money owed them, so they quit.

BASS. Just like that . . . they quit?

PIANO. This is our last night here, too. Deeny's in trouble with the union. No more gigs here until the hearin'.

BASS. Awww, man . . . there's always some shit with that jive-ass sucker. Is we gettin' our bread from Deeny tonight?

DRUMMER. Who knows? He don't have to pay until the last performance, and the union says stay on the gig until tonight.

BASS. We always gettin' put in some cross . . .

PIANO. Yeah, man. But juke boxes don't go on strike and Deeny knows we know it, so let's take care of business.

BASS. Man, don't tell me that . . . the broads can't dance to no juke box.

PIANO (*seriously*). Why not, man?

BASS. It just ain't done, man. No machine ain't never goin'a take a musician's play from him when it comes to providin' music for shows.

PIANO. Don't believe it, baby . . . in a couple of mo' years they'll find a way. Broads will be shakin' their cans to canned music just as good as to your playin' or mine and the customers will be payin' even higher prices . . . nobody wins, man. Least of all us. C'mon, let's hit it . . .

(*He begins playing "Delilah" as* PANDORA, MAMMA TOO TIGHT, *and* CURT *make their entrances. The girls wave at the musicians and stop at the bar, then move to a table near the bandstand.* PANDORA *places her costumes on an empty chair of a nearby table.* CURT *stands with his back to the bar.*)

PIANO. Okay. That's better . . . c'mon . . . Cook! . . .

BASS (*not enthused, to* MAMMA *who waves again*). Hey, pretty girl . . .

(ART *walks in, saunters to the cigarette machine;* CURT *joins the girls.*)

CURT. Hey, I wonder where everybody's at.

DRUMMER (*stopping, followed by others*). Hey . . . hey . . . what's the use of this fuckin' shit . . . ?

PIANO. What's happen'n now, man?

(DRUMMER *hops from stage.*)

MAMMA. Damn . . . Stew and Ronny must be late, Pan.

PANDORA (*to* BARTENDER). What happened to your boss, Deeny, Chico?

(BARTENDER *ignores her.*)

DRUMMER (*to* PIANO PLAYER). Not a thing, man . . . everything's cool . . . (*Goes to bar, to* BARTENDER) Hey, Chico. Give me a screwdriver and charge it to your boss.

BARTENDER. Deeny ain't in the charity business, baby.

(ART *sits down with his friends. One of the customers leaves.*)

PANDORA (*to* BARTENDER). Yeah, baby, give me the usual and give my friends what they want. Put it on my tab.

DRUMMER (*to* BARTENDER). You let me and Deeny worry about that, cool breeze. Give me a screwdriver like I said.

(BARTENDER *goes behind bar and begins mixing* DRUMMER'S *drink.*)

BARTENDER (*sullenly, to* PANDORA). When you gonna take care of that tab, sweetcake?

PANDORA (*angry*). When your fuckin' boss pays me, mister! Now get us our drinks, please!

CURT (*to* BASS PLAYER *who stands beside instrument*). Where's Deeny?

(PIANO PLAYER *has gotten off of stage and talks to* DRUMMER *at the bar. A customer goes to jukebox and looks over the selections.*)

PIANO. What's happen'n, man? We got to make this gig . . . that's what the union says.

DRUMMER. Fuck the union.

BASS (*to* CURT) It's a mystery to me, Curt.

MAMMA (*to* BASS PLAYER). That number's a gassy one, honey. Pan's gonna work by that, ain't she?

BASS. Looks that way, Mamma, if anybody works at all tonight.

PIANO (*to* DRUMMER). Awww, man . . . you know I know how you feel . . .

DRUMMER. Well, just don't run that crap down to me. I'm just fed up. The union screws you out of your dues and the clubs fuck you every chance they get . . .

PIANO. It ain't exactly that way . . . now if . . .

MAMMA. Don't you like Pan's new number, Art?

(ART *doesn't answer. The customer drops a coin into the jukebox and punches a selection; "Something Cool" sung by June Christie is played.*)

PANDORA (*to* ART *and* MAMMA). Can't come in here one day without some shit goin' down. Where's the brass so I can rehearse?

MAMMA. They better get here soon, honey. It'll be too late after a while.

BASS (*to* PAN). Forget about it, Pan. They ain't no brass tonight.

DRUMMER (*to* PIANO PLAYER). Well I know all that, but it's no use rehearsin' without any brass and if this is our last night anyhow . . .

CURT (*rising and going to the bar*). You said this is the last night, man?

PANDORA (*to* BASS PLAYER). NO BRASS!

MAMMA (*to* ART). You hear what he said?

BASS (*putting down instrument*). Hey, fix me a C.C. and ginger ale, Chico!

(*Customer who played record goes to the bar and sits down.*)

PANDORA (*to* BARTENDER). Hey, what about our drinks, man?

BARTENDER. Okay, Pandora . . . just a minute.

CURT. Hey, fellas . . . what's goin' down?

(*The musicians tell* CURT *about the trouble as the scene plays on in center stage at the table. The conversations should overlap as they have but become increasingly rapid and confusing if necessary. After the musicians are served the* BARTENDER *takes the orders at* PANDORA'S *table as* CURT *continues to talk at the bar.*)

PANDORA. Shit . . . no brass . . . musicians quittin' . . . I ain't got no job no more.

MAMMA. Yeah. It don't look so good but perhaps Deeny can do somethin' when he comes in . . .

PANDORA. Deeny . . . shit . . . Deeny . . . all he can do! . . . (*furious, searching for words*) Why, shit, woman! Deeny can't even do numbers and shit cucumbers!

ART. Thanks for the drink, Pan.

PANDORA. Is that all you can do, man? Say thank you?

ART. No. It's not the only thing.

(MAMMA *gets up and goes over to the* BASS PLAYER *who drops out of the conversation between* CURT, *the other two musicians, and the* BARTENDER. *Another customer leaves, leaving only one sitting upon a stool, attempting to get the* BARTENDER'S *attention.*)

BARTENDER. Well look, man, I only work here. You better settle that with Deeny.

(*Behind the bar the phone rings. The* BARTENDER *answers.*)

CURT. If that's Deeny I want to talk to him.

BARTENDER. Hey, man, I'm talkin' on the phone.

DRUMMER. Let me talk to the mathafukker! (*He tries to reach across the bar.*)

BARTENDER (*backing off*). Hey, cool it! Wait!

PIANO (*grabbing* DRUMMER'S *arm*). Hold it, man!

DRUMMER. Take your fuckin' hands off me, baby!

BARTENDER. Wait, I said.

CURT. Tell Deeny I'm waitin' for him.

(DRUMMER *breaks away from* PIANO PLAYER *and begins around the bar.* BARTENDER *reaches under bar for a weapon.*)

BARTENDER (*shouts*). Wait!

(*The scene freezes in tableau except for the* BARTENDER, PANDORA, *and* CURT. *Lights go down to purples and deep shadow shades as an eerie spot plays upon the table. Occasionally from the shadows voices are heard.)*

BARTENDER *(in shadows)*. Okay, Deeny. I'll be expectin' ya.

PANDORA *(to* ART*)*. So he's comin'.

ART. Yeah, no need to wait for very long now.

PANDORA. What else can you do, Art?

ART. What else can I do except say thank you, you mean?

PANDORA. Yeah. That's what I mean.

ART. I can wait, Pandora.

PANDORA *(jolly)*. What's the good of waitin' when things have ta be done? Is that why you have to eat at Rescue Missions and get favors from friends, baby? Cause you waitin'? Tell me. What are you waitin' on, Art?

ART. Me? I'm just waitin' so I won't jump into somethin' too fast and I think you should do the same.

PANDORA. I didn't know you gave out advice too. But I wish I could take some of it. Ya see, we're already in the middle of some deep shit . . . There just ain't time to sit back and cool it, honey . . .

ART *(disregarding the ridicule in her voice, soothing)*. Yes you can . . . just sit back and look around and wait a while. You don't have to do anything . . . baby, the whole world will come to you if you just sit back and be ready for it.

PANDORA *(serious)*. I wish I could. But so much has to be done and we keep fallin' behind.

BARTENDER *(in shadows)*. Now what can I do, man? Deeny left with Pete and he said he'd be right back and for you guys to practice with the girls.

(One of the customers who walked out enters with a SHOW GIRL. *She is dark and thin and pretty in a tinseled way. They stop in the shadows and whisper and the girl separates from him, enters the light, passes through and heads toward the dressing rooms in the rear. The* CUSTOMER *takes a seat at the bar. He is engulfed by shadows and becomes frozen in place like the others.)*

PANDORA (*nodding to show girl as she passes*). Hi, Cookie. I really dig that dress, baby.

ART. Things can always get worse, Pan.

PANDORA. Oh, you're one of those? How can they? Just lost my job. This was to keep me goin' until you guys turned up somethin' big and I didn't even get paid from the last two weeks so I know this just means another great big zero.

ART. What do you think will happen now?

PANDORA. I don't know . . . the job Curt's got planned can't be pulled off until three more days and in a week we got to have all our money together for the restitution and juice . . . not to mention the goin' away money. And I'm not even goin'a get paid for this gig.

ART. Haven't you got any now?

PANDORA. Just a couple of hundred but we can't go into that. Got to hold onto it. We wouldn't eat if we didn't have to. We got to hold on to every cent.

BARTENDER (*in shadows*). Do you want that scotch with anything?

(DRUMMER *momentarily breaks out of position.*)

DRUMMER. I ain't finished talkin' yet, Chico.

BARTENDER. Just a minute, man.

(MAMMA *breaks out of position and goes to* PANDORA.)

MAMMA. Lend me a dime, Pan. I got to call Shaky.

PANDORA (*fishing in her oversized purse*). You got somethin' workin', baby?

MAMMA. Yeah. Slim's gonna get somethin' from Shaky.

PANDORA. That's workin'.

(*She gives* MAMMA *a coin.* MAMMA *enters the shadows and walks to the rear of the club.* PANDORA *notices* ART *looking at her.*)

PANDORA. Forget about her. Shaky's got her up tight. All you could do is play young lover a little. You can't support her habit, Art.

ART. She can't have a habit if she's just hit the street.

PANDORA. She's got one. What do you think they came in high on? In a couple more days she'll be hooked as bad as before. Shaky'll see to that.

ART. What does she do it for?

PANDORA. What does . . . ? Awww, man . . . what kinda question is that? I thought you knew somethin', baby.

ART. I tried to ask an honest question, Pan.

PANDORA. Is it an honest question when you don't have anything to go by to compare her experience with yours?

ART. I don't know. Is it?

PANDORA. Do you know how it feels havin' somebody paw all over you every day?

ART. Well, no . . .

PANDORA. Then you don't know that she has to use that stuff to put off the reality of it happen'n?

ART. Oh, I see.

PANDORA (*bitter*). Yeah, you see. Do you see her givin' up her body every day and murdering herself every day? Is that what the world has brought to her, Art? That's all she can look forward to each day . . . killin' herself with that needle by inches. She has her fix, and maybe a bust and she has keepin' her man. She just takes her fixes to get through the day and Shaky keeps her on it so she'll need him more.

ART. That's too bad.

PANDORA. Wait a minute, Art. Don't sing no sad songs for that woman, you understand? She's not askin' for your pity. She's a real woman in some ways and she won't let you take it away from her by your pity. She'd spit on your pity.

ART (*annoyed*). And you?

(*Lights change.*)

PANDORA (*fantasy*). And me? . . . Well I ain't no whore . . . I'm just makin' this money so Curt and me can get on our feet. One day we gonna own property and maybe some businesses when we get straight . . . and out of this town.

ART. In Buffalo?

PANDORA. Maybe if we decide to stay there but I'm really an entertainer. I'll show you my act one day and Curt's got a good mind. He's a good hustler but he's givin' that up after a while. He can be anything he wants.

(*Lights change.*)

ART. What does he want?

PANDORA. He wants what I want.

ART. How do you know?

PANDORA. He tells me . . . We talk about it all the time.

ART. Can you be sure?

PANDORA. Sure?

ART. Yeah . . . like Mamma's sure she'll always get her fix and her bail paid.

PANDORA. You little smooth-faced punk . . . wha . . .

ART (*cutting*). Some guys are really lucky.

PANDORA. Kiss my ass, sucker!

ART. Curt and Shaky are really into something.

PANDORA. Yeah! Because they're men!

ART. Is that what bein' a man is, bein' lucky?

PANDORA. No. It's from gettin' what you want.

ART. And how do you get what you want, Pan?

PANDORA. You go after it.

ART. And after you have it.

PANDORA. Then maybe it's yours and you can do whatever you want with it.

ART. And what if I wanted you, Pandora?

PANDORA (*three-beat pause*). You don't have enough to give me, Art. What could you give me that would make things better for me?

ART. I'm not a giver, Pan. I'm a taker.

(*Lights go up evenly. Figures become animated and resume activities. The* BARTENDER *pours drinks and nods to grumbling musicians and to* CURT. *A customer goes to jukebox and drops coin in. "Parisian Thoroughfare" plays. The* SHOW GIRL, *in thin robe, revealing skimpy costume, walks from the rear and takes seat beside customer she entered with.* MAMMA TOO TIGHT *goes to the table and sits.*)

MAMMA (*brightly*). What you guys been talkin' bout so long?

PANDORA. Nothin' much, why?

MAMMA. Oh nothin' . . . just thought I'd ask. But the way you and old fuzz wuzz was goin' at it and lookin' at each other . . .

PANDORA. Looks can't hurt you, Mamma, but your big mouth can.

MAMMA (*fake surprise*). Pan . . . I didn't mean . . .

PANDORA. I'm sure you didn't, Mamma!

MAMMA (*now hurt*). Now listen, Pan. If you can't take a little teasin' . . . What's wrong with you? This is my first day home and you been on my ass all the time. Girl . . . you been the best friend I ever had, but lighten up.

PANDORA. Awww, Mamma . . . let's not you and me start in actin' flaky . . .

ART. Would you like a drink, Mamma?

MAMMA (*pleased*). Yeah . . . but you can't pry Chico from behind that bar.

(ART *stands and places hand upon* MAMMA's *shoulder.*)

ART. That's okay. Just sit. (*He goes to bar and stands beside* CURT *who has his back to him, drinking and brooding.*)

MAMMA (*to Pandora*). Hey, he's so nice.

PANDORA. See . . . I told you I wasn't tryin' to steal your little playmate.

MAMMA (*serious*). If I didn't know you was kiddin' I wouldn't take that, Pan.

PANDORA. You wouldn't? . . . Well, I wasn't kiddin', broad!

MAMMA (*half rising*). Hey, check yourself, girl. This is me! Remember? Mamma Too Tight. Don't you know me? Lil ole Queenie Bell Mack from Biloxi, Mississippi.

PANDORA. Okay. Sit down before you trip over yourself. I know who you are.

MAMMA (*sitting*). And I know you too, baby. Remember I

was the one who was there those times so many yesterdays ago. Remember? I was there with you holding your hand in those dark, little lonely rooms all them nights that your man was out on a job . . . Remember how we shivered together, girl? Remember how we cried together each time he got busted and sent away again . . . I'm your friend, baby . . . and you actin' like this to me?

PANDORA (*genuine*). I'm sorry, Mamma. It's just that Art. He's different. Everything seems different when he's around.

MAMMA. I think I know what you mean, Pan. I think I know . . .

(*Lights dim; color wheel still throws pastel shadows.* CURT *and* ART *stand in spot at end of bar. In the shadows there are rustles from the other people and lighted cigarettes arc through the gloom toward mouths which suck at them like spiders draining fireflies.* CURT *turns.*)

CURT. Hey, Art. Sorry to put you through all this hassle but some bad shit is goin' down, man. I'm really gettin' worried . . . If things keep breakin' bad like this . . .

ART. Don't worry about me, Curt. I'm just along for the ride. Try and get yourself together. It don't matter to me what you have to go through to get yourself straight, man. Just work it on out.

(*Spot off* ART *and* CURT. *Spot on* SHOW GIRL *and* CUSTOMER.)

CUSTOMER. How 'bout it, sugar?

SHOW GIRL. Are you kiddin', man?

CUSTOMER (*whining*) Well christ . . . twenty-five bucks . . . what's it lined with . . . gold or somethin'?

SHOW GIRL. You see those two broads over at that table?

(*Lights on* PANDORA *and* MAMMA.)

CUSTOMER. Yeah. You suggestin' that I hit on them?

SHOW GIRL. Yeah. Do that. The one in the black dress won't even speak to you unless you're ready to leave a hundred or more . . . and besides . . . she has to like your type first. The other one might consider it for fifty.

CUSTOMER. Who's the girl in the black dress?

(*Lights change.*)

SHOW GIRL. That's *Pandora*. She headlines the Revue. You have to give her twenty bucks just to get her phone number. So why don't you go hit on her?

(*Lights off. Spot on* BARTENDER.)

BARTENDER. You call yourselves artists and then you want me to bleed for you? What kinda crap is that?

DRUMMER (*in shadows*). Listen you jive-time whiskey-pourer. We are artists and I don't care what you call us or how you bleed. It's cats like you and your boss who make us all the time have to act like thugs, pimps and leeches to just make it out here in this world.

BARTENDER. So why ya tellin' me? So make it some other way?

PIANO PLAYER (*in shadows*). It's just impossible to talk to you people . . . it's just impossible to be heard any more.

(*Spot off* BARTENDER. *Spot on* CURT *and* ART.)

CURT. Yeah . . . when I first met her, Art. You should of seen her. It was in a joint somethin' like this . . .

(*Light off; spot picks up* PANDORA *standing in the door looking younger, nervous.* CURT *crosses stage to meet her as he speaks.*)

CURT (*entering light*). She was just eighteen . . . had the prettiest little pair of tits poking right out at me . . . sharp enough to put your eyes out. (*He takes* PANDORA *in his arms and kisses her violently. She resists but he is overwhelming.*)

PANDORA (*young voice*). I beg your pardon, mister.

CURT. I said that you're beautiful . . . that I want you . . . that you are mine forever . . . that it will always be this way for you, for you are mine. (*He brutally subdues her. Her hair falls across her face. Her face has that expression that prisoners' sometimes have when they are shifted without prior explanation from an old cell to an unfamiliar cell, equally as old.*)

PANDORA. Are you the man I'm to love?

CURT (*dragging her into the shadows*). Don't talk of something you'll never know anything about . . .

(*They speak from the shadows now, facing the audience.*)

PANDORA. I can't love you? I can't love if I even wanted . . . ?

CURT. You are mine . . . my flesh . . . my body . . . you are in my keeping.

PANDORA. Is it so much to ask for . . . just to be your woman?

CURT. You will do as I say . . . your flesh, your soul, your spirit is at my command . . . I possess you . . .

PANDORA. First there were others . . . now there is you . . . always the same for me . . .

(*Lights change.*)

CURT (*in shadows, walking toward* ART). Yeah . . . she was ready . . . has always been.

(*Spot on* ART. CURT *enters light.*)

ART. Pandora's a beautiful girl, Curt. You're lucky, man, to have her. I envy you.

CURT. Thanks, Art.

ART. Don't mention it, don't mention it at all.

(*Lights go down. Come up with* SHAKY *sitting at the table with* MAMMA *and* PANDORA.)

SHAKY. What's happen'n, baby?

MAMMA. Nothin' yet, Shaky. Give me time. The joint ain't even open yet.

SHAKY. Don't take too long, woman.

MAMMA. Give me time, Shaky. Why you got to come on so strong, man? You know I always take care of business. You know I got to get used to it agin. Didn't I set up that thing between you and Slim?

SHAKY. Yeah, baby. But that's my department. You take care of business on your side of the street. (*The* BASS PLAYER *comes over to the table. To* BASS PLAYER) Let's take a walk, poppa.

BASS. After you, Shake Shake.

MAMMA. I'll be here, Shaky.

SHAKY. Let's hope you're either here or there . . . okay?

MAMMA. Shaky . . . you're goin' too fast. Don't push me so hard.

SHAKY (*leaving*). Tonight, baby. One hundred stone cold dollars, baby.

(*Light on* SHOW GIRL *and* CUSTOMER.)

SHOW GIRL. They're alone. Why not now?

CUSTOMER. Okay . . . okay . . . twenty-five you get . . . after the show tonight.

(*Lights off; spot on* CURT *and* ART.)

CURT. When I saw you in action, Art, I said to myself I could really use that kid. Man, you're like a little brother to me now, man. I watch the way you act around people. You think on your feet and study them like a good gambler does. You're like me in a lot of ways. Man, we're a new breed, ya know. Renegades. Rebels. There's no rules for us . . . we make them as we break them.

ART. Sounds kind'a romantic, Curt.

CURT. And why shouldn't it? Man, this ain't a world we built so why should we try and fit in it? We have to make it over the best we can . . . and we are the ones to do it. We are, man, we are!

(*Spot on* MAMMA.)

MAMMA. I don't know why I'm this way . . . I just am. Is it because my name is different and I am different? Is it because I talk like a spade?

PANDORA (*from shadows*). Take a look at that! Just because this white broad's been hangin' out with us for a couple of years she's goin' ta blame that bad talk on us.

(*Light on table.*)

PANDORA (*to* MAMMA). When you brought your funky ass from Mississippi woman we couldn't even understand you . . . sheeet . . . we taught you how to speak if anything!

MAMMA (*out at audience*). All I know is that I'm here and that's where I'm at . . . and I'll be here until somethin' happens . . . I wish Shaky wouldn't push me so . . . I want to be good for him . . . I want him to be my man and care about me a little . . .

(ART *brings* MAMMA *her drink.* CURT *sits with him at the table.*)

CURT (*to* PANDORA). Don't look so pissed off, honey.

PANDORA. Why shouldn't I? Everything's gone wrong.

(CURT *stands and takes* PANDORA'S *arm.*)

CURT. C'mere, baby. Let me talk to you. (*They walk into the shadows.*)

ART. Just saw Shaky. He didn't stay long.

MAMMA. Nawh. He's gone to take care of some business. Wants me to stay here and take care of mine.

ART. I guess that's what you should do then.

MAMMA. Should I? He's rushin' me too fast, that's what he's doin'. He knows I take a little time gettin' right inside before I can go back to work but he's pushin' me. It's Curt's and Pan's fault . . . they're desperate for money and they're pressin' Shaky.

ART. Maybe you should try and talk to him or to Curt.

MAMMA. It wouldn't do any good!

ART. It wouldn't? If you were my girl I'd listen to what you had to say.

MAMMA. Oh, man, knock off the bullshit!

ART. But I would, really.

MAMMA (*hesitant*). You would? I bet you're full of shit.

ART. Sure I would. I look young but I know what you need . . . and I know what you want.

MAMMA (*giggling*). You do? (*Peering over her glass*) What do I need and want, fuzz wuzz?

ART. Understanding.

MAMMA. What?

ART (*soft*). Understanding.

MAMMA. Sheeet . . .

ART (*softer*). Understanding.

(*Lights down; spot on* CURT *and* PANDORA.)

PANDORA. I'm gettin' fed up with this shit, Curt. We seem to be goin' backwards, not forward.

CURT. I know that, baby. But things will get straightened out. You know it has to. When the job . . .

PANDORA (*cutting*). The job! Yeah . . . it better be somethin', Curt, or you're in some big trouble . . . We're both in some big trouble . . . what'd I do without you?

CURT. If anything happens, baby . . . let Art take care of things . . .

PANDORA. Art?

CURT. Yeah.

PANDORA (*afraid*). But I'm your woman, remember?

CURT. He's like a little brother to me. I've already spoken to him about it . . . you can get a real gig in a show or somethin' and share an apartment with him. He'll look out for you while I'm away. Go up to Frisco and wait for me . . . Art's got a head and he can look after things until I get out . . . then things will be okay again. But that's if the worst happens and we don't get the juice money . . .

PANDORA (*struck*). You think that much of him, Curt?

CURT. I told you he's like my brother, baby. I've been waitin' a long time for a real cat to come along . . . we're on our way now . . .

(*Lights lower; spot on table as* SHAKY *enters.*)

SHAKY (*to* ART). Hey, what you say your name was?

ART (*smiling, holding out his hand*). It's Art, Shaky, you know I met . . .

SHAKY (*cutting*). Yeah, I know . . . what you doin' takin' up my ole lady's time?

(BASS PLAYER *enters.*)

ART. I was only sittin' here and bought her a drink. She rode over in my car with Curt and Pan.

SHAKY. That's what I mean, man . . . takin' up her time.

MAMMA. Shaky . . . stop it! He wasn't doin' nothin' . . . he's a friend of Curt's and . . .

SHAKY. Shut up!

MAMMA. You don't understand . . .

(*He slaps her.* ART *grabs his arm and pushes him sprawling across a chair.* SHAKY *regains his balance and begins to lunge but is caught by* CURT.)

CURT. Hey, cool it, man! What's goin' on?

SHAKY. This little punk friend of yours doesn't like what I do with my woman.

BASS PLAYER. Why don't you forget it, Shaky. If it had been me I would of done the same thing. Forget it. It ain't worth it.

MAMMA (*scared*). He don't understand.

SHAKY. You'll see what I understand when we get home, bitch!

ART (*putting out his hand*). I'm sorry, man. It was my fault. I had . . .

(SHAKY *knocks* ART's *hand aside and turns, being led toward the door by the musician.*)

SHAKY (*to* ART). I'll see you later.

CURT. Hey, Shaky. C'mere, man. It don't mean nothin'.

(*They exit.* PANDORA *takes a seat.* CURT *goes to the bar and answers the questions of the musicians and the* BARTENDER. *The* SHOW GIRL *goes to the rear of the club and the* CUSTOMER *orders another drink.*)

MAMMA. He just don't understand . . . he can't understand and he can't give me any understanding . . .

PANDORA. Who don't understand, Mamma?

MAMMA. Shaky . . . he just don't understand . . . he should try and understand me more.

PANDORA. Girl, you so stoned you're not makin' any sense. He understands, Mamma. He understands you perfectly.

MAMMA. He can't, Pan. He can't or I wouldn't feel this way about him now.

ART. Maybe you're changin'.

PANDORA. Oh, man, you're full of it!

ART. You're cynical but not that hard, Pandora.

PANDORA. Man, I've seen it all. I don't have to be hard . . .
I just use what I know.

ART. Have you seen everything, Pan?

PANDORA. Yes!

ART. Then you've seen me before?

PANDORA (*staring*). Yeah . . . I've seen you before. There's a
you standin' on every corner with his hands in his pockets and
his fly half unzipped . . . there's a you in every drunk tank in
every city . . . there's a you sniffin' around moochin' drinks and
kissin' ass and thinkin' he's a make-out artist. Yeah . . . I've
seen you before, punk!

MAMMA. He just don't understand . . .

ART. No, you've never seen me before, Pandora. I'm goin'a
tell you something.

PANDORA (*sarcastic*). What are you goin'a tell me, Art?

ART. That I'm goin'a change your life.

PANDORA. *What?*

(*Lights go up with a startling flash.* DEENY *and the* BOUNCER,
Pete, enter. DEENY, *in black glasses, sports an ascot and a cum-
merbund under his sport coat. In the thin dress she entered in,
the* SHOW GIRL *walks from the rear and takes a seat beside the*
CUSTOMER. MAMMA TOO TIGHT *stands and* CURT *nearly bowls
over a customer on his way to meet* DEENY *in center stage in
front of* PANDORA'S *table.* PANDORA *jumps to her feet beside*
MAMMA, *followed by* ART.)

CURT. Deeny!

(*The* BASS PLAYER *enters, and the* DRUMMER *and* PIANO PLAY-
ER *hurry over. Behind the bar the* BARTENDER *stands tensed;
the* BASS PLAYER *climbs upon the stage and begins zippering his
bass fiddle into its cloth bag.*)

DEENY. Keep it, Curt! I don't want to hear it. I just come
from the union and I've taken all the crap I'm gonna . . . the
show's closed.

(*Chorus of yells.*)

CURT. Deeny, what you take us for?

PANDORA. Hey, man . . . let's go in the back and talk . . .

DRUMMER (*pushing his way around the* PIANO PLAYER). Yeah, Deeny, I want to talk to you!

DEENY. I just don't want to hear it from any of you. Okay? . . . Okay! Now everybody . . . this club is closin'. Ya hear? Everybody out inside of ten minutes . . . understand? This is my property. Get off it inside of ten minutes or I'm callin' the cops . . . your things and you out . . . hit the street . . . that means everybody!

(*Another chorus of yells from nearly everyone. The customers hurry out the exit and the* SHOW GIRL *joins the group.*)

BASS PLAYER (*to other musicians*). Hey, fellas, I'm splittin' . . . what about you?

(MAMMA *turns and goes over to him.*)

DRUMMER. Man, what about my pay?

DEENY. Take your bitchin' to the union, fellah. They instigated this hassle.

PANDORA. We don't know nothin' bout no union, Deeny . . .

DEENY (*sarcastic*). I know you don't, sugar. But you girls should get organized . . . try to get paid hourly and get off the quota system and you'd . . .

CURT. Watch your mouth, mathafukker!

BOUNCER. You'd better watch yours!

DEENY (*to* BARTENDER). Hey, Chico, call the cops! You just can't reason with some jerks! Call them now!

(*The* BARTENDER *dials.*)

PANDORA (*to* CURT). What we gonna do, baby . . . ?

CURT. Quiet!

PANDORA. But your case, honey . . .

BARTENDER (*on phone*). Yeah . . . there's trouble at the Strip Club on Western . . . yeah . . .

(DEENY *tries to push his way past but* CURT *blocks him. The* BOUNCER *moves to shove* CURT *out of the way but* ART *steps in as the four confront each other, and the girls back off. The* PIANO PLAYER *has coaxed the* DRUMMER *to join the* BASS PLAYER *upon the stage, packing away his equipment. At a run, the* SHOW GIRL *rushes to the rear of the club as the* BARTENDER *hangs up the phone. As the other musicians pack up, the* PIANO PLAY-ER *comes back to the group.*)

PIANO. Deeny, you just can't do this. This ain't right about us. We stuck by you for below scale wages, riskin' our own necks with the union to keep you in business, until you got on your feet. And still we never got paid on time. Now I hear you gonna put some names in here and clean up on the rep we made for you.

BOUNCER. Shut up, mister. You're not supposed to be here right now, remember?

PANDORA (*furious*). You owe me for two and a half weeks, man!

DEENY (*trying to get by again*). Sorry, baby. Come around some time and maybe we can work out somethin'.

CURT. I know why you doin' this, Deeny. Don't pull that union shit on me! You want all the girls to work for you . . . on the block like tramps for ten and fifteen dollars a trick. Pan, Mamma and all the other broads. I'd die before I'd let you put my woman on the street for ten tricks a day. Why you got to be so fuckin' greedy, man? You ain't right! You already got six girls now.

BOUNCER. Just say he has taste and discrimination, Curt. You know he wants your old lady because . . .

DEENY (*cutting*). Shut up all of you! And are you goin' to get out of my way?

MAMMA (*from bandstand*). Deeny. Who you think you are?

DEENY (*to* MAMMA). You know who I am, you stupid country cunt. And if you want to stay on the streets and keep that junkie ole man of yours cool, just keep your mouth out of this! That way you won't get your legs broke and . . .

CURT (*cutting*). I know why you doin' this, Deeny.

(SHAKY *enters. The* SHOW GIRL *rushes from the rear with costumes in arms and exits, speaking to no one.*)

SHAKY. Did I hear somebody say they gonna break Mamma's legs?

(*There is general bedlam with shouts and near screaming.*)

DRUMMER (*exiting*). I'm goin' ta take this farther than to the union, Deeny!

BOUNCER. You can take it to your mother, punk!

(DRUMMER *drops equipment and lunges toward* BOUNCER *but* PIANO PLAYER *grabs him and holds.* BASS PLAYER *helps.*)

BASS PLAYER (*exiting with* DRUMMER). Hey, Deeny, you're wrong! You're dead wrong, man!

PIANO (*to* CURT *and* PANDORA). Cool it. Let's all split. This ain't nothin' but a big bust. (*It becomes suddenly quiet and the* BARTENDER, *a club in hand, comes around the bar and stands behind* CURT *and* ART. SHAKY *stands to the side of* DEENY *and the* BOUNCER. MAMMA *is on the bandstand, wide-eyed, and* PANDORA *is downstage glowering at her enemies. Leaving*) I'll see you guys. (*Seeing* SHAKY) Hey, man. It ain't worth it.

SHAKY. I'll get in touch with you, okay?

PIANO. C'mon, man. I don't like what I see.

SHAKY. Make it! Be a good friend and make it.

(PIANO PLAYER *exits. It is even more quiet. Very low, from somewhere outside, the theme is heard as each group eyes the other and tenses.*)

PANDORA (*spitting it out, violent as unexpected spit spattering a face*). Fuck you, Deeny! Fuck you! Fuck you! *Fuck you!*

DEENY (*frenzied*). You little trampy bitch . . . you . . .

(CURT *smashes him in the mouth as he reaches for* PANDORA. DEENY *falls back beside the table, grabs a glass and hurls it into* CURT'S *face, shattering it.* CURT *launches himself upon him and pummels* DEENY *to the floor. Meanwhile, the* BOUNCER *and* ART *fight in center stage.* SHAKY *is struck almost immediately from behind by the* BARTENDER'S *club.* ART, *seeing the* BARTENDER *advancing on* CURT'S *rear, breaks away and desperately kicks out at the* BARTENDER. *With a screech he doubles over and grabs his groin. The* BOUNCER *seizes* ART *from behind, about the*

206 / ED BULLINS

throat, in an armlock, and begins strangling him. PANDORA, *who has taken off her shoes after kicking* DEENY *several times as* CURT *beats him upon the floor, attacks the* BOUNCER *from behind and repeatedly strikes him about the head with her shoe heels. The* BOUNCER *loosens his grip on* ART *and grabs* PANDORA *and punches her. She falls.* ART, *gasping, reaches down for the* BARTENDER'S *dropped club, picks it up and turns and beats the* BOUNCER *to the floor. All the while* MAMMA TOO TIGHT *screams. With face bloodied from splintered glass,* CURT *has beaten* DEENY *into unconsciousness and staggers over and pulls* PANDORA *up. Sirens, screeches, and slamming car doors are heard from outside. Shouts.*)

CURT (*towing Pandora*). C'mon, Art! Pull yourself together. The cops are here.

(ART *staggers over to* SHAKY *and tries to lift him but he is too weak.* MAMMA, *crying and screaming, jumps from the bandstand and pulls at* SHAKY.)

CURT (*heading for the rear*). He's too heavy, Art. Leave him. Grab Mamma and let's get out the back way. Move! C'mon, man, move!

(*Dazed, but following orders,* ART *grabs* MAMMA'S *arms and struggles with her.*)

MAMMA (*resisting*). No! No! I can't leave him like that!

CURT (*exiting*). Bring her, Art. Out the back way to the car.

MAMMA (*being dragged out by* ART). My first day out . . . my first day . . .

(*They exit and immediately the stage blackens, then the rumble of running feet.*)

VOICE. CHRIST! (*More heavy running, then stop.*) Hey, call a couple of ambulances . . . Emergency!

CURTAIN

ACT III

Scene I

Time: Three days later. Afternoon.
Scene: CURT'S *apartment. He and* RICH *play chess as in Act I.*
The bed is lowered and MAMMA TOO TIGHT *sleeps with the*
covers pulled up to her chin as if she is cold. The radio is off
and the California sunshine glistens in the clean room. The
room looks sterile, unlived-in and motel-like without the light-
ing of the first act.

CURT *wears two band-aids upon his face, one upon his fore-*
head, the other on the bridge of his nose.

CURT (*bored*). It'll be mate in two moves, Rich. Do you want
to play it out?

RICH. Nawh, man. I ain't up to it.

CURT (*sitting back*). The last three day have just taken everything out of me, man.

RICH. Yeah. They been pretty rough. (CURT *stands, stretches,*
and walks across the stage.) Hey, man. Is there any more beer?

CURT. Nawh. Pan and Art's bringing some in with them
when they come.

RICH (*muttering*). Yeah . . . when they get here.

CURT (*noticing* RICH'S *tone*). What did you say, man?

RICH. Oh. Nothin', man.

CURT (*sharply*). You're a liar . . . I heard what you said!

RICH (*sullen*). I ain't goin'a be many more of them liars, Curt.

CURT (*gesturing*). Awww, man. Forget it . . . you know how I
feel with Deeny in a coma from his concussion for the past
three days and me not knowin' if he's goin' ta press charges
finally or die.

RICH. Yeah, man. I'm a bit edgy myself. Forget about what
I said.

(CURT *returns to the couch and sprawls back.*)

CURT. But I'd like to know what you meant by it, Rich.

RICH (*seeing no way out*). Now, Curt. You and I been friends since we were young punks stealin' hub caps and tires together, right? Remember that time you, me and the guys gang-banged that Pachuco broad? . . . And the Dog Town boys came up and we had that big rumble and they killed Sparky?

CURT (*sensing something coming*). How can I forget it . . . I served my first stretch behind it for stabbin' that Mexican kid, Manuel.

RICH. Yeah. That was a good time ago and Manuel ain't no kid no more . . .

CURT. Yeah. But, tell me. What do you have to say, good buddy?

RICH (*pausing, then serious*). It's about this guy Art and Pandora, man.

CURT. What do you mean, man?

RICH. Man . . . I don't mean there's anything goin' on yet . . . but each afternoon he's taken Pandora out for the past three days they been gettin' back later . . . and . . .

CURT. And what, Rich?

RICH. And the way she looks at him, Curt.

CURT (*disgusted and angry*). Awww, man . . . I thought I knew you better.

RICH. Well I told you that I didn't think that they were doin' anything really.

CURT. But, what? That he drives her up to Sunset Strip to keep her dates with the big tricks . . . you know how much dough she brings back, man?

RICH (*resolutely*). Yeah, man. Sometimes over a hundred dollars for one trick.

CURT. So you can't hurry those people for that kinda bread, man.

RICH (*trying to be understood*). But I wasn't talkin' about the tricks, Curt. I don't think they're holdin' back any money on you.

CURT. Then what are you talkin' 'bout?

RICH. About that little jive-ass square gettin' next to your woman, that's what!

CURT. Now listen, Rich. We're friends and all that but that little jive-ass square as you call him is just like a brother to me . . . and we been in some tighter things than you and me will ever be in.

RICH (*obviously hurt*). Well, forget it!

CURT. No, let's not forget it. You're accusing my wife of jivin' around on me. You know that Pan's the straightest broad you'll ever find. That's why I married her. You know if we couldn't have gotten another man that she would have gone on the job and been as good as most men. She and I are a team. What could she gain by messin' 'round on me with my ace buddy?

RICH. Forget it, I said.

CURT. Nawh, Rich. I don't want to. I know what's really buggin' you. Ever since Shaky got busted at the Club and they found all that smack on him you been buggin' Mamma to be your woman 'cause you know that with Shaky's record he won't be hittin' the streets again for at least ten years. But you're wrong on two counts cause we're bailin' out Shaky tonight and takin' him with us and Mamma don't want you cause she wants Art but he don't go for her.

RICH (*getting to his feet*). I'll see you, man. Between your broad and that cat you can't think any more! (CURT *reaches for* RICH's *shirt front;* RICH *throws his hands off.*) Take it easy, Curt. You already won a close one this week. And your guardian angel ain't round to sneak-punch people.

(CURT *stares at him and steps back.*)

MAMMA (*from bed*). Hey, what's all that shoutin' about?

CURT. Nothin', baby. Rich and I are just crackin' jokes.

MAMMA (*sitting up*). Curt, I wonder if . . .

CURT. No, Mamma. You can't have no fix. Remember what I told you? You don't turn no tricks in town cause you're hot behind Shaky's bust so you don't need any heroin, right? You're on holiday and besides, you're full of codeine now . . . that's enough . . .

MAMMA. But I would be good if I could get some. I wouldn't worry about Shaky so much and I'd feel . . .

CURT. You just come out of the joint clean, Mamma. You don't need anything but to keep cool.

MAMMA (*pouting*). But I got the sixteen hundred dollars that Shaky had stashed at our pad. I could buy it okay, Curt.

CURT. Forget it. That money is with the other bread. We all takin' a trip with that. Besides . . . Shaky had over two thousand bucks worth of stuff in the pad and we sellin' it tonight so we can bail him out so he can leave with us . . .

(MAMMA *jumps out of bed in a thin gown.*)

MAMMA (*delighted*). You are? Then he'll be home soon?

CURT. Yeah. Then we all make it before Deeny comes out of his coma or croaks. Now get back in bed before Rich grabs you!

MAMMA (*playful*). Rich, you better not. Shaky will be home soon.

RICH (*teasing*). Sheeet, woman. I don't care about old ass Shaky. C'mon, baby, why don't you get yourself a young stud?

MAMMA (*getting in bed*). When I get one it won't be you.

RICH (*serious*). Then who?

CURT (*mutters*). I told Art and Pan that we need the car this evening to drop off the stuff. After that it'll be time to get ready for the job.

RICH (*bitterly, to* MAMMA). So he's got to you, too.

MAMMA. Nobody's got to me. What'chou talkin' 'bout, Rich? Art's been stayin' over to Shaky and my place for the last couple of nights while I stayed here. How can he get . . .

RICH (*cutting*). How did you know I was talkin' about Art?

MAMMA. Cause you got Art on the brain, that's why!

CURT. I thought we dropped that, Rich.

RICH (*to* MAMMA). If you're goin'a get somebody young . . . get a man . . . not some little book-readin' faggot . . .

MAMMA (*red-faced, to* RICH). Oh, go fuck yourself, man! (*She covers her head.*)

RICH. Okay, man. We got a lot to do tonight, so I'll lay off.

(*Through the back curtain the outside kitchen door can be seen opening. Dusk is come and* ART *enters first with a large bag;* PANDORA *follows, closes the door, and purposely bumps against him as she passes. She wears dark glasses, her pants, and boots.*

ART. Hey, you almost made me drop this! Where should I put it?

(PANDORA *enters front room smiling.*)

PANDORA. Hi, honey. Hello, Rich. (*She walks over to* CURT, *kisses him, and places money in his hand.*)

CURT. Hey, pretty baby. (*He pulls her to him, gives her an extended kiss, and breaks it, looking over* PANDORA'S *shoulders at* RICH *who looks away.*)

CURT. Everything okay?

PANDORA. Smooth as Silky Sullivan.

(*In the kitchen* ART *is taking items from the bag.* CURT *hands back the money to* PANDORA.)

CURT. Here, Pan, put this in the box with the rest.

PANDORA. Okay. (*She walks past bed and looks down.*) What's wrong with Mamma?

CURT. Rich's been tryin' to love her up.

RICH. She won't go for my program, baby.

PANDORA (*entering the kitchen*). That's too bad . . . you better cultivate some charm, Rich.

RICH. Yeah, that's what's happen'n. I'm not one of the lucky ones . . . some people don't need it.

PANDORA (*going to* ART). Let me take in the beer, Art. You put the frozen food in the refrigerator and the canned things in the cupboard.

(ART *pulls her to him and kisses her.*)

PANDORA (*taking breath*). Hand me the glasses, will ya?

(*They kiss again, she responding this time, then she pushes him away and begins fixing beer for* CURT *and* RICH.)

CURT. Hey, Mamma. You want any beer?

MAMMA (*under the cover*). No, no.

(PANDORA *serves* CURT *and* RICH, *then climbs the stairs and enters the dressing room.* ART *comes out of the kitchen.*)

RICH. How you feel, Art?

ART. Okay. Hollywood's an interesting place. First job I ever had just drivin' somebody around.

CURT. Hope it's your last, Art. With this job tonight and my cut from sellin' Shaky's heroin we'll be just about in. Might even go into business back East.

ART. Yeah? I hope so.

CURT. We already got almost twenty-four hundred with Shaky's money we found at his place and the bread we've been able to hustle the last few days. After tonight we'll be set.

RICH. Yeah. After tonight you'll be set.

CURT (*looking at* RICH). It's too bad you won't come with us, Rich. But your share will fix you up out here okay.

RICH. Fix me up? Ha ha . . . I'll probably shoot that up in smack inside of several months . . . but if I make it I'll probably be lookin' you up in two more years when my probation's up. No use ruin'n a good thing. When I cut this town loose I want to be clean. I just hope all goes well with you.

ART (*smiling*). Why shouldn't it?

CURT. Yeah, Rich, why shouldn't it?

RICH. Funny things happen to funny-style people, ya know.

CURT. Yeah. Too bad you won't be comin' along . . . we need a clown in our show.

(RICH *watches* ART *studying the chess game.*)

RICH. Do you see anything I missed, good buddy?

ART. Oh. I don't know.

RICH. You know I seldom beat Curt. Why don't you play him?

ART (*still looking at board*). Maybe I will when we find time.

CURT. What would you have done from there, Art?

ART. It's according to what side I'm on.

CURT. You have the black. White's going to mate you in two moves.

ART. He is?

RICH. Yeah. He is.

(ART *reaches over and picks up the black king.*)

ART. Most kings need a queen to be most powerful but others do the best they can. (*He places the king upon another square.*) That's what I'd do, Rich.

CURT (*perceiving*). Yeah. I see . . . I see . . .

RICH. Say, why'd you move there? . . . He can't move now . . . he can't put himself in check . . .

ART (*as* RICH *stares at him*). Yeah, Rich?

CURT (*matter-of-factly*). A stalemate.

RICH (*muttering*). I should of seen that. (*To* ART) How did you . . . why . . .

ART. When you play the game you look for any break you can make.

CURT. We should play sometime, Art.

ART. I'm looking forward to it, Curt. But you name the time.

CURT (*standing*). I'll do that. Hey, Pandora! We got to go! (PANDORA *comes to the top of the stairs. She has changed into a simple dress.*)

PANDORA. We goin' some place?

CURT. I got to drop Shaky's stuff off and go down to the bail bondsman and the lawyer. I want you to drive. C'mon, Rich. Pan will sit in the car down the street in the next block and you and me will walk up the street talkin' about baseball, understand? On the corner of Adams and Crenshaw we'll meet a man and hit a grand slam.

RICH. Yeah, I hope so, brother.

CURT. It's trip time from here on in, baby.

PANDORA (*excited*). Wait until I get my coat.

CURT (*in good humor*). Let's go, woman. It's eighty degrees outside and we might be the hottest thing in L.A. but it just

ain't that warm. Let's go, now. See you, Art. (*Going to* ART)
Oh, I almost forgot the car keys.

ART (*handing him the keys*). See you guys.

CURT (*hands keys to* PANDORA). You'll watch the phone, okay?

ART. Sure, good buddy, I'll see to the phone.

CURT. If Mamma wakes up and wants a fix don't give in to
her.

ART. I'll try not to.

CURT (*serious*). I mean it, Art.

ART (*smiling*). I'm dead serious, man.

PANDORA. See you later, Art.

ART. See you later, Pan. Good-bye, Curt. Good-bye, Rich.

(*The trio exit and* ART *goes to the radio and switches it on.
It plays the theme as he enters the kitchen and gets himself a
beer. He comes from the kitchen drinking from the bottle and
climbs the bathroom stairs. His shadow is seen lifting and then
dialing. His voice is muffled by the music and by his whisper;
nothing is understood. After the shadow hangs up,* ART *returns
to the living room and descends the stairs. He sits upon the bed
and shakes* MAMMA TOO TIGHT.)

MAMMA (*being shaken*). Huh? I don't want any beer. (ART
shakes her once more. She uncovers her head.) Oh, Art. It's you.
Where's everybody? (*He doesn't answer, looks at her. Evening
comes and the room blackens.*) I'm glad you woke me. I always
like to talk to you but I guess I bug you since you don't say
too much to me. Why ain't you sayin' nothin' now? (*Three-
beat pause.*)

ART (*laughing*). Ha ha ha . . . ha ha . . . Ma-ma Too Tight!
. . . ha ha ha . . .

MAMMA. You said it! Sometimes you have such a nice look
on your face and now . . . you look different . . . (*Pause*) like
you so happy you could scream . . . You never looked at me
like this before, Art, never. (*In total blackness as the music
plays*) You said Shaky wouldn't be back? . . . You won't? . . .
I don't care as long as you don't go away . . . You know . . . you

understand me. It's like you can look inside my head . . . Oh how did you know? Just a little bit? More? You say I can have a fix any time I want? . . . Oh! . . . You understand me, don't cha? Don't let Curt know . . . you say don't worry about Curt . . . don't care what anybody thinks or says except you? (*Silence, pause*) Oh I feel so good now . . . I didn't know but I was hoping . . . I didn't know, honey . . . Oh, Art! . . . Ahhhh . . . now I can feel you oozing out of me . . . and I'm glad so glad . . . it's good . . .

ACT III

Scene II

PANDORA *leans against the kitchen door as the lights go up. The atmosphere of the first act is recreated by the lights and music. The bed has been put up and* ART *sits upon the couch.* PANDORA *has been crying and what can be seen of her face around her dark glasses appears shocked.*

She walks to the center of the room and faces ART.

PANDORA. Art . . . Art . . . they got them. They got Curt and Rich . . . with all that stuff on them. The cops were waitin' on them. They busted them with all those narcotics . . . we'll never see them again.

ART (*rising*). We're hot, Pandora. We got to get out of town.

PANDORA. They got 'em, don't you hear me, Art? What can we do?

ART. Nothin' . . . we got to make it before Curt or Rich break and the cops are kickin' that door in.

PANDORA. You said nothin'? But we . . . what do you mean? We got to do somethin'! (*Crying*) We can't just let it happen to them . . . we got to do somethin' like Curt would do if it was one of us . . . Art! Art! Don't just stand there! Do . . . (*He slaps her viciously, knocking off her glasses, exposing her blackened eyes.*)

ART (*commanding*). Get a hold on yourself, Pandora. You've had a bad experience. (*She holds her face and looks dazed.*) Now listen to me. Mamma has gone over to her place to pack and as soon as she gets back we're all leaving.

PANDORA (*dazed*). Mamma is packin'? . . . Did Curt tell her to pack?

ART. You know he didn't. Now as soon as she gets here I want us to be packed, okay?

PANDORA. But . . . Art . . . packed . . . where we goin'?

ART. To Buffalo, baby. Where else?

PANDORA. To Buffalo?

ART. That's what I said. Now go up in your dressing room and get your suit case . . . (*A knock comes from the front door.*) That's Mamma already . . . we're runnin' late, woman. C'mon, get a move on. (*He shoves her.*) Move! Get a move on, Pandora! (*She stumbles over the first step, catches her balance and begins climbing.* ART *looks after her.*) Oh . . . Pandora . . . (*She turns and looks vacantly at him.*) Don't forget your box!

(*As she turns and climbs the last steps* ART *saunters to the radio as the knock sounds again. Instantaneously, as he switches the radio off, the stage is thrown in complete blackness.*

THE END

Family Meeting

A Play in One Act

WILLIAM WELLINGTON MACKEY

Cast of Characters

FATHER LOVE: *A very proud and successful Negro capitalist. He was born and shall die in the great land, America.*

MOTHER LOVE: *His precious wife.*

BROTHER LOVE: *His precious son.*

PRECIOUS LOVE: *His precious daughter.*

LILLIE OF THE FLOWERS: *His precious maid.*

FOUR TO EIGHT MIDDLE-AGED LADIES: *The precious sorority sisters of Mother Love. Old bags, really, who are unworthy of further description.*

A COLORED BOY OF THIRTEEN

TWO TO FOUR WOMEN DRESSED IN WHITE

A YOUNG MAN DRESSED IN WHITE

THE TIME: Yesterday and today

THE PLACE: Heavenly Heights, U.S.A.

AUTHOR'S NOTES

Staging

There need only be a suggestion of elegant furnishings. I envision painted abstract caricatures depicting various pieces of furnishings either suspended or hanging from the flies. A spiral stairway which appears to be extended up into the flies is the focal point of the set.

A bier is located at upstage center. Its coloring is blood red. The body of a very black Negro woman who is hideously obese lies on the bier. Her hair is extremely bushy and wild-looking. It is pure white. The woman, who is very dead, appears to have lived for a million years.

The Characters

We are dealing, I believe, with exaggerated caricatures. The characters are frightfully Southern in manner. It is suggested that the two PRECIOUS LOVES *be dressed in very gay, sprightly looking outfits. A little-girl simpleness must be achieved if these roles are to come across correctly.*

FATHER LOVE'S *and the two* BROTHER LOVES' *appearances should further add to the absurdity of the "funny house" situation which evolves as the play develops.* FATHER LOVE *is probably fiftyish and is probably overbearing and endowed with a somewhat snobbish effrontery. The* TWO BROTHER LOVES *are in their middle or late twenties and are simply the sons (or son, as the case may be) of their father.*

MOTHER LOVE'S *first entrance down the spiral stairway should indeed be an almost blinding experience for the audience. She is probably attired in an unusually loud-colored, extraordinarily flamboyant-looking outfit. Her every move, her every mannerism to the nth degree is that of a grand duchess.*

Note: In Act I, the roles of PRECIOUS LOVE *and* BROTHER LOVE *should be played by Negroes.* LILLIE OF THE FLOWERS *during this act is played by a white actress. In Act II the roles reverse.*

PRECIOUS LOVE *of Act I (the Negro actress) assumes the role of* LILLIE OF THE FLOWERS. LILLIE OF THE FLOWERS *of Act I (the white actress) assumes the role of* PRECIOUS LOVE. BROTHER LOVE *in Act II (first sequence only) is played by a white actor.* MOTHER LOVE *is played by a Negro actress and* FATHER LOVE *by a white actor.* MISS P. P. *is played by a very fat, very black Negro woman. The other sorority sisters are played by white actresses. In the final scene, the Negro and white* BROTHER LOVES *play the scene as one.*

Re: Final Scene. The Apotheosis

A true montage effect suggested. Quick and precise collection of scenes; sequential enticement of movement and speech —almost precision choreography. Possibly the use of visual projections during the monologue of the BROTHERS, *projecting the best pictorial images that may be pulled from the text for good effect, i.e., the funeral processions down Washington's Pennsylvania Avenue of both F.D.R. and J.F.K., the bombing of Hiroshima, the 1963 march on Washington, and such lines as sit-ins, stand-ins, etc.*

Indeed, for the final scene, a staccato effect; full percussive catharsis—total collage staged to the nth degree of perfection.

ACT ONE

Part One

Darkness for a second or so. Enter music—the melody to a minuet. Lights enter PRECIOUS LOVE *dancing about in a minuet routine. Lillie adjusting something on the bier.*

LILLIE. Good morning, Miss Precious.

PRECIOUS LOVE. Good morning, Lillie, dear Lillie of the Flowers. Isn't it a loverly day?

LILLIE (*a slight pause, and somewhat hesitantly*). You dance divinely, Miss Precious.

PRECIOUS LOVE. Yes I do, don't I, I'm sure.

LILLIE (*curtseying*). Oh my, indeed you do, Miss Precious. Indeed you do, like an angel, like one of God's own angels, you do.

PRECIOUS LOVE (*curtseying*). Why thank you, Lillie. I do thank you ever so kindly for your sweet compliment.

LILLIE. Miss Precious Love! Now don't you go curtseying me none. Shucks, I's only Lillie the maid. Your mother'd have a plum fit if she saw you bowing down to me. Now you stop that foolishness and go on with your dancing lessons.

PRECIOUS LOVE. Lillie you are a dear; a dear darling angel.

LILLIE. No I ain't either. I's only Lillie. Better not let your mama hear you talking that kin'a talk.

PRECIOUS LOVE. But Lillie . . .

LILLIE. Now you just hush now. Don't you vex me none. I's only Lillie, the maid. And you for shorenuf is Miss Precious Love. I knows my place and you should know yours too; least by now you should.

PRECIOUS LOVE. I suppose you're right, of course. Though sometimes it rightly seems just as silly as all hell, it does. I mean it really does. Seems just as silly as all pure hell, it does sometimes. It really does.

LILLIE. Miss Precious Love!

PRECIOUS LOVE. Oh my goodness gracious. I said a bad word, didn't I? Tee hee hee . . .

LILLIE. Glory sands alive! If your mama's anywhere near listening breath . . .

PRECIOUS LOVE. Precious sakes! You don't have to tell me about it if you don't want to. (*Teasingly*) Besides . . . I'm gonna let you in on a lil ole secret, Lillie, dear Lillie of the Flowers. Want me to tell you what I know, what I done just gone and done all by my lil ole precious self?

LILLIE. *Glory Jesus above!*

PRECIOUS LOVE. I did! I did! Yes I did too. I've seen it all with my own lil ole precious eyes, I did. And I heard it all with my own two lil ole precious ears, I did! Yes I did! And Lillie, I swear to Sweet God Above, I shorenuf ain't never seen or heard nothing like it in all of my lil ole precious seventeen years, I haven't. Ohhhh, Lillie, it was just the most exciting experience I have ever encountered in all of my precious seventeen years, it was. It really was! Why them ole nasty dirty niggers over there in Goodbread Alley are just exactly like Mother Love and Father Love say they are, they really are! And Lillie, they actually really do smell too! Ohhhhh it was just so exciting, Lillie. It really was! Lillie, you just have to; if you really love me at all, you just have to let me come and visit you some precious Sunday. You just have to! Why I ain't never seen nothing so mysterious and exciting as them old dirty ordinary niggers in all of my precious seventeen years, I haven't. Promise . . . you promise, Lillie?

LILLIE. Now I don't know bout that, Miss Precious. Seems like that's asking for shorenuf trouble. (*Slight pause*) No, Miss Precious. No Mam! Your daddy ain't gonna kill me. And your mama ain't gonna be spreading the word round to all these other precious people up here in Heavenly Heights and cause me not to git my steady employment. No Mam! That'd be trouble for shore, Miss Precious. If I had anything to do with tainting those precious ears and those lil old precious eyes of your precious self, ain't no telling what would happen to me.

PRECIOUS LOVE (*babyishly*). But Lillie, it ain't fair. It ain't fair at all. I want to see Goodbread Alley.

LILLIE (*snappingly*). Thought you said you'd seen it. Thought you said you been there. I done caught you in one, ain't I? Done caught you in one.

PRECIOUS LOVE. But I . . . I . . .

LILLIE (*angered*). Where you learn them bad words from? You ain't been to no Goodbread Alley. Where you learn them alley words from?

PRECIOUS LOVE. I . . . I . . . No, I was just fibbing. I haven't been to no Goodbread Alley. Shucks! I thought I could fool you, Lillie. I was just fibbing. (*Like a little baby*) I'm sorry, Lillie, I'm sorry. (*She sniffles.*)

LILLIE (*moving and comforting the girl*). Now don't cry none, Miss Precious. Hurts my heart to see those precious tears falling like that.

PRECIOUS LOVE. But I do awful-like want to see for myself, Lillie. I honest-to-goodness do. Cross my heart, I do. Just don't seem fair not to ever be able to see what those poor colored people are like. Miss Blessingful at school says that just as sure as all us precious children sitting there in her classroom, one of these days, we're all going to have to be sitting in the same room with those people; and maybe even eating in the same room with them, Lillie; even living with them. Can you imagine that? Ain't that something, Lillie?

LILLIE. Honey child, that's one thing you and your precious self needn't ever fear. God give a special blessing a long, long time ago to you folks up here in Heavenly Heights. Not that I rightly know what it was, or anybody does for a fact. Yes mam! Long, long ago, he planted that seed, and he says: "Now these people is gotta be different from these people." And he says, "And there's a reason. There's a reason. People just gotta be different."

PRECIOUS LOVE. But . . . But I didn't ask to be born, Lillie. It ain't my fault I was blessed to be born in Heavenly Heights.

LILLIE. Well, the sun don't ask to shine and the rain don't ask to fall, either.

PRECIOUS LOVE. Lillie . . .

LILLIE. Yes, Miss Precious Love.

PRECIOUS LOVE. You don't suppose . . . Well, you don't suppose that . . .

LILLIE. What is it, Miss Precious Love?

PRECIOUS LOVE. Well that ole nasty Billie Joe Hankerson over in Goodbread Alley told me that . . .

LILLIE (*shocked*). Miss Precious Love! What are you doing talking to that lil ole nasty Billie Joe Hankerson?

PRECIOUS LOVE. Oh, I ain't done no talking to him, Lillie. It's him. He's always a'talking to me. He's always picking on me all the time.

LILLIE. Well you just stay away from him. He ain't nothin' but old common nigger trash. Even worse than me, thinking of what part of the Alley he's from.

PRECIOUS LOVE. I still wants to tell you what he says, Lillie. Listen. He says that . . .

LILLIE (*placing her hands to her ears*). Can't be worth listening to.

PRECIOUS LOVE. Lillie, please. It's important. I got to know something. 'Cause I'm rightly confused and upset about what Billy Joe Hankerson said to me, with his disgusting self.

LILLIE. Well what did that old nasty Billie Joe Hankerson, with his disgusting self, say to you honey?

PRECIOUS LOVE. Well . . . He said that God . . . Lillie, he said that God—

LILLIE. Lord! What in glory's name that old nasty nigger done said to my baby?

PRECIOUS LOVE. He said that God ain't rightly as white as precious ivory. He said that God ain't necessarily as preciously fair and golden ivory as the color of my precious self. Lillie, he said . . . (*Frightfully*) He said that precious God above is just as black as he is, Lillie. Ain't true is it, Lillie? Ain't true, is it? God ain't black, Lillie, is he? God ain't black! Not precious God the Father. (*Shouting*) God ain't black! He ain't black! He ain't black! Is he Lillie?

LILLIE (*tenderly*). Honey, come here to Lillie.

PRECIOUS LOVE. But he ain't black, is he Lillie? God can't be black, Lillie. He can't be black. That'd make everything about almost everything wrong. He ain't black, is he Lillie?

LILLIE. Honey, you shorenuf putting your Lillie on the spot. I don't know what God is like. Nobody know that. Ain't nobody yet seen the face of God. Ain't nobody yet touched him or really rocked in his bosom the way the Bible says it is.

PRECIOUS LOVE. But is he black, Lillie? Is he black like that dirty ole Billie Joe Hankerson? Or is he . . . (*Hesitantly*) Is he ever precious white and ivory . . . like the color of my precious self?

LILLIE. Miss Precious—God is just God. He's what you believe He is.

PRECIOUS LOVE. But, Lillie . . .

LILLIE. No. No Miss Precious. I guess you is right. No, He . . . God ain't nasty. And he ain't dirty, either.

PRECIOUS LOVE. Like that old Billie Joe Hankerson?

LILLIE. Like that old Billie Joe Hankerson.

PRECIOUS LOVE (*embracing* LILLIE). Oh, Lillie! You are so good. I love you. I love you. I love you.

LILLIE. And your Lillie loves you, little darling.

PRECIOUS LOVE (*again babyishly*). Lillie . . . Do me a sweet lil ole favor, please.

LILLIE. Anything your precious lil heart desires, Miss Precious.

PRECIOUS LOVE. I have got the silliest ole desire for some of that precious gumbo you've been cooking in there. Would you be a dear and fix me up a lil ole serving of it? I am positively frightfully starved.

LILLIE. Well Lillie had better do something bout that, hadn't she? (*Leaving*) Ain't gonna just stand round here and see her precious angel starve now, is she? (*She exits.*)

PRECIOUS LOVE (*as* LILLIE *is leaving*). Oh Lillie . . . Dear Lillie of the Flowers! You are so sweet to lil ole undeserving me. (*The music from the minuet enters again.* PRECIOUS LOVE *begins the dance routine again. Again, perhaps a minute or so of the dancing.* PRECIOUS LOVE *then glides very gracefully towards the bier and stops there. The music continues.*) Did you hear, Grandmother? Did you hear? God ain't black! God ain't black! Ain't it just wonderful, grandmother? Ain't it just wonderful? (*A loud crash is heard offstage.* PRECIOUS LOVE *stares frightfully and speaks toward the direction of the sound. Down music.*

Calling frightfully) Father . . . Father . . . Father Love . . . Is anything wrong?

FATHER LOVE (*offstage, hauntingly*). No. No dear. Nothing is wrong. Everything is in order. I . . . I was asleep. Asleep. No. Nothing is wrong with the world today. I was asleep. Must have been dreaming. Yes—dreaming. An accident. I was asleep.

PRECIOUS LOVE. Father . . . Father Love . . . Are you sure? Is everything all right? (*A second of quiet.*) Poor Father. Poor Father Love. (*She begins dance routine again. Up music, full and voluminous. A full minute of the dancing. The telephone rings.* PRECIOUS LOVE *dances toward the telephone and answers. Down music. Like all precious Southern Belles*) Heavenly Heights Manor—One, One, One. Precious Love speaking.

FATHER LOVE (*offstage*). If that is for me, I'm not in today.

(*The music stops.*)

PRECIOUS LOVE. Oh hello, Dr. Successman. However are you doing? Well isn't that just loverly. I do declare. And how is Mrs. Successman, these loverly days? Oh really, she is? Well I do declare. Isn't that just loverly. I shall certainly tell Mother Love. She will be positively delighted to attend, I'm sure. No. No sir. I am so sorry, but Father Love isn't in as of yet. I can't imagine what has detained him. He should be in shortly, I'm sure. The family is scheduled to attend the baccalaureate this afternoon. We never miss going, you know. Yes, I understand he is supposed to be the speaker. He is so divine, isn't he? Such an eloquent speaker. I do look forward to hearing him again. I beg your pardon. Why Dr. Successman! You ought to be ashamed of yourself. Tee hee . . . Well maybe he is and maybe he isn't. Mother Love doesn't allow us to cater to rumors, you know. (*She laughs again.*) Perhaps so. Perhaps so. I agree, I'm sure. Well, we all do have our moments, don't we, we do. All right then. I shall be more than delighted to do just that, I shall. As soon as he arrives, I'll give him your message, I'm sure. Bye now. (*To Father Love*) That was Dr. Successman.

FATHER LOVE (*offstage, hauntingly*). What did he have to say?

PRECIOUS LOVE. Nothing.

FATHER LOVE (*offstage*). What did he want?

PRECIOUS LOVE. Nothing, I'm sure. Perhaps you will call him when you arrive.

FATHER LOVE (*offstage*). I shall call him when I arrive. (*A pause*) Precious . . . Precious Love . . .

PRECIOUS LOVE. Yes, Father Love.

FATHER LOVE (*offstage*). Perhaps you had better remind me when I arrive. I may forget.

(BROTHER LOVE *appears at the top of the stairway. He moves halfway down the stairs and stops. He remains unseen by* PRECIOUS LOVE.)

PRECIOUS LOVE. I shall certainly will do just that, Father Love, I shall.

FATHER LOVE. Promise?

PRECIOUS LOVE. I promise, I do.

FATHER LOVE. Cross your heart and hope to die?

PRECIOUS LOVE (*doing it*). Cross my heart and hope to die.

FATHER LOVE. Like dear Grandmother Love?

PRECIOUS LOVE (*crossing her heart again*). Cross my heart and hope to die.

FATHER LOVE. You're a good daughter. A fine, fine . . . A good daughter. A good . . .

(BROTHER LOVE *springs across the railing of the stairway into the main level of the stage mimicking very loudly the sound of a whinnying jackass. Music continues, but down.*)

BROTHER LOVE. Hee haw, hee haw . . .

PRECIOUS LOVE (*overlapping, screaming*). Ayeeeeeeeeee! Ayeeeeeee!

BROTHER LOVE (*overlapping, roaring*). Ha ha ha ha ha ha ha . . . .

PRECIOUS LOVE (*infuriated*). Damn-it-to-hell all, Brother Love. Don't you do that to me. What is ever the matter with you? You plum crazy or something?

(*Up music.*)

FATHER LOVE (*offstage, somewhat disturbed*). Precious . . . Precious Love!

PRECIOUS LOVE (*clutching to her heart as if out of breath*). My precious self is all right, Father Love. It's just your crazy son out here acting like some clowning nigger! Sneaking up on me and scaring the living daylights outta me precious self.

FATHER LOVE. I was afraid. You had crossed your . . .

PRECIOUS LOVE (*still angered*). I'm exhaustedly all right now, Father Love. You go on back and get your precious rest.

FATHER LOVE. Very well. I need . . . to rest.

PRECIOUS LOVE. Promise?

FATHER LOVE. I promise.

(*The music begins to fade.*)

PRECIOUS LOVE. Cross your heart and hope to die? (*Music fading out.*) Cross my heart and hope to die . . . (*The music stops. Very bitterly*) Now just look what you done gone and done. You done upset Father Love. Ain't you ashamed of yourself?

BROTHER LOVE (*teasingly and imitating* PRECIOUS LOVE). You done gone and upset Father Love. Ain't you ashamed of yourself?

PRECIOUS LOVE (*somewhat disgusted*). Brother Love, I have for all of these precious seventeen years of my livelihood on this precious earth tried to understand how you could have possibly ever been so preciously deserving to be a member of this precious family.

BROTHER LOVE (*outrightly clowning*). Well Precious Love, I tell you. It was like this. It was a long cold night and all. And Father Love just couldn't stand it for another minute. And so he just tiptoed on down to Mother Love's room, and patted her on the behind, and whispered ever sweetly in those precious ears . . . (*Now, rather Amos and Andyishly*) "Honey, I'm sorry. I know this is Tuesday and that us upper-class folks cohabitate only on Monday, Wednesday, and Friday . . . But like honey love, I know this is off-schedule and all . . . But

sweet love, I just got the hots tonight, I does. And I just got
to have a lil bit, if you and your precious self don't mind . . .
(*A slight pause*) "Goddammit! Move over Woman!"

PRECIOUS LOVE. Brother Love! You are acting like some common nigger now. This, this Alley Talk! I will not let my
precious ears be subgeecated for another precious minute to
such crude and savage jungalism!

BROTHER LOVE. Ha ha ha ha ha . . . Little Sister. Little Precious Love . . . Haven't you learned yet? Don't you know?
(*Slight pause*) No. I guess not. (*Slight pause. In a more serious
vein*) And to think . . . All those precious seventeen years too.
(*Moving toward the coffin. The music enters again.*) But you
will. Yessiree you will. Ole Granny did. (*He is now standing
by the head of the bier.*) Yessiree she did. Bless her sweet lil
ole concubining soul. (*He directly addresses the bier.*) Granny!
Grandmother Love! It was rough, wasn't it?

(*Up music.*)

PRECIOUS LOVE (*frightfully*). Brother Love! You should be
ashamed of yourself. Addressing the dead in such an unholy
manner. Now you just stop that now! Sure as you're standing
there, God Almighty's gonna strike you down with a bolt of
lightning so powerful . . . so powerful . . .

BROTHER LOVE (*continuing, rather maudlin*). Yes . . . Here
within lies the genesis of mankind; histories, counterpoints, a
thousand civilizations; rectal flowerings and births of a thousand nightmares. (*Slight pause*) Beginnings and endings; non-
sensical ambivalences . . . (*Pause*) Mother earth, a trillion to-
morrows, for nothing ends that begins.

PRECIOUS LOVE (*even more frightened*). My sands alive! Brother Love, what on earth are you ever talking about?

BROTHER LOVE (*in the same mood*). God. Seeds of time . . .
the earth, life, death. (*Pause*) *Anything*. Take your pick. (*He
takes a deep breath.*) And . . . *nothing*. Nothing is everything.
Anything is nothing. Nothing is anything. Right Granny?
(*Speaks to the bier again*) You gotta burn, girl. Yessiree, you

gotta burn. Don't give a damn if they held a thousand pistols at your skull. You shouldn't have done it. (*Bitterly*) There are Heavenly Heights all over this goddamn world now because of bitches like you. *Mother whores!* Damn pity. Rottenness goddamn shame of the world.

PRECIOUS LOVE. Now you just hush that kinna talk. You ain't got no right mocking Precious Grandmother like that. No right at all. And don't think you ain't mocking your ownself, either. If you don't hush talking this vile talk into my precious ears, I am going to call Mother Love downstairs this very minute.

BROTHER LOVE (*pondering*). Yes, I had better, hadn't I? Behave, that is, in the customary manner more properly befitting our rather caecilian ancestral heritage.

PRECIOUS LOVE (*puzzled*). What? (*They stare at each other for a long second; and then as if finally understanding,* PRECIOUS LOVE *speaks.*) Why, Brother Love! I do declare! I really do declare!

BROTHER LOVE (*smiling, a slight pause*). Here. (*Extending his hand*) Dance with me, Precious Love. Dance with me. (*He snaps his fingers and simultaneously the pompous and grand beat of the music of a waltz enters.*) Dance with Brother Love (*Precious Love curtseys.*) Dance with Brother Love. (*He bows.*) Mother Love could never understand the action on this level at any rate. So it doesn't really matter despite the circumstances. Nothing really matters at any rate. And besides, it is twelve o'clock. (*He bows again.*)

PRECIOUS LOVE (*happily*). Yes . . . It is twelve o'clock. (*She curtseys again.* BROTHER LOVE *takes* PRECIOUS LOVE *and they merrily waltz about the room. Overlapping as they dance.*)

BROTHER LOVE. Twelve o'clock it is. Twelve o'clock at Heavenly Manor. One, One, One. Time for the afternoon. Beeeeeeeee Mmmmmmmmm . . .

PRECIOUS LOVE (*happily*). Brother Love! I do beg your pardon.

BROTHER LOVE. And I yours, dear sister. (*Louder and in the direction of the bier*) AND YOURS TOO, GRANNY. (*Still louder and towards offstage*) Your pardon too, Father Love. (*And still louder toward the top of the stairway*) And of course, I do beg your pardon, dear, dear Precious Mother Love. To all of you: A pardon for everything. For the breath of foul air that binds us together! For life and its hideous aftermaths and afterthoughts! For yesterday's miseries and today's happy sadness! For the trillion smelly farts that tomorrow will bring! Tomorrow . . . Tomorrow . . . Tomorrow . . .

PRECIOUS LOVE (*elated*). Oh this is fun! This is fun! Are you going to do it? Are you going to do it?

BROTHER LOVE. Well . . . only for you, of course. Only for you. (*He releases* PRECIOUS LOVE *and bows.*)

PRECIOUS LOVE (*enthralled*). Oh goody! Oh goody! (BROTHER LOVE *moves near the stairway and begins mimicking rather profusely a punch-drunk boxer. The speech is purposely exaggerated. The music continues.*)

BROTHER LOVE. Oh yes . . . the afternoon B.M. I am my mother's keeper. We must remember the *schedule. Aukaudin tu this guyh, Dahtau Successman.* Well nawh come on, lisn youse guyhs. Ahmm tryin tuh talk some sense tuh youse guhys. Nayh anybody whose got any sense atahl; who wants tuh keep emself in good fisical coindision gonna take a B.M. three toines a day; when youse wake up in the moining, thas when youse rise and shine; and then youse take anuther round twelve a'cluck like the ole lady's doing now; and then ONE MORE in before youse tuck in tuh bed at night. Now lisn youse guyhs, lisn! I knows! Hell! I got the best trainer in this here camp. (*Points toward the top of the stairs*) And this here broad *always knows* what's best fer you, cause this broad is *Mother dear.* And there ain't nothing like *Mother dears.* Right, Miss Precious?

PRECIOUS LOVE (*clapping her hands*). Well I'm sure that I just have to agree, I'm sure.

BROTHER LOVE.* So fer the betterment of yer fisique and yer whole self, be sure and git in them three B.M.'s a day, and always on SCHEDUALEE. (*The word schedule is exaggerated.*)

PRECIOUS LOVE (*still clapping*). Hurrah for our leader! Hurrah! Hurrah! On with the movement. (*The "a" in Hurrah is pronounced as "a" in May or Day.*)

BROTHER LOVE* (*vindictively*). On with the movement! Before the dush . . . The movement! We must have movement! A hot steaming shower, orders to the maid . . . (*Pause, and then very sadly*) Lillie . . . Dear lillie of the flowers. Orders! Orders! And then the movement! We must have movements!

PRECIOUS LOVE (*still clapping, but now somewhat sadly.*) Hurrah for the movement! Hurrah! Hurrah!

BROTHER LOVE.* Hurrah for the movement! Orders for the day. A cooling refreshing hour resting comfortably, blissfully there! On top of the world, the commode, the drain. Down, down, down it comes. There is peace. The movement commences. There is silence. There is peace.

PRECIOUS LOVE. Hurrah for the movement! Hurrah! Hurrah!

BROTHER LOVE. There is *peace. There is peace.*

PRECIOUS LOVE (*sadly*). Mandy Luther King of Spades, I salute you. (*She curtseys.*)

BROTHER LOVE (*puzzled*). Who dat?

PRECIOUS LOVE (*equally as puzzled*). I don't know. Don't you?

BROTHER LOVE. There is something strikingly familiar about the meter.

PRECIOUS LOVE. Napoleon, do you suppose?

BROTHER LOVE. Could be. Something or other at least.

PRECIOUS LOVE. It's probably important.

BROTHER LOVE. Probably. Perhaps so. But does it really matter? In time we'll remember if it's important. Takes time for everything you know.

* Brother Love's lines in these three speeches spoken as if he were reciting a television commercial.

PRECIOUS LOVE. Takes time.

BROTHER LOVE. Takes time.

PRECIOUS LOVE. I suppose you're right.

(*There is a long pause. They stare at each other.*)

BROTHER LOVE. I suppose we could do the thing again.

PRECIOUS LOVE. I suppose.

(BROTHER LOVE *moves toward* PRECIOUS LOVE. *He bows. She curtseys. After a second or so, he snaps his fingers and the music goes up. And again they dance about the room. The lights begin to dim.*)

DARKNESS

ACT ONE

PART TWO

Scene 1

THE SCENE: The same. The play continues as if there has been no break between scenes.

Music enter; lights up, and PRECIOUS LOVE *and* BROTHER LOVE *still dancing about.*

MOTHER LOVE (*calling from offstage*). Precious . . . Precious . . . Precious Love . . . Are you still practicing?

PRECIOUS LOVE (*still dancing with* BROTHER LOVE). Yes Mother Love. My precious self is still practicing, I'm sure.

MOTHER LOVE (*a clock is heard being wound*). Very good girl. You still have a few minutes of practice time remaining.

BROTHER LOVE (*jokingly*). Home sweet home! (*He sings to the beat of the music.*) "There's no place like home for the holidays . . ." Clutz! Damn!

PRECIOUS LOVE (*teasingly*). Well! I do ever declare, Brother Love. Clutz! My, my, my. I do ever declare! What those Yankee schools won't do for you precious Southern Boys. I do declare!

FATHER LOVE (*entering*). *Clutz*? *Clutz*? What is wrong? What is wrong with the world today? Is the precious world coming to an end?

BROTHER LOVE (*jokingly*). Only as close as Brother Dante managed to get, Father Love.

FATHER LOVE. Is that a fact? Hmph! Well, I do declare. How about that. How about that.

PRECIOUS LOVE (*moving and kissing* FATHER LOVE). Miss Blessingful did, as I recall, speak ever so highly of the *devine* Comedia.

FATHER LOVE. Is that right? Is that a fact? Well, well, well.

BROTHER LOVE. Fare thee well, Grandmother. Father thee well (*to the coffin*).

PRECIOUS LOVE. Oh yes indeed. A most interesting and enlightening symposium.

FATHER LOVE. No doubt, I'm sure. (*Pondering*) Strange though. I'm sure the journey was a rewarding one. We all have our journeys . . . our retributions . . . . our dreams.

PRECIOUS LOVE. How was baccalaureate, Father Love?

FATHER LOVE. Baccalaureatish, dear. Baccalaureatish. Same old rigamarole. Everything on schedule. Speeches, tears, glorified tributes, dressed-up gobbledygook. Master Degreed and PhDeed Precious Colored People parading in all their glory. The Pope on the day of Ascension.

MOTHER LOVE (*calling*). Father Love . . . Father Love . . . Is that you, dear?

FATHER LOVE (*hesitantly*). Yes, Mother Love, dear. It is I. I have arrived.

MOTHER LOVE (*still calling*). Father Love . . . Are you there? Have you arrived, dear?

FATHER LOVE (*a little louder*). I have arrived, Mother Love, dear. I am home . . . (*Not quite as loud*) Home . . . Sweet home.

MOTHER LOVE. Very well. I shall be down shortly. Tell Precious Love that she may stop practicing now. (*Simultaneously,* FATHER LOVE, BROTHER LOVE, *and* PRECIOUS LOVE, *look at their watches and then at each other smiling.*) I'll be down in a minute or so. Please see to it that Brother Love has arrived by the time I come down. Family meeting, remember?

FATHER LOVE. Yes, Mother Love, dear.

BROTHER LOVE. Yes, Mother Love. I have arrived.

PRECIOUS LOVE. Yes, Mother Love.

MOTHER LOVE. Very good then. Everything is in order. I'll be right down.

BROTHER LOVE. And what is this all about, Father Love? Family meeting . . .

PRECIOUS LOVE. I thought all the arrangements were complete, I'm sure, I thought they were.

BROTHER LOVE (*sudden exasperation*). Are we bankrupt again?

PRECIOUS LOVE. Oh goody!

FATHER LOVE. Don't be impetuous, the two of you. We're going to have a little family meeting, that's all. There is no crisis, no great problem. Your mother and I have already taken measures about the little incident.

PRECIOUS LOVE (*pondering*). Hmmmmm . . . Little incident, little incident, incident . . . Hmmmmm. (*Very quickly*) Father Love! Oh my gracious Lord, No!

BROTHER LOVE (*sprightly*). Hopeful's pregnant again?

FATHER LOVE. I didn't say that. You said that.

MOTHER LOVE (*appearing at the top of the stairs*). Oh Father Love, dahhlinggg, don't play tiddle-le-winks with the children. Of course she's pregnant, dahhling. What else could it be? (MOTHER LOVE *moves grandly down the stairway.*)

BROTHER LOVE (*to the bier*). Well, Granny . . . Here we go again.

MOTHER LOVE. And how was Baccalaureate, dear?

FATHER LOVE. Baccalaureatish, dear.

MOTHER LOVE. Wonderful. Wonderful! And your address, how did it go?

FATHER LOVE. The usual response: mild, appropriate, receptive as usual. Dear, let's get on with this, shall we. We must be getting ready for the funeral, remember?

BROTHER LOVE. Is it necessary to go through this routine again? Thirteen times! Thirteen times in three years we've been through the same routine. Good Lord! Call Dr. Successman.

MOTHER LOVE (*somewhat aggravated*). Brother Love, will you please be quiet and listen, stupid son of mine. The matter has been attended to. Dr. Successman has been informed. In fact, well, Hopeful is at his office now. See . . . See . . . If you'd only wait and not jump to conclusions about things, you'd understand.

BROTHER LOVE (*sarcastically*). Yes, I know. Understand that everything is in order. Understand that we're right on schedule.

MOTHER LOVE. Understand that you have a family. Everyone isn't as fortunate as you, Brother Love; to have a family that share and resolve their problems as a unit, as we do.

BROTHER LOVE. Mother Love, you are vague . . . very very vague. (*Slight pause*) But what does it matter. An abortion's an abortion. Hmph. And life goes on.

MOTHER LOVE (*tearfully*). Yes dear, another abortion. It hurts me to my heart to have to say this again. But your sister . . . your sister, Hopeful, has disgraced us again.

FATHER LOVE. There, there, dear. Try to bear the pain. These things do happen occasionally, and to the best of families. Children are expected to make a few mistakes. Our children are no exception.

MOTHER LOVE. But that's not true, Father Love. Mistakes! Mistakes! Every time Hopeful does this to us, it's a catastrophe. These things are not supposed to happen to better families. Certainly never before in this family. Nowhere in my family tree is there an inkling of such behavior and catastrophe.

BROTHER LOVE (*adjusting something on the bier*). Hear that, Grandmother?

PRECIOUS LOVE (*as if to be helpful*). We understand, Mother Love. We do know how fortunate we are. We understand the importance of these delicate matters. (*The little girl again*) I certainly know how blessed I am to have a precious family that loves me, I do.

MOTHER LOVE (*near tears*). Oh, Hopeful, Hopeful, Hopeful! That daughter of mine. If she'd only listen. If she only had your attitude, Precious Love. Your father and I understand how it is with young people, in these modern times, we do. Seven years! Seven Years of Columbia's Child Psychology wasted! Wasted on that foolish ungrateful child. If she'd only listen. I've told her. I've told that girl time and time again, as only a precious mother who loves her precious daughter would do, I have. If she'd only listen. Then . . . Then, these little incidents, these catastrophes would never happen.

PRECIOUS LOVE (*quickly taking out her purse*). See, Mother Love. See, Father Love. I remember. I remember. I carry my materials with me everywhere. I always remember what you've told me. You can never be too careful in this wicked, wicked world. There are vileful evil spirits everywhere.

FATHER LOVE. Yes and we're right proud of you, Precious Love. Right proud of you. One would think that you were the oldest, at times.

MOTHER LOVE (*crying now, very melodramatic*). Oh what are we ever going to do? What are we ever going to do?

BROTHER LOVE. Well for one thing, we need to stop having these family meetings. That's for sure. We should let Hopeful have this baby.

PRECIOUS LOVE. But Brother Love. Hopeful is entirely too awful young to have a baby. Why . . . Why she'd have to get married.

BROTHER LOVE. Well whose baby is it, Hopeful's or ours?

MOTHER LOVE (*with nervous exasperation*). Brother Love! Father Love, am I hearing correctly? Do you hear our son? After all that we've done for him, he has the unmitigated gall to suggest that, that I become a grandmother before any of my precious children are even grown. (*She starts to cry again.*)

FATHER LOVE (*comforting*). There, there, dear. There, there. He's only a child.

MOTHER LOVE. Why, why, what would I be able to say at sorority meetings? Why, my own baby, my precious little daughter who was a debutante. (*Frightfully*) Oh my God! They'd discontinue my membership.

FATHER LOVE. There, there dear. Try to bear the pain. Everything will be all right, I'm sure.

MOTHER LOVE (*almost hysterical*). But, But . . . Can you imagine me at the convention next year? "Oh yes, Mrs. *Happy Hollow*, didn't you know? I'm a grandmother. Yessssssss . . . a Grandmother! Hopeful is married. She's been married for more than a year now. That dear, dear, daughter of mine. She just went off and eloped and didn't even let us know. Isn't that just too cute? These modern children are just always so full of surprises, aren't they? My son-in-law? Oh he's just the nicest young man. A gay young blade if I've ever seen one. His name? (*Very nervously*) Henry . . . Yes, Henry, Henry something or other. Or is it Joe? Or Amos? Or is it . . . Is it . . . (*She starts to cry again.*)

PRECIOUS LOVE (*comforting* MOTHER LOVE). Father Love, does Hopeful know? Does she know who he is?

FATHER LOVE. I'm not sure. Your mother and I called Sinners at the University last evening. He mentioned that Hopeful has been seen in the company of a young man there quite often as of late. Let me see now. His name was . . . It was . . . Henry something or other. Yes, Henry. That's it. Henry Joseph Hankerson!

PRECIOUS LOVE (*surprised*). Henry Joseph Hankerson!

BROTHER LOVE. You're joking of course. Whoever heard of anyone with a name like that?

MOTHER LOVE. Oh! My gracious alive! How ordinary sounding.

PRECIOUS LOVE. Joseph? How biblical. Henry Joseph Hankerson. That's cute. Is he a darkie, Father Love? The name sounds rather Africana.

FATHER LOVE. Can't be sure. Can't be sure. Sinners mentioned that he was originally from Miami, Florida.

PRECIOUS LOVE (*elated*). Miami, Florida! You mean Miami Beach, Florida?

BROTHER LOVE. Don't be ridiculous, Precious Love. There aren't any Heavenly Heights at that place.

MOTHER LOVE. Don't stop there, Father Love. Tell all! Tell them the rest.

FATHER LOVE. Well I don't rightly think that the other part's that important, dear.

MOTHER LOVE (*snappingly*). Tell them! Goddamn it! Tell them! They may as well know what's in store for them if we don't do something about this matter.

FATHER LOVE (*somewhat reluctantly*). Well it seems as if this Henry Joseph Hankerson is, well, is just a NOBODY! JUST A NOBODY! I understand that he's related to the Hankersons from round these parts, the Hankersons over in Goodbread Alley.

PRECIOUS LOVE (*frightfully*). Billie Joseph Hankerson.

MOTHER LOVE (*overlapping*). Goodbread Alley! Ugghh! Precious Love, you can't imagine the kind of people, you can't imagine the kind of people that live over there. They're . . . They're animals! Savages!

PRECIOUS LOVE (*just above a whisper*). Billie Joe Hankerson.

FATHER LOVE. And, who, Precious Love, is Billie Joe Hankerson?

PRECIOUS LOVE. He . . . He's one of them old dirty nasty niggers over there in Goodbread Alley. He's always teasing me and calling me awful names, and saying vile terrible things into my precious ears.

MOTHER LOVE (*horrified*). What kinds of things, Precious Love?

PRECIOUS LOVE. Real, real, dirty, nasty, vileful things, Mother Love. Real, awful, terrible things; terrible things like *hell, damn, sonuvabitch*, Mother . . .

BROTHER LOVE (*overlapping, roaring*). Ha ha ha ha ha . . .

MOTHER LOVE. Oh my precious, precious little baby. (*She embraces* PRECIOUS LOVE.) Your precious ears have been tainted by vileness. My precious, precious baby.

FATHER LOVE (*infuriated*). The blackheart must be punished. He must be dealt with immediately. How dare he taint the precious ears of my precious daughter. How dare he! Damn nigger!

BROTHER LOVE (*still laughing*). Her precious ears have been tainted permanently.

FATHER LOVE (*scornfully*). Brother Love! Acquit yourself of this unbrotherly behavior or leave the room immediately.

BROTHER LOVE. I'm sorry, Father Love. (*Whispering towards the bier*) Like Hell I am, eh, Granny?

FATHER LOVE. What did you just say?

BROTHER LOVE (*catching himself*). I . . . I said, I said . . . Like hell will Henry Joseph Hankerson be afforded the honor of affiance with the likes of my precious fair sister, Hopeful. Like hell will the blackheart do such, as would well be the case, if the matter is not attended to at once! It is not the time for the bloods to become one. (*Slight pause*) And besides, I understand that they stink.

PRECIOUS LOVE (*crying now*). And . . . And, Father Love, and precious family of mine, that old nasty Billie Joe Hankerson told me, he told me . . .

FATHER LOVE (*like a knight in shining armor*). What else did that old nasty dirty Billie Joe Hankerson tell you, precious daughter?

PRECIOUS LOVE. He told me, precious family of mine, that, that God Almighty and powerful above was, was a black God! (MOTHER LOVE *screams*.) He said that God was as black as he was and as black as all them people over there in Goodbread Alley.

MOTHER LOVE (*bursting, almost to the point of hysteria*). Enough! Enough! I can't take it! I can't take it! I can't take it! Give me strength! Father Love! I suggest that we vote immediately! Before the very foundation to this holy and precious establishment crumbles away to precious nothingness!

FATHER LOVE. I agree, Mother Love. I agree! (*Slight pause*) And this is no dream. Then is it unanimous? Say aye, if it is so, precious family.

MOTHER LOVE. Aye.

PRECIOUS LOVE (*tearfully*). Aye.

BROTHER LOVE (*somewhat hesitantly*). Aye.

MOTHER LOVE. And you, Father Love?

FATHER LOVE (*moving toward the bier*). Grandmother Love and I vote . . . vote, aye.

MOTHER LOVE. Poor Grandmother. Poor, poor, Grandmother.

PRECIOUS LOVE. Dear, dear Grandmother.

BROTHER LOVE. A mighty fortress is our . . .

LILLIE (*entering*). Mrs. Love . . . Madam . . .

MOTHER LOVE (*tearfully*). Yes, Lillie.

LILLIE. The ladies from your sorority are entering the driveway.

MOTHER LOVE. Oh dear, dear, dear. They're here. I'll have to hurry. (*She starts to leave—and stops.*) Father Love . . . THE MATTER IS SETTLED?

FATHER LOVE. Yes, dear. The matter is settled.

MOTHER LOVE (*approaching the stairway*). Very well then. And please, Father Love, try not to be impertinent to P.P. and the girls. They're only trying to be helpful.

FATHER LOVE. I won't, dear.

MOTHER LOVE. Lillie . . . Have the ladies come in. Give me a moment or so to change before you send them up.

BROTHER LOVE. Mother Love, you're having them come up? Why up rather than down . . . here?

MOTHER LOVE. Brother Love, we are in mourning, remember? How would it look for us to receive people who have come to comfort me, down here?

BROTHER LOVE. Yes, but I still don't . . . But what does it matter, really? What does it matter?

MOTHER LOVE. Yes, you're quite right, I'm sure. (*Affirmatively*) Your Grandmother is dead, Son. She is resting in Abraham's bosom at this very moment. We are in mourning, remember? We are in mourning. Come, Precious Love.

(*The two women exit up the stairway.*)

FATHER LOVE (*leaving*). Your mother says that we are in mourning, son. Please . . . Try to understand that we are in mourning. (*He exits.*)

(*The sorority sisters enter. There are from two to four women at the most. They are gaudily made up. Cheap fur pieces and excessive jewelry add to the absurdity of their appearance.*)

MISS P. P. (*in a high falsetto*). Brother Love! Girls, will you just look at Brother Love. I do declare this precious child has certainly grown. I have been hearing great things about you, Brother Love. When are we going to get a peek at this novelette we hear you've been writing?

BROTHER LOVE. Oh it's nothing, Miss P. P., nothing at all. Just throwing around some ideas on paper. Mother Love shouldn't have mentioned it yet. It's really nothing.

MISS P. P. Ohhhhhh, now don't be so modest with us, Brother Love. Remember, I taught you English Literature. I taught you English Literature. I know your talents, boy, I do. I know your abilities. Girls, I have always said that this young man was exceptionally talented. I have always said so, I have. Isn't that right, Brother Love?

BROTHER LOVE. Yes, Miss P. P. Yes mam. Still . . . What I'm doing amounts to little or nothing, really. Ideas mainly. Ideas that have yet to be . . .

MISS P. P. Well I'm sure that we will just not listen to any of that kind of talk, will we, girls? And before we leave, you had better read some of this lil ole novelette to us, or I swear to God that we'll just never forgive you, will we girls?

BROTHER LOVE. Well . . . Maybe a few lines. But it's really nothing, ladies; really nothing.

PRECIOUS LOVE (*appears at the top of the stairs*). Miss P. P. Ladies . . . Mother will see you now.

(*Almost ritualistically, the mood of the women shifts to one of sadness.* MISS P. P. *begins to cry. The other women, as if cued, take handkerchiefs out and sniffle.*)

MISS P. P. Precious Love . . . Dear, dear Precious Love. How is the dear?

PRECIOUS LOVE. She's taking it well, I'm sure, Miss P. P. Won't you ladies please come up now?

(*The ladies solemnly file up the stairway. The lights begin to fade and focus on* BROTHER LOVE *who has moved beside the coffin. Off stage the women are heard singing.*)

WOMEN (*offstage*). The hymn (*To the melody of "America the Beautiful"*).

Sorority . . . Sorority,
The Sisters in the bond.
Sorority . . . Sorority,
The bond so big and strong.
Sorority . . . Sorority,
And we shall move along.
Sorority . . . Sorority,
We'll even stand the bomb.

(*The song is repeated a second time.*)

BROTHER LOVE (*overlapping, during the second chorus; to the bier*). Hear those bitches. Hear them, Granny. Listen to them. "Sorority, the sisters in the bond; the bond so big and strong; they'll even stand the bomb." Isn't that absurd? Stupid fools. Fighting to hold on to a dream. Some dream. Some dream. (*A pause*) Oh I wish . . . I wish . . . (*Angrily*) You old cold bitch! (*He spits onto the bier.*) Why didn't you die? Goddamn you! I hate you! Why didn't you die? Why didn't you die? Why didn't you die?

(*The lights begin to fade out. The singing of the sorority sisters is now overlapped and drowned out by other voices singing the old Negro spiritual, "I've Been Buked."* BROTHER LOVE *backs away and exits. Only the bier is seen until the complete blackout.*)

>I've been buked and I've been scorned.
>Yes, I've been buked and I've been scorned,
>>children.
>I've been buked and I've been scorned.
>I've been talked about sho as you born.
>There is trouble all over this world.
>There is trouble all over this world,
>>children.
>There is trouble all over this world.
>There is trouble all over this world.
>Ain't gwine lay my ligion down.
>Yes, ain't gwine lay my ligion down,
>>children.
>Ain't gwine lay my ligion down
>Ain't gwine lay my ligion down.

DARKNESS

ACT ONE

PART TWO

Scene 2

The stage is dark for only a moment or so between the division of scenes.

What is most important, for staging this scene, is that the mystic quality of a dream be established. We are concerned with a sequence of sensations, images, thoughts, etc. passing through a sleeping person's mind.

Author's suggestions about staging: (1) A white spot (dimmed a bit) on the BOY *who is located at downstage right. (2)* BROTHER LOVE *(white) off to the right side of the bier. He recites the dialogue of the narrator. A blue spot is on him. (3)* BROTHER LOVE *(Negro) off to the left side of the bier. He is almost unseen. A purple spot is on him. (4) The sorority sisters are seated in chairs at center stage. They face the bier with their backs to the audience.*

NARRATOR (*passionately*). An open field stretched for miles about. Red clay hills in the distance. An early morning breeze —central Georgia. A colored boy of thirteen standing upright— a mule grazing nearby. A blood-red sun blazing overhead. An occasional rumble-like sound from above.

THE BOY. Lord have mercy! It's gonna rain. (*Pause*) Well ain't that one. The devil and his wife shorenuf must be fighting now with the sun up there a'blazing like that. (*To the mule*) Jinny—guess we'd better git going now or we'll shorenuf drown, gal.

NARRATOR. A crackling of thunder—and the boy looking hesitantly in various directions; and then kneeling and picking up a wrapped package. The boy unties the package. A revolver is revealed. The boy faces the animal and points the weapon in its direction.

THE BOY (*jokingly*). Shoot, Jinny! I ain't gonna kill you, girl. I shore wouldn't git no gun to run off and kill no dumb jackass. You don't think I'd take and shoot you, do you, girl? *With this gun?* Lord, no, Jesus! Mama'd kill me for shore if I went off and did something as stupid as that. Hmph! Sides—done all we could to git her to let me keep the damn thing. So you needn't worry none, girl. You just sit there and keep still now so I can git the feel of this thing.

NARRATOR. The boy raises the gun as if preparing to fire it.

THE BOY. Now see . . . See, Jinny. All you got to know about this thing is that you ain't suppose to pull this here click here unless you really want to kill something. See . . .

NARRATOR. It begins to rain. The boy lowers the weapon and then raises it again. The animal moves about. The boy abruptly, but proudly, paces off thirteen steps, shouting aloud the numbers in cadence. He stops and brings the weapon to his side. He ponders to himself for a moment and raises the gun again—pointing it toward the beast.

A piercing bursting eruption from above. And the boy moving away from the beast in fear.

THE BOY (*frightfully*). Lord, Jesus! I ain't got no business being such a scaredy cat. I'm thirteen years old today. Pa says I's a man today. He says Ahm almost a man today.

NARRATOR. The sound of thunder again. Spasmodic ejaculations from the sky above—entering and subsiding. A branch from a tree falling to the ground. And the animal moving about frightfully in meaningless directions. And the boy—terrified and falling onto the ground. And the crackling outburst of a beast in pain. And the sound of the rain seemingly amplified a thousand times over. (*Pause*) And the boy—horrified, and grabbing ahold of his arms; examining them closely, as if they were torn away from his body . . . and then tenderly squeezing his fingers and hands between his legs for a long second. (*Pause*) And the boy placing the damp hand that held the weapon into his mouth, as if to warm it; to stop the pain.

And the surmounting cries of the beast—the beast in pain. And the boy staring sadly at the animal . . . a sickening sight. The boy, looking, wanting not to believe . . . And the boy finally overcome to the state of vomit at the sight of the very red blood, pouring away from the dying body; fast—very fast, and then settling into a pool of murky red liquid; the blood of life, being sucked away into the bowels of a very black and uneasy earth. (*The second verse of the Negro spiritual enters and overlaps the remaining action.*)

There is trouble all over this world.
Yes, there is trouble all over this world,
children.
There is trouble all over this world.
There is trouble all over this world.

NARRATOR (*continuing, overlapping*). And the boy panics. He takes a handful of black wet earth and frantically attempts to insert it into the animal's wound. (*Pause*) And then . . . a final cry from the animal. The beast dies. (*The lights begin to fade. Continuing*) And the boy slowly rising with the gun in the hand that destroyed the beast.

THE BOY (*sadly*). Oh, Lord! Damn! Damn! Damn!

NARRATOR. And the boy firing the weapon; emptying it of its entrails into the animal's body, and then slowly walking toward the tree. He kneels there, at the foot of the tree and hurriedly buries the weapon.

And the rain and the thunder and the cries of the boy become one.

THE BOY (*cryingly*). Mama . . . Mama . . . Mama . . .

DARKNESS

(*A quick count and then back to main set and final scene.*)

ACT ONE

PART TWO

Scene 3

APOTHEOSIS

Lights up. The sorority sisters are now congregated together. They listen in delight as BROTHER LOVE (*both Negro and White* BROTHER LOVES *play as one*) *recites to them a brief synopsis of the novel he is writing.*

It must be established through direction and acting that the vignette of the colored boy killing the mule has been a part of

BROTHER LOVE'S *monologue. The first lines of the monologue should begin during the change of scenes.*

This final scene requires a staccato effect; full percussive-like carthartic resolution.

BROTHER LOVE BLACK (*abruptly, resoundingly*). And so this slow purge towards meeting the reality . . . the life . . . explodes into painful understandings and knowledges as the boy emerges into adolescence. For then, the reality of the life can no longer be kept hidden behind the veil of the dream which has been the very essence of his existence up to this point.

(*The change of scenes is complete. The sorority sisters listen, entranced by the eloquence of the brothers who are now one.*)

BROTHER LOVE WHITE. And . . . my protagonist, dear ladies, is thrown, his eyes wide open, plum smack damn into the middle of the forties. And . . . And . . . well I haven't given him a name yet, mind you. So let's just call him . . . Clutz; yeah . . . Clutz! Let's just call him Clutz. Clutz it is! And so Clutz lives . . .

BROTHER LOVE BLACK. He suffers . . .

BROTHER LOVE WHITE. He dreams . . . Imagine if you will, Miss P. P., Clutz is in an elementary school. The school bell starts a'ringing like all hell that day. Something very terrible has happened. Sirens are blasting away all over the city every which-a-way. Cars on the streets are honking their horns something mighty frightful. Remember . . . Clutz is just a lil olé child now. And that poor boy is as scared as all pure hell. And that poor boy says to himself, "My God! Has the world gone plum crazy?"

BROTHER LOVE BLACK. But then . . . just as quick as all the confusion had started, everything is all quiet again. Quiet like a hush-a-bye lullaby. The world just stops completely still. And you can't even hear the sweet sound of a baby sucking away at his mammy's nipple. The whole world is silent. Stilled faces . . . glazed eyes seem to devour that boy as he makes his way

home. Home to his mama—his sweet mama. A nation is mourning. A nation eulogizes with ramifications of love and honor
and respect for *that man* . . . *that man* who had just a while
ago stole his way to the sweet bosom of Abraham. When the
boy gets home, his mama makes some sense of all the confusion
for him. She says to him those words in such a terrifying way
until he knows for sure that he ain't gonna ever forget them
words for as long as he lives on God's sweet earth. With all
them tears falling down that woman's face, she says to him:
"Honey, git down on your knees and pray! Mr. Roosevelt is
dead! Mr. Roosevelt is dead!"

BROTHER LOVE WHITE. And Clutz mourns for his first hero.
(*Slight pause*) How emotional the times are during that poor
boy's childhood, Miss P. P.

BROTHER LOVE BLACK. TERRIFYING!

BROTHER LOVE WHITE. And there was that other time. Yes,
that day too. And Clutz's mama crying and carrying on all over
again. When was it—before that man died, or was it after he
died? It was something awfully mysterious about this bomb;
this great big old powerful bomb that is set off somewhere and
kills thousands and thousands of people . . .

BROTHER LOVE BLACK. Slant-eyed yellow people!

(PRECIOUS LOVE *appears. The white* PRECIOUS LOVE. *She stands
and listens.*)

BROTHER LOVE WHITE. "Those dirty Japs! Those damn dirty
Japs!" Miss P. P., this is all them poor helpless children heard
everywhere during those times. "Those goddamn Jap sonsav-
bitches! Good for them! They were warned! They were
warned!"

BROTHER LOVE BLACK (*sarcastically*). The American Dream is
saved again.

BROTHER LOVE WHITE. Yes, my brother! Yes! Yes! Yes! That
dream is saved again. (*Slight pause*) And this is when that
child gets his first hearing about this dream.

BROTHER LOVE BLACK. Yes . . . but again—Clutz's mama crying again. "Lord, when is my mama gonna stop crying?" that boy says. But then he finds out the woman's crying because she's happy. The boy's daddy is coming home. The boy's daddy is on his way home; coming clear across all that water to his sweet wife and child. Coming home to his home sweet home.

BROTHER LOVE WHITE. But when his daddy gets home, he's acting differently from the way he acted before he went across that ocean to fight those dirty, those dirty Japs. He's acting mighty, mighty strange now. Clutz ain't never seen his daddy act like he acted now. Something mighty terrible must have happened to that man while he was over there in that war. Something terrible had hurt that boy's daddy. Took Clutz a long time before he figured out what had happened to that man. It all started that morning when his mama told him that his daddy had been called practically outta his senses by some white men cause his daddy had refused to sit in the colored seats on the city bus.

BROTHER LOVE BLACK. Lord oh Lord, Clutz's daddy, that man! Everybody in the neighborhood called him the craziest man. But he wouldn't stop. No, he just wouldn't stop. He got beat and kicked around so much up to the time Clutz was in high school, until that big pretty man that had come back from that war wasn't nothing but a cringy bag of bones. Yeah . . . Clutz's daddy shorenuf wasn't a man no more. But he just kept on fighting and causing trouble until a 38-caliber bullet found its way clear through his cringy boney skull one dark Saturday night. (MOTHER LOVE *appears.*) And then the craziest thing happened, Miss P. P.

BROTHER LOVE WHITE. The damnest craziest thing! In no time at all, back across the waters went a couple of Clutz's cousins to some godforsaken place called Korea. (*Slight pause*) And neither of them ever came back. They never came back. Though he was only a child, Clutz couldn't help but think to himself . . .

BROTHER LOVE BLACK. "This ain't right! This ain't right at

all! Seems like those poor boys just ain't never got a chance to live. They ain't never got a chance to live."

BROTHER LOVE WHITE. But by then, the boy was finally beginning to understand what everything was all about. Now Miss P. P., that boy certainly did love America, his country . . . They, his country, America—they had seen to that. But the Dream? The Dream? My country 'tis of thee and all that, that . . . crap? Well none of it seemed to have had any kind of meaning to him any more. No goddamn meaning at all. (*With nervous exasperation*) Yet . . . Yet, his teachers at school were beginning to act very peculiar about something. There was something very strange going on; something that had to do with this dream . . . Again! All over again. Something about that goddamn dream! (*The last lines antagonize the sorority sisters. They begin to fidget and move about.*) What a mess of a world to be living in!

BROTHER LOVE BLACK. A goddamn funny house!

BOTH BROTHER LOVES. A mess of mass chaotic confusion leading here and there and absolutely no goddamn where!

(MOTHER LOVE *gives with a sharp, piercing scream. She then starts to moan, as if she were experiencing labor pains. This business of hers will overlap the monologue to* CURTAIN. PRECIOUS LOVE *at this point begins to laugh. Her laughter and giggling produces a rather sickening sound. It becomes evident at this point that she is near madness. The music from the minuet enters again. Occasionally,* PRECIOUS LOVE *enters into the ballet routine which began the play.*)

BROTHER LOVE BLACK (*overlapping*). But then . . . then . . . a lull; a quiet hush-a-bye baby lullaby.

(*The sorority sisters are now crying. They make occasional outbursts and screams which depict intense inner suffering and turmoil.* FATHER LOVE *enters at this point. He goes to the bier and kneels before the body and clasps his hands together in prayer. We vaguely hear him reciting the child's prayer.*)

FATHER LOVE (*just above whisper, overlapping*). "Now I lay

me down to sleep, I pray thee Lord my soul to keep. If I should die before I wake, I pray thee Lord my soul to take." (*He continues to end of play.*)

BROTHER LOVE BLACK. My God! What was happening now?

BROTHER LOVE WHITE. Had the world gone plum crazy again?

BROTHER LOVE BLACK (*resoundingly*). Goddammit! Clutz had had it!

BROTHER LOVE WHITE (*with fervor*). He was damn tired of being a boy!

BROTHER LOVE BLACK. Despite the fact that certain species of people had other ideas in mind.

BROTHER LOVE WHITE. He remembered his daddy!

BOTH BROTHER LOVES. He was tired of being a boy child! (*Slight pause, then sadly*) Boy child.

(FATHER LOVE's *chanting,* MOTHER LOVE's *moaning, and* PRE-CIOUS LOVE's *dancing about and laughter continue to overlap the monologue. The sorority sisters are now walking aimlessly about the room. They are beginning to undress.*)

BROTHER LOVE BLACK. And then Miss P. P. . . . . (*Slight pause*) Miss P. P.

BROTHER LOVE WHITE. Miss P. P. . . . .

BROTHER LOVE BLACK. Miss P. P. . . . .

BROTHER LOVE WHITE. Miss P. P. . . . .

BROTHER LOVE BLACK. Miss P. P. . . . .

BOTH BROTHER LOVES (*screamingly*). Miss P. Peeeeeeeeeeee . . . (MISS *P. P. screams frightfully. She then enters into a rather catatonic state of uneasy quivering and jerking-like bodily movements.*) Then, Miss P. P. You know what happened? What happened after that. You know goddamn well, you do!

(MISS P. P. *screams again. The other sorority sisters scream. They too now enter into catatonic bodily movements. Now enter the sounds of ringing chimes. The following series of lines to accompaniment of an effect full, voluminous, staccato. Almost equivalent to that of a constant drum roll.*)

BROTHER LOVE WHITE. Sit-ins . . . .

BROTHER LOVE BLACK. Stand-ins . . .

BROTHER LOVE WHITE. Walk-ins . . .

BROTHER LOVE BLACK. Wade-ins . . .

BROTHER LOVE WHITE. A bald-headed madman slamming away his shoes on a table.

BROTHER LOVE BLACK. A bearded beatnik and other hairy apes a'comin' down the mountains.

BROTHER LOVE WHITE. Hands across the sea . . .

BROTHER LOVE BLACK. My country tis of thee . . .

BROTHER LOVE WHITE. Sit-ins . . .

BROTHER LOVE BLACK. Stand-ins . . .

BROTHER LOVE WHITE. Walk-ins . . .

BROTHER LOVE BLACK. Ride-ins . . .

BROTHER LOVE WHITE. God bless the Pope.

BROTHER LOVE BLACK. May he rest in peace.

BROTHER LOVE WHITE. The nation must move forward with vigahhh . . .

BROTHER LOVE BLACK. Vigahhhhhhhhh . . .

BROTHER LOVE WHITE. Vigahhhhhhhhh . . .

BROTHER LOVE BLACK. God bless America and all that jazz.

BROTHER LOVE WHITE (*singing*). "There is trouble all over this world . . ."

BROTHER LOVE BLACK (*singing*). "We shall overcome. We shall overcome . . ."

BROTHER LOVE WHITE. Bullshit!

BROTHER LOVE BLACK. Bullshit! Amen! Turn thy cheek, fool! Don't mind the dogs. They're only animals. They're just playing.

BROTHER LOVE WHITE. Bullshit! I'm getting tired of this crap! (*Resoundingly*) Forward with vigahhhhhhhh . . .

BROTHER LOVE BLACK (*religiously, like an old Southern Baptist preacher*). With vigahhhhhhhhhhhh . . .

BROTHER LOVE WHITE. Burning flesh!

BROTHER LOVE BLACK. A heifer!

BROTHER LOVE WHITE. Hands across the sea.

BROTHER LOVE BLACK (*joyfully*). And we just march along.

BOTH BROTHER LOVES. March on, darkies . . . March, darkies, march!

BROTHER LOVE WHITE. On to the promised land of nowhere!

BROTHER LOVE BLACK. And that big, fat, big-mouthed black pretty woman leads us on in song.

BROTHER LOVE WHITE (*singing*). "I've been buked and I've been scorned. I've been buked and I've been scorned . . ."

BROTHER LOVE BLACK (*cantoring*). "There is trouble all over this world . . . There is trouble all over this world . . ."

BROTHER LOVE WHITE (*now cantoring, as if answering the cries*). "What does it mean . . . Where is it leading us . . ."

BOTH BROTHER LOVES (*snappingly, directly to audience*). Nowhere! My brothers! Here and there and absolutely no goddamn where! (*After a pause*) And then . . . Prayer!

BROTHER LOVE WHITE. Prayer from your leader.

BROTHER LOVE BLACK. Prayer from that man.

BOTH BROTHER LOVES (*chantingly*). I have a dream . . .

THE OTHER CHARACTERS. Aaaaaaaamen, brother!

BOTH BROTHER LOVES. I have a dream . . .

THE OTHER CHARACTERS. Aaaaaaaamen, brother!

BOTH BROTHER LOVES. I have a dream . . .

THE OTHER CHARACTERS. Aaaaaaaamen, brother!

BOTH BROTHER LOVES (*with joyful passion*). Requimmmmmm-mm . . .

(*The other characters stop their movements. There is a full minute of quiet. Only the ringing chimes are heard.* LILLIE OF THE FLOWERS, *played by the Negro* PRECIOUS LOVE, *enters. Two other women escort the sorority sisters off the stage. One of them will return and take* PRECIOUS LOVE *away.* PRECIOUS LOVE *hums the melody to the minuet as she is leaving. A man who is also dressed in white will enter and take* FATHER LOVE *away. He returns and escorts the two* BROTHER LOVES *off the stage after their monologue is completed.*)

(*Following monologue overlapping the business.*)

BOTH BROTHER LOVES. The heifer is still bleeding.
Passion! Beautiful pain. A hush-a-bye baby lullaby.
The nation, my country tis of thee, is silent again.
The world is stilled.
Another man is dead.
Another hero has stole his way to the bosom of Abraham.
Another man is dead.
For a moment—a pitiful handful of seconds . . .
Hands across the sea . . . and the world is silent.
There is peace . . . There is peace . . . There is peace . . .
There is peace . . . There is peace . . .
(*The last lines are repeated as the* BROTHERS *are taken off the stage.* LILLIE OF THE FLOWERS *gestures towards* MOTHER LOVE. LILLIE *is smiling.*)

MOTHER LOVE (*frightfully*). I won't go! I will not go back there! I won't go without Hopeful Damn-it-to-hell-all! I won't go without Hopeful! You can't make me go. (LILLIE *moves towards* MOTHER LOVE.) You black nigger! Take your black hands off of me! I won't go! I won't go! I will not go back there! (LILLIE *takes her away. Lamentfully, as she is taken away*) Hoooooooooooooooopeeeeeeefulllllll . . . Where is Hopeful? Where is Hopeful? Hooooooopeeeeeeefulllll . . .

(*A dim light beams on the bier for a long second before fading. The clanking sounds of iron doors being closed are heard.*)

DARKNESS

CURTAIN

Notes on Contributors

ED BULLINS lives in San Francisco, California, where he has been associated with the Black Arts Theatre. He has received grants from the Rockefeller Foundation and from the American Place Theatre.

Three of his short plays, *The Electronic Nigger, Clara's Old Man,* and *Son, Come Home,* produced in New York in 1968 by the American Place Theatre, have won excellent critical reviews. A full-length play called *In New England Winter* is scheduled for a 1968 production in New York City. A talented creative writer, Mr. Bullins is also an able spokesman for the revolutionary theater, and his provocative essays have appeared in several publications.

LONNE ELDER has written five plays in addition to *Ceremonies in Dark Old Men,* in this volume, which won the Stanley Drama Award at Wagner College in 1965. He has been a recipient of a John Hay Whitney Fellowship in playwrighting; an alternate winner of the ABC Television Writing Fellowship Award at the Yale School of Drama, 1965–66; and "playwright in residence" on a fellowship with *Fiddler on the Roof* during rehearsals and out-of-town tryouts of the production.

In 1964 Mr. Elder wrote a documentary teleplay for CBS's *Camera 3*, and a special play, *The Terrible Veil*, for NBC's *Kaleidiscope*. His one-act play *Charades on East Fourth Street*, commissioned by the Cultural Arts Department of New York's Mobilization For Youth, Inc., was performed at Expo 67 in Montreal.

Mr. Elder is currently director of the Playwrights-Directors division of the Negro Ensemble Company in New York.

ADRIENNE KENNEDY, the daughter of a school teacher and social worker, was born in 1931 in Pittsburgh and grew up in Cleveland, Ohio. After high school she attended Ohio State University but found the social structure there during the fifties "so opposed to Negroes" that she hardly did any academic work and started writing at twenty. She has written two novels, as well as stories and poems. Her plays include *Funnyhouse of a Negro* (1962), *The Owl Answers* (1963), *A Lesson in Dead Language* (1964), *A Rat's Mass* (1965), and *A Beast's Story* (1966).

Although her first idol in the theater was Tennessee Williams, Miss Kennedy acknowledges Edward Albee as a major influence in her playwrighting career. She has been a member of Mr. Albee's Playwright's Workshop, where she has received, and continues to receive, much encouragement from him.

The Owl Answers was produced for the first time at the White Barn Theater in Westport, Connecticut, sponsored by Eva LeGallienne, Ralph Alswang, and Lucille Lortel. The play was directed by Michael Kahn. *A Rat's Mass* was performed by the Theater Company of Boston in April, 1966. Her play

Funnyhouse of a Negro won an Obie Distinguished Play Award in 1964.

Miss Kennedy's play *In His Own Write*, an adaptation of John Lennon's book, was presented earlier this year by the National Theatre in London. *The Owl Answers* will be produced late in 1968 by the New York Shakespeare Festival Public Theatre. Miss Kennedy is presently living in London and is working on a play which the New York Shakespeare Festival has commissioned her to write.

WILLIAM WELLINGTON MACKEY is from Louisiana and attended Southern University in Baton Rouge. After graduation in 1958 he taught high school in Miami, Florida. With money earned during summers as a waiter and bellhop in the Catskills—a job Cab Calloway helped him land—he entered the University of Minnesota, where he earned a master's degree.

While working as a recreational therapist at the Colorado State Hospital in Pueblo, Mr. Mackey completed his first full-length play, *Behold! Cometh the Vanderkellans*, begun when he was a graduate student at Minnesota. The play, "an attack on the black bourgeoisie" done in avant-garde manner, was performed by the Eden Workshop, the Negro theater group in Denver, in 1965. *Cometh the Vanderkellans*, which is particularly satiric of a Negro college president and his family, has attracted a great deal of attention.

Mr. Mackey's next two plays, *Requiem for Brother X, A Homage to Malcolm X* and *Family Meeting*, will be produced off-Broadway.

DOUGLAS TURNER WARD was born on a plantation at Burnside, Louisiana, and grew up in New Orleans. In 1948 he came to New York and worked as a journalist for three years. To learn the actor's craft as an aid in his ambition to become a playwright, he enrolled in Paul Mann's Actors' Workshop. From this grew a successful acting career. He made his debut at off-Broadway's highly esteemed Circle in the Square in *The Iceman Cometh*. Next he was featured in the New York City Center production of *Lost in the Stars*, under the direction of Jose Quintero. He then won the position of understudy to Sidney Poitier in *A Raisin in the Sun* and assumed this leading role opposite Claudia McNeil during the ten-month national tour of the play. On Broadway he has also been seen in *One Flew Over the Cuckoo's Nest* with Kirk Douglas, and with Jean Simmons and Raf Vallone in the pre-Broadway tour of *Rich Little Rich Girl*. Off-Broadway he gained critical acclaim in *The Blacks* and *Blood Knot*, playing the latter in Chicago and Washington as well. His Shakespearean credits include *Coriolanus* for the New York Shakespeare Festival. On television, Mr. Ward has been seen on many of the leading network shows, including *East Side, West Side, The DuPont Show of the Month*, and *The Edge of Night*, and as co-star of a television special on CBS's *Look Up and Live*.

Mr. Ward's first produced plays, *Happy Ending* and *Day of Absence*, were presented at the St. Mark's Playhouse with Mr. Ward acting in one of the major roles. The satiric double bill, which won praise from critics and audiences alike, received the Vernon Rice Drama Award and the Obie Award in 1966, and had a run of well over a year.

In August, 1966, Mr. Ward wrote an article for the New York *Times* in which he called for the establishment of a Negro-oriented theater in New York. He envisioned it as combining professional performance by a resident company and an extensive training program for promising actors, playwrights, directors, and managerial and technical personnel. It is that vision which has been realized in the establishment of the Negro Ensemble Company, which under the guidance of Mr. Ward and Robert Hooks launched its first highly successful season in January, 1968.